A11Y Unraveled

Become a Web Accessibility Ninja

Dimitris Georgakas

Apress®

A11Y Unraveled: Become a Web Accessibility Ninja

Dimitris Georgakas
Oldham, UK

ISBN-13 (pbk): 978-1-4842-9084-2
https://doi.org/10.1007/978-1-4842-9085-9

ISBN-13 (electronic): 978-1-4842-9085-9

Managing Director, Apress Media LLC: Welmoed Spahr
Acquisitions Editor: Divya Modi
Development Editor: James Markham
Coordinating Editor: Divya Modi

Cover designed by eStudioCalamar

Cover image designed by Freepik (www.freepik.com)

Distributed to the book trade worldwide by Springer Science+Business Media New York, 1 New York Plaza, Suite 4600, New York, NY 10004-1562, USA. Phone 1-800-SPRINGER, fax (201) 348-4505, e-mail orders-ny@springer-sbm.com, or visit www.springeronline.com. Apress Media, LLC is a California LLC and the sole member (owner) is Springer Science + Business Media Finance Inc (SSBM Finance Inc). SSBM Finance Inc is a **Delaware** corporation.

For information on translations, please e-mail booktranslations@springernature.com; for reprint, paperback, or audio rights, please e-mail bookpermissions@springernature.com.

Apress titles may be purchased in bulk for academic, corporate, or promotional use. eBook versions and licenses are also available for most titles. For more information, reference our Print and eBook Bulk Sales web page at http://www.apress.com/bulk-sales.

Any source code or other supplementary material referenced by the author in this book is available to readers on GitHub via the book's product page, located at https://github.com/Apress/A11Y-Unraveled-by-Dimitris-Georgakas. For more detailed information, please visit http://www.apress.com/source-code.

Printed on acid-free paper

To my two families.

Table of Contents

About the Author

 **Dimitris Georgakas** is originally from Greece and has been living in the UK for about 8 years now. He started working as a graphic designer around 2004 doing mostly print work, had his own business along the way, and is now working as a senior designer on web and digital products. He considers himself as a hobbyist designer, since he has not been formally educated in the subject (he holds a degree in geography and is now finishing a degree in biology). However, Dimitris does love all things about design and has managed to transform his hobby into a profession, so he considers that as a win.

Dimitris likes to think that the fact he is interested in multiple subjects allows for a more spherical, multivariate approach to solving (design) problems, and natural curiosity is one of the main reasons he decided to write this book. While working as a designer, he always thought to himself, "Why do I do this?", "Does it matter?", "How will this affect usage?" So when he started learning about web accessibility, he naturally went in there 100% ready to make sense of it all. Combine that with the fact that he was appointed as the main accessibility person in the company he works for, he had to educate himself on the subject. Now, Dimitris would like to share what he has learned and make digital professionals see that it's actually pretty easy to make something accessible.

About the Technical Reviewer

Shanma Ahmed is a digital designer, born and raised in the beautiful isles of Maldives. Her love for design is fueled by her passion to bring ideas to life as user-centric and engaging experiences. In her day-to-day work, she has curated resources to inspire and create awareness on the importance of creating barrier-free designs that are accessible and can be used by all. When she's not mixing espresso shots with tonic, you can probably find her binge-watching *Friends* for the gazillionth time.

Acknowledgments

I'd like to think that, for anything, the first people one should thank is the mum and the dad. So thank you. The genes you passed on hopefully didn't go to waste.

Mum, thanks for making me see that kindness and understanding is the way to go forward. It has made me re-evaluate criminal behaviors that pop in my head every now and again.

Dad, thanks for making me think we were lost when I was five years old and allowing me to take lead, taking us back home. It has sparked the spirit of adventure and the curiosity in me.

Awesome sister Sofia, you deserve a place in here too, for some reason. I've always liked to share things with you, be it a chocolate, a room, or a book you haven't written.

This book would not have been a reality if it hadn't been for the support and encouragement of my superhero, AAA conformance level, and soon-to-be wife, Shirley, who, for some reason, is willing to suffer through all of my weird endeavors and even weirder quirks. But she says she loves me, so it's not really suffering, is it?

Special thanks to my stepdaughter for keeping it down while gaming on a PC or a console and for providing me with material to include in this book.

Of course, this section of the book would not be complete if I didn't thank the design crusader from the Maldives, Shanma, who, as the technical reviewer, ensured information was always accurate and presented in a meaningful manner.

ACKNOWLEDGMENTS

Second special thanks to Darryl who, through his confident mannerism and endless supply of design justifications, gave me some of his ability to explain design decisions in a way that people can understand.

You all didn't help me write the book, but you definitely played your part in starting this. Not sure if this needs to be said, but the fact that my work allowed me to work remotely played a huge role, not in starting, but definitely in finishing this book. Thanks, Access.

Finally, the support of Divya and Shon from Apress, as well as their constant ~~mithering~~ reminders, helped to keep me in place, ensuring that this book would finish on time.

Introduction

This book is a comprehensive gui– Wait a minute. This seems so strange. Have I read this before? Oh, silly me. I must have mistaken this for all the other thousands of "comprehensive guides" out there. Seems that this phrase is becoming too familiar.

This book is probably not going to end up being a comprehensive guide; it was written in an effort to help web designers and people who work in the "Internet business" (is that even a thing?) of any level or experience understand (myself included) if what we do in our designs matters, in terms of accessibility and usability, and how much. It was also written in a non-pretentious, light-hearted way that hopefully puts some fun back into this job as I try to stay away as much as possible from long, incomprehensive lingo that might frighten new web or digital designers.

"Container? It's just a box, mate."

It is primarily addressed to the poor professionals mentioned before, but hopefully anyone within the digital industry, whether a manager, a web developer, or a business owner with a web presence can find something helpful within these pages. Lastly, it was also written to provide a more layman's approach to terms like web accessibility, user-centric design, ARIA (Accessible Rich Internet Applications) practices, markup language, CSS, XML, FMCSJRB and TOISBCE (no, these don't exist, luckily), and other terms and acronyms that we know or don't know or don't want to know. There's an abundance of information out there about web accessibility, usability, and so many other beautiful and somewhat incomprehensible terms that it's very easy to get lost thinking, "What on Earth am I even doing?" Through many, many, many pages, we will try to create some order from the chaos (mainly for web accessibility) having everything in one place, so the next time we go about our business to design a beautiful website, we can be sure that it will also be accessible, and usable, in the best possible way for the goals that we have set for our audience.

You don't have to be an expert to follow this book. I don't claim to be one, and my purpose is not to dictate what you should be doing. You need to figure that out for yourself. In fact, your level of experience doesn't even matter. If you're just starting your career in web or digital design, maybe you can expand on a thing or two, or maybe reading through this book will make you think differently on how you approach your designs and your quest for client feedback. If you're an experienced web/UI/UX/insert-appropriate-title-here designer, this content might make you see things differently and might spark a healthy debate with your fellow coworkers. Or I could be completely wrong in everything, and it can spark a joke or two. Regardless, as long as it makes you feel, learn, or experience anything, I will consider it successful. Like a wise man once said: "Failure is always an option" (bonus points if you know who it was). Even if this book is a total flop, I will have gained the knowledge of what not to do next time.

In any case, through my years as a professional designer of all things pretty (that sometimes might miraculously work), I've seen and done too many designs to count, and often, through feedback or personal curiosity, I've wondered, what am I doing, or what's the reason for doing this? Is it really that important? Is my client bonkers? Or maybe they know something I don't. The frustration is real.

Especially with web accessibility, as it is a huge matter, and for the right reasons since everyone deserves access to the same information in the same way. However, in many cases, we usually design websites that are going to be used by very specific people. So, for the websites and the audiences that we cater and design for, I'm also posing the question: Does accessibility really matter, or do accessibility features add anything to the user's experience if they're not needed? Are there any areas of web accessibility that we can fail to comply with or don't need to use? And how would that affect usability? Would it make the world stop?

In other words, how much does following web accessibility and usability guidelines and rules around digital and web design (written or unwritten, proven or nonproven) matter for our success, a website's success, and the overall product's success? Does it even matter at all? Don't get me wrong. I'm not against developing accessible websites and digital applications nor following design fundamentals and guidelines, rather the actual opposite. In fact, in some countries accessible websites are required by law. Aside from that though, it's also ethical to make sure that every user is able to use a product that interests them or get access to information in the same way. Still, putting legislation purposes to the side, if we know that our audience will not be people with disabilities and we specifically know that our users won't be using any assistive technologies or have any other cognitive, motor, or visual impairments (assuming we've done correct market and audience research), should we be obsessed with accessibility, and would it add anything to user experience?

Well, yes and no, it depends. That's usually the answer in any design-related question, and that seems like an easy one, but in order to get to that conclusion, we need to go through some definitions and over several points in each area – primarily accessibility, usability, and user-centric design, among others. Because if we don't know what we're talking about, then, what are we even discussing?

If you manage to reach the end of the book and think "well, d'oh! Yes, Sherlock, all this is pretty darn obvious, so this was a waste of time" you'd be right surprised as to how easy it is to not use our common sense, even in everyday tasks, or how easy it is to ignore the obvious, just because it didn't fit our way of thinking at some particular time. Our brains are pretty smart, but quite oblivious at the same time. Finally, the content that follows would be more beneficial to a web or digital designer rather than a developer, although there are a few bits of web development wisdom here and there that some amazing people have come up with (not me).

If you're wondering why I chose this job if it brings me to a point I want to pull my hair out one by one, I didn't. It just happened. And I love it.

Or do I...?

How to Use This Book

Who needs instructions when it comes to reading a book, you ask? No one, I'd answer. This awkwardly small "subsection" of this book is entirely dedicated to my stepdaughter who, once, when I got her a book for her birthday (don't remember the exact age but still teenage years), asked me with no hesitation whatsoever, "How do I use it?" To you, my beloved child, and to anyone out there that might have the same question in their head, the answer is simple. You pick it up, flip the pages, and read through them.

I am really sorry if this seems condescending; that was my intention. But this is not addressed to you, dear reader. If my stepdaughter is by some miracle reading this, this is only a joke (although she's made great progress since then).

CHAPTER 1

When the Amazon Was Nothing but a River

April 22nd, 1962 (date totally random)

"Aah, today's paper, right on time as every morning. Thanks, Johnny!"

What a lovely kid, thought Fred while sitting on his withered wooden chair in his front garden, enjoying his fresh breakfast (Frosties) and a cup of coffee (if you lived in the 1960s and didn't have cereal and coffee for breakfast, don't really know what to tell you; you were missing out). The newspaper was the way for Fred to learn about what had happened in the world, the country, and his local community the day before (or many days before) and what might happen in the days ahead. That was actually *The People* newspaper's slogan back then: "The paper that looks ahead." Newspapers were one of the few ways people were able to get access to information (along the TV, the radio, or Suzie and Frank, the next-door neighbors who liked to stick their noses into other people's business), be it news, gossip, sports, science, and so on.

All these different mediums weren't that inclusive. The content of a newspaper was only accessible to people who could, firstly, buy one and then, to the ones that could hold it, see what was on it and read it. Contents of a TV were (and pretty much still are) only accessible to people who could see what's on the screen or hear the sounds coming out of the device.

D. Georgakas, *A11Y Unraveled*, https://doi.org/10.1007/978-1-4842-9085-9_1

But then, if someone couldn't hear or see, they would only get half the information at any given time. Similarly, the contents of the radio were only accessible to people who could hear. All in all, there was no one medium that had information accessible to everybody. That is, until the Internet and the World Wide Web came along.

The first functional and programmable computer that kind of resembles the ones we know today (very loosely though) was invented in the mid- to late 1930s, and by the 1960s much progress had been made in this new computer science field along with a small progress in the size of computers, since the first ones occupied pretty much entire rooms, so they weren't very convenient to use or carry around like today's laptops. It was around that time that the idea of the Internet was just starting to emerge. Fred was in for a big change in his life.

A member of the Internet hall of fame, American psychologist and computer scientist (what a strange combination) Joseph Carl Robnett Licklider (simply known as J.C.R.) was the first to talk about the idea of an "intergalactic computer network." Not sure why he chose that name, but it's a really cool one. There's no doubt about that. He popularized the idea that computers could be devices that communicated with each other and that we could use them to transfer information. Up until that time, such devices were only used for mathematical problems, in a way to speed up computations. But how would computers communicate? Well, with packet switching.

I had no idea what packet switching was. But thanks to the Internet, I can now look it up and come up with the answer in less than a minute, which is far less than the time it took me to write this information down. Packet switching is a method to group electronic data and transmit them through a digital network as small chunks of data or "packets." The first paper about packet switching was published in 1961 by Leonard Kleinrock, and after a few experiments and lots of trial and error, DARPA (Defense Advanced Research Projects Agency) funded the creation of ARPANET (Advanced Research Projects Agency Network), which used this method of packet switching so that multiple computers could communicate over a single network. The first message that was communicated was the word "LOGIN."

However, that wasn't a total success as the network crashed and the message was only partially delivered as "LO," which, thinking about it nowadays, was not much, but it was a first step toward that "intergalactic computer network."

The experiments and research continued, and during the 1970s the TCP/IP (Transmission Control Protocol/Internet Protocol) was developed, which set the standards on how the small pieces of data would be transmitted across the networks. The TCP bit would collect and reassemble the packets of information, while the IP part would make sure that the packets were sent to the correct recipient. ARPANET started using this protocol in 1983, and from there on the "one network to rule them all" took shape and became the Internet as we know it today.

Its more recognizable form, though, came in 1990 with the invention of the World Wide Web (or www for short or simply "Web") by Sir Tim Berners-Lee, a British computer scientist working as a software engineer at CERN (the world's largest particle physics laboratory, located in Geneva, Switzerland) at the time. While he worked there, he became aware of how hard it was to share information between computers. To solve that, he exploited "hypertext," a term invented by Ted Nelson, another pioneer of technology, who used hypertext as part of a model for linking content together (hypertext is basically text that links to other text[1]).

By October 1990, Tim Berners-Lee had developed the fundamental technologies that still underpin today's Web: the HTML, which is the formatting language for the Web; the URL (then named URI for Uniform Resource Identifier, which is a form of address used to identify resources on the Web); and the HTTP (Hypertext Transfer Protocol), which allows to retrieve linked resources from all over the Web. Sir Berners-Lee created

---

[1] www.w3.org/WhatIs.html

the first browser that also worked as a web page editor and the world's first web server. In 1993, the web code was made available to the public, and the rest is history. Shortly after, in 1994, the World Wide Web Consortium (W3C) was founded, an international organization on a mission to develop the web standards, and the rest is history (how original). Too bad Fred was long gone by then, and he didn't get a chance to see and experience this new wonder that contained a wealth of information.

CHAPTER 2

Be a Designer, They Said. It'll Be Fun, They Said.

The year was 2004. I can't really tell what the weather was like, but given the fact I was born and grew up in Athens, Greece, you can pretty much assume it was a nice, warm, and bright morning. One of the modules I had to do as part of my geography studies was web mapping, and what we had to learn to complete the course was HTML and CSS. Web mapping is basically using any map you have produced, on the Internet. We'd take the spatial data, visualize them, and then use a web-based platform to view and analyze whatever we created. And we had to make that platform ourselves (which back then was basically an iframe[1] on a web page with basic controls, like zoom in/out and pan up and down).

Learning about HTML and CSS opened up a world of possibilities. I no longer needed a pen and pad to make a box (or many boxes) and create something that might make sense. I could now use words (code) to create something that I could visualize on a screen, and that was amazing (I would be lying if I said it didn't make me feel like a hacker). Little by little,

---

[1] An iframe is an HTML element that literally puts a web page inside a web page (or "embeds" it, if you want to be posh). As if onc wasn't enough.

© Dimitris Georgakas 2023
D. Georgakas, *A11Y Unraveled*, https://doi.org/10.1007/978-1-4842-9085-9_2

I practiced a bit more on my own after finishing the course, and by the end of the module, I thought I could be a web developer. I tried. I failed.

You see, when you start working as a graphic or web designer (or straight as a developer if you're feeling hardcore), you make these pretty compositions: a box here, a box there, some words on one side of various sizes and styles, images to "make things pop," colors everywhere because that's what you think attracts attention. Then, you stand back, look at your work, and think, "Okay, I've created a masterpiece!" But then, reality comes in.

You present your work to the client, and for some inexplicable reason (after all, you know better; you followed all those Internet tutorials), the client doesn't like it, or they think that your work is not something that will be usable for their purpose because "It doesn't represent our brand," "The colors are too pale," or my own personal favorite "It doesn't have the wow factor" (whatever that wow means). What all these things actually mean is that

a) Fonts are too small.

b) Colors are used the wrong way.

c) You really are not a web designer/developer simply because you can use a software or create a box by writing <div> ... </div>.

Some work and more training are needed – specifically, to learn about the fundamentals and the standards that we need to adhere to, to produce something that might potentially work in the real world (I'm still trying; hopefully, I'll get there at some point).

There is no doubt that typography; color theory; compositions; design models; rules of 3rd, 5th, 128th, and so on are all concepts a designer needs to be aware of (even if they don't know they know). You can't really have white text on white background because no one can see it, you can't have a font that's too small because no one will be able to read it, and you can't have a button that looks like a link because chances are no one is going to click it, if they're looking for a button.

Following the Rules

When it comes to web design, specifically, there are certain rules and guidelines that one must adhere to, in order for the end result to be usable and, most of all, accessible. At least, in theory. I'm one that keeps moaning about guidelines and rules all the time, as I don't like feeling constricted in what I create. On the other hand, certain standard practices can probably make the difference between success and failure of a digital product. One of these practices are web standards.

But what are web standards? The World Wide Web Consortium, or W3C in short, is an organization whose members are responsible for developing web standards. A research study carried out using Twitter in 2018 from Amy Dickens, a PhD researcher in the Mixed Reality Laboratory at the University of Nottingham, showed the remarkable results that a bit over 43% of the more than 500 people who took part in the poll knew little or nothing about web standards (Figure 2-1).[2]

---

[2] What do you know about web standards? https://twitter.com/ RedRoxProjects/status/1063435079559581696, accessed November 5, 2020.

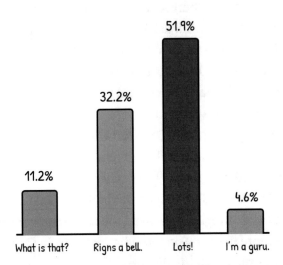

What do you know about web standards?

Figure 2-1. *Final results (as of November 2018) of a study around knowledge of web standards (source: Twitter)*

When you are a professional who designs or builds websites, following standards and adhering to fundamentals matters. To be completely honest, fundamentals matter in any profession or career. Even when you're doing advanced mathematics, unless you have practiced over and over and over again the four basic operations, there is no way you will be able to make sense out of anything. But if you have mastered the fundamentals, then you realize that even when there is an equation with no numbers in it, but only x, y, z, ω, or θ, you will still find it "easy" enough to do, since at the end of the day, any mathematical problems, even the most advanced ones out there, will have a solution that is still based on the four fundamental operations: addition, subtraction, division, and multiplication.

In the same sense, web standards set the fundamental rules that professionals in the web design and development industry need to follow (ideally).[3] In other words, they are a set of tools and practices that make sure we design and develop high-quality web applications that will benefit the people who use them in some way. Besides, the W3C's key purpose revolves around the message "Leading the Web to its full potential." And, in that sense, this is what these standards help achieve. How did they come to be, though?

So far, we've covered that the Internet is a network and that the World Wide Web is the things you see when you're on that network. As BBC content has beautifully put it, "The Internet is the roads you drive on, and the World Wide Web is the houses and buildings you see as you travel along the road network."[4]

Turning Something into Something

In a nutshell, what happens online is that people will create "something" that will go on the Web and people will find their way to access that "something" through an application called a browser. Before the birth of web standards, there was no certain way as to how these contents, the web pages, were created and no specific way on how the browser would give that information to people. That was so awkward, to the point where a page made for the early, for example, Internet Explorer would not really work on any other browser and the developers of the time would have to create different versions of their content for the different browsers (how personalized). This led to the browser creators adding features to their browsers to make them different, and they used these features to get ahead of the competition. However, this led to problems. The more features added to browsers, the more complex they got. The more complex the browsers got, the harder it was for content creators to develop their pages

---

[3] W3C's list of web standards, www.w3.org/TR/
[4] www.bbc.co.uk/newsround/47523993

for every browser out there, at the time. At the end, we reached a point where a simple update to a specific browser could mean that your page wouldn't work on it anymore. So what do you do?

We stop the personalization and make everything (every browser) follow the same rules and work in a more standard way that ensures compatibility of the content with past, current, and future versions of the browsers.

If you visit the page listed in this footnote[5] that lists out all the standards (Figure 2-2), you might get overwhelmed by the enormous amount of information. It takes about 26 scrolls on a 15.6" screen to reach the end of the article, and you can imagine the wealth of information behind each one of them. So how can a web designer, a web developer, or anybody who has to deal with all that, be it a business owner or a one-man band, make sense out of it all? Should we use a checklist? Should we consider each one of these standards when we design or build our products? Should we just quit, go out in the woods, and enjoy what nature provides while acting like mad people?

---

[5] www.w3.org/TR/

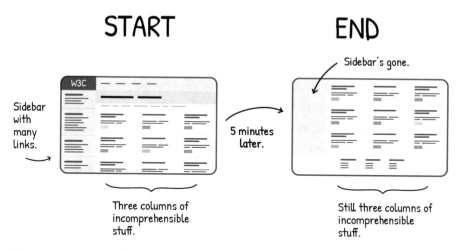

Figure 2-2. *Graphical representation of the first and last screens of the web standards page, graciously annotated. If you're feeling brave, go and have a look on the W3C's website (link in the footnote)*

The Value of Standards

The truth is that most of these standards are second nature to professionals (i.e., for the 57% of them) and they conform to them even without realizing it (at least, I hope). For example, a web designer would never use white text on a white background, because that would make the text not readable by the average user. In some extreme cases, however, it might be accessible in some sense, and this is where some of the confusion comes in. If a user is using a text-to-speech software, that text will still get read, and the user will still get that information, provided the page has been built properly. In other words, the text is accessible *for them*. More specifically, however, that text is partially accessible since an average user who doesn't use a text-to-speech software won't be able to see it. What do we do in this instance? ~~We jump in the river.~~ We make sure that the text is fully accessible for everybody. And that's what web accessibility is all about, not jumping in rivers or pulling our hair trying to make things work, but to ensure that everyone gets access to the same information equally. Does that, ultimately, matter though?

"Everyone gets access to the same information equally." And that's an absolute truth as it makes sense wanting everybody to benefit from some sort of information. However, the question that comes to mind is: Does everyone need that information? Will that information benefit everyone in the same way? Will a vegetarian be benefited if they're included in a meat-eater group? Is someone looking for a job as a doctor ever going to visit a website that recruits for engineers? Posing these questions brings us to one of the most fundamental aspects of web, UI, and UX design (or whatever kids call these things these days): the importance of knowing your audience.

And I mean really know your audience, down to the last detail (personas help with that; will explain more in Chapter 9). I often get clients who need, let's say, a recruitment website, and when I ask them to please define your audience, what I sometimes get is "people who are looking for work." Err... okay. Anything else? No?

Well, thank you, Captain Obvious. That's been very helpful. Joking and sarcasm aside, this is where a gap in fundamental web knowledge exists in the part of the client (sometimes even in the part of the designer/manager or whoever is asking a vague question), and we, as respectable professionals (insert smiley giggly face here), need to make sure that we ask the right questions in order to get the right answers from our clients. If that felt like a weird unrelated pair of parentheses to the rest of the paragraph, it's probably because it was.

Websites that provide information needed by a broader audience, such as Wikipedia or a website of a public service, need to conform to accessibility guidelines fully in order for their information to be readable and accessible by everybody, literally everybody on the planet Earth. Other websites that have a very limited and very specific audience may not have to. Why? Because it might not benefit their audience in any way. I think you know where I'm going with all this by now, and we're only a few pages in. But bear with me. It's worth it.

Maybe. We'll see.

CHAPTER 3

One Standard at a Time

First things first, what is this elusive thing called accessibility? According to the W3C, web accessibility is a set of techniques and practices in web design and development to ensure that a website is effectively accessible by all people, regardless of their physical or cognitive abilities. This way everyone can have access to information equally.[1] In this chapter we'll first define web accessibility and then look at the specific guidelines that help govern this requirement.

Defining Web Accessibility

Like any other accessibility definition out there, accessibility is about being able to use something, regardless of your physical or cognitive status, regardless of how well you can hear, move your hands, or understand information. It's the process of making sure that we have elements in place that will make the content accessible for everybody and bring down any barriers in interaction, much like having a ramp outside of a store, to make sure that people in a wheelchair can go in and buy whatever they want and satisfy a need.

---

[1] World Wide Web Consortium, www.w3.org/standards/webdesign/accessibility

© Dimitris Georgakas 2023
D. Georgakas, *A11Y Unraveled*, https://doi.org/10.1007/978-1-4842-9085-9_3

To make sure that a website is accessible, we first need to break down web accessibility in different bits and make sure we address each one individually. We know of a general term about web accessibility, but what does that really mean and how can we break it down?

Firstly, in order for someone to access a website, all they need to have is access to the Internet, so that's the first requirement for accessibility, much like there needs to be a store that can be easily located by a person in a wheelchair so that person can enter the store. However, access to the Internet is not our concern, so we can skip that, and we can assume that for the purposes of this example, Internet access is a given. One thing that matters here though is Internet speed.

If someone's Internet connection is dodgy or slow, how do we help them? In short, we design our website in a way that when it's developed it is going to be as light as possible, using optimized images, minified codes, caching pages, and so on. So we need to provide these people with a way to access that information in the best possible way.

Then, we have the requirement that the website needs to be easily located, and that's where search engine optimization (SEO) comes into place, making sure that we get the best possible ranking in search engines so our website can be discovered. Search engines take a user's query and present the best possible results for them, based on how relevant a web page seems to be, compared with that query. Whether our website is going to be at least in the first page of results is another issue.

Accessibility doesn't really affect SEO directly, since SEO refers more to individual practices that are involved in creating the most accessible websites, like clarity of content, captions, meta-descriptions, and so on, which in essence is content, and content, most importantly properly structured content, affects SEO.[2]

---

[2] Lisa McMichael, Does Website Accessibility Benefit SEO? https://blogs.perficient.com/2018/01/12/website-accessibility-benefit-seo, accessed November 6, 2020.

Ultimately, it turns out web designers don't really have to do much work in the accessibility area, as they (we) only need to follow certain specific design fundamentals, which, after some time, become second nature in designing anyway, so we don't really have to think about it too much. Similarly to walking, it happens on a subconscious level, and we don't even realize we are doing it. Web accessibility is more of a set of practices that need to be implemented at a web development level, for example, proper tagging of elements and labeling, proper markup as the professionals call it. Be that as it may, a good design is the first step toward an accessible website as it lays down the foundations for the rest of the build, up until the release of a product.

What is a "markup"? Well, it's a computer language, much like HTML or XML. It's called markup because a website is basically content (text, images, etc.) that is marked up (get it?) using a set of instructions that tell the browser how a web page is supposed to look and function. Actually, that's exactly what HTML stands for: HyperText *Markup* Language.[3]

This will allow a screen reader to go through all the different elements, identify them, and announce them to a user who might have, for example, visual difficulties. In this case, something that us designers need to have in mind, like color contrast, doesn't matter fully, or at least in the way that is presented in the W3C's accessibility guidelines, because the users won't be able to see colors or the correct colors anyway. And this kind of potential contradiction is where the fun is! Or the frustration for some people.

---

[3] Definition of Markup, https://makeawebsitehub.com/terms/markup/, accessed November 6, 2020.

Web Accessibility Guidelines

The W3C separates accessibility guidelines into three groups: Authoring Tool Accessibility Guidelines (or ATAG), User Agent Accessibility Guidelines (or UAAG), and the focus of this chapter, as it's more closely related to web designers' work, Web Content Accessibility Guidelines (or WCAG). All these three components, ideally, need to be implemented together to ensure maximum accessibility so the web is fully (or as much as it can be) accessible to people with disabilities.

For the sake of information, the Authoring Tool Accessibility Guidelines refer to a set of standards that need to be followed on software and services that "authors" use when they produce web content, for example, a content management system or a what-you-see-is-what-you-get (WYSIWYG) editor (so many acronyms). The User Agent Accessibility Guidelines refer to standards to make sure that user agents are accessible to people with disabilities. In computing, a user agent is "*any software that retrieves and presents Web content for end users or is implemented using Web technologies.*"[4] A user agent includes a browser, its extensions, media players, or any software that renders web content.

The Web Content Accessibility Guidelines refer to standards that need to be followed on web content, which according to the W3C is defined as any information on a web page or application, which includes the content that the users see, such as text, images, or sounds, as well as the code (or markup) that defines how the preceding content will be structured and presented. Currently we are in version 2.1 of the WCAG, with a view on releasing a 2.2 version within 2022 (the official version might have already been released by the time this book is out as procrastination is my friend; a draft version of WCAG 2.2 is already available as well as one of WCAG 3.0).

---

[4] W3C Definition of a User Agent, www.w3.org/WAI/UA/work/wiki/Definition_of_User_Agent, accessed November 10, 2020.

Web Content Accessibility Guidelines Sneak Peek

The following are a tiny taste of (mostly) web design and development practices that are covered in WCAG 2.1 and 2.2 and what you should expect from them.

Animated Graphics

Who doesn't like flashy, blinky things? Not everybody. In fact, it can be so hard on some people that it might even cause them to experience epileptic seizures aside from being distracting, making it harder to concentrate on what you're looking at. To be a good designer, you need to ensure there aren't any animated bits that overlap important content and that anything you do have doesn't flash for more than three times a second, or anything that flashes to begin with. If you really have to, the flashing elements would need to have low contrast so they're not as visible.

Color

"She comes in colours everywhere, she combs her hair, she's like a rainbow..."

I'm sorry, I got distracted. The WCAG specify that any information conveyed by color also relies on other aspects in order to be understood. For example, use an icon alongside a red border if you need to indicate an error in a form. Users who won't be able to see the color properly will get the hint by your intimidating graphic indicating that something has gone wrong there.

Contrast

You'd be surprised to know that, for some reason, sufficient contrast is not a requirement for the lowest level of accessibility conformance (the W3C has set different levels of compliance with accessibility standards based on certain requirements). Be that as it may, going crazy using white text color on a white background still makes content inaccessible for the majority of people. Colors that have enough contrast when they are side by side should be used, ensuring that people with visual impairments can make sense of what they're looking at, whether it's text or any other user interface element.

Content

If your content is such that cannot be understood by a 12-year-old, chances are your audience will give up on trying to understand what you mean and what you offer while lost within your long and incomprehensible sentences. The WCAG recommend to always use plain and easy-to-understand language. That's not only beneficial to users who might have lower cognitive abilities but to everyone that will be scanning your website trying to find out what they're looking for in a quick and easy way. Guidelines recommend having our sentences 25 words or fewer and, if we really have to use harder-to-understand language, making sure we provide our users with an alternative that is not written in whatever they speak in planet Gliese 581 in the Libra constellation.

Focus States and Focus Order

A focus indicator highlights an interactive element (like a button, a form field, or a link) when it is selected by using either a keyboard or a voice command, and it's pretty much just a shape on or around the element emphasizing it. Don't forget to design them in, and make sure they have sufficient contrast with their surroundings, wherever they appear. Pay attention to the order of focusable items. All you need for your website to be a little bit accessible is to ensure that all functionalities can be performed through a keyboard, all focus states are visible enough, and going through all the focusable elements follows a logical order. For instance, if you're exiting from an otherwise hidden burger menu, the next focused item should come after the menu icon and not before it.

Forms

Logical and usable forms are what the WCAG recommend. Avoiding overcomplicated layouts, having clear labels for any fields, and making sure any errors will be presented in an easy-to-understand way are all included in the Web Content Accessibility Guidelines. Any instructions should be given outside the form field in plain language, and any field should be able to receive sufficient focus. Required fields should be clearly defined either by an asterisk of a different color (okay) or by simply adding the word "Required" next to your labels (best).

Page Layout

Nobody likes a mess. And the W3C is on it like a car bonnet. Unless we're specifically aiming for mess in various aspects of our lives (like a sloppy burger that leaves your t-shirt needing three washes to get rid of the extra sauce; otherwise, it's not a burger – it's a failure). Designing simple and clear layouts that are easy to follow is a must according to the WCAG. Make sure that your content follows a logical order and that each section is clearly defined by an introductory heading, as this will potentially be used by assistive technologies to announce the start of each section making it easier for the users to know where they are and what to expect. Oh, and use headings that are in a sequential order, from H1 to H6, to avoid confusion. But more on that later on.

Tables and Lists

A few cells here, a few cells there, and boom, there is your layout. Luckily, we've got CSS now for that, so make sure you only use tables to present data and not for layout purposes. When you design tables, the WCAG suggest including headers and perhaps alternate colors between rows as this will make them easier to read. And remember, always include a caption as this would provide context for the users and help them decide if they want to go through the whole thing. A few bullets here, and a few bullets there, and there's your list. Keep it simple by using bullets for unordered lists and simple numbers for ordered lists. No need to be fancy here. This way, a screen reader will have no problem picking up a properly structured list and announcing its items.

Typography

Let's face it; it's all about content. And the best presented content is always with written words. According to the WCAG, text on our pages should be presented in a hierarchical way that conveys meaning in the easiest possible way. Make sure you're flexible with your typography to make your design work on any device and in any way the user will choose to view your content.

A requirement for web accessibility is that text needs to be able to resize up to 200% without any loss of content or function. To cater to people with lower cognitive abilities or difficulty in reading as well as anyone that scans your content, text boxes should be kept narrow enough, and line heights should be at least 1.5 times the size of your font. Sometimes. Other times and depending on the chosen font, we don't really need to adhere to an absolute number as legibility and readability are more important than conformance. Speaking of fonts, don't go crazy; use easy-to-read fonts and avoid sketchy, badly written typography, similar to how you used to write in the second grade before you became this awesome designer. At least, that's what they say. I like sketchy fonts.

These are only a handful of what's included in the endless pages that revolve around web accessibility guidelines. As someone would expect, following these suggestions would produce content that is accessible to a wider range of users with disabilities, including best practices for users with blindness and low vision, deafness and hearing loss, limited movement, speech disabilities, photosensitivity, and any combinations of these and some accommodation for learning disabilities and cognitive limitations. Obviously, it's hard to cater for every person and every disability that exists, but following the content accessibility guidelines ensures that almost everybody can access and comprehend the same information equally. Furthermore, following these guidelines, as we will see further down, has a direct positive impact on usability. So why question them?

There is no question about it. Some web content accessibility standards do need to be implemented, but the truth is that not all of the guidelines are necessary at any given time and any application and content should be designed and developed on a case-specific basis, to address the needs of a very specific audience. In other words, everybody deserves equal access to information. However, some information might not be of interest to everybody, but only to the selected few who fit our target audience. In this case, maybe we shouldn't strive to make a website 100% accessible; rather, maybe we should be making something as accessible as it can be for our particular needs and purposes.

At the moment this book was written, the way these guidelines are presented can be a bit daunting and intimidating, with numerous pages and even more click-throughs to different pages in a seemingly random order (it's not, but at times the back-and-forth can be quite confusing). What follows is an effort to make this as easy to digest as possible.

Accessibility Guideline Principles

As stated in the accessibility guidelines, in order for a website to be accessible, it needs to follow a certain number of principles. Therefore, web content needs to be

Perceivable

In other words, the content must be presented to the users in a way they can understand it. An example of this is the use of captions in a video; users who are not able to listen to the audio can read the captions and still get access to the information. Happy days.

Operable

Meaning a user interface, a website, a web app, or anything web related must not include interactions that cannot be performed. In other words, can people use what you want them to use (e.g., buttons or links)? Disabled buttons and the like, this one is for you.

Understandable

The content presented and the way the user interface is operated must be easy to understand and appear in a predictable way (menu on the top left, anyone?). Imagine Chris Tucker in *Rush Hour* while he was yelling, "Do you understand the words that are coming out of my mouth?" We're talking about content on a screen, but still.

Robust

Content must be robust, meaning that it can be interpreted in a reliable way by a bunch of user agents, which also include assistive technology software.[5] Maximizing compatibility with future versions of software is a way to make sure we satisfy this principle. If you've ever found yourself asking (while mumbling profane language), "Why is this not working? This tablet, I swear it's @#%!..." then someone hasn't made their content robust enough.

Conformance Levels

To be successful in these principles (some people like to call it POUR for short; I find it a rather unfortunate acronym), a "few" criteria need to be followed that will allow the content to be fully accessible and ultimately determine the "level of conformance" as they call it, meaning how accessible our web content is.[6] At the moment, there are three levels of conformance: level A, which needs to satisfy all level A success criteria; level AA, which needs to satisfy all level A and AA criteria; and, you guessed it, level AAA, which needs to satisfy all the preceding criteria and the AAA criteria as well.

---

[5] You might have come across this term before, but for the sake of information and as its name implies, assistive technology can be considered anything that helps users who might be experiencing a disability by improving their capabilities. This technology can include anything from a screen reader, which is basically a software that reads text aloud, to a screen magnifier or a voice-over software that we can give commands to by using our voice.

[6] When these lines were written, WCAG 2.1 included 78 success criteria in total. WCAG 2.2 is set to have an additional 9 success criteria; nonetheless, these guidelines are pretty similar.

Note that conformance with accessibility criteria can only be achieved if our content does not violate any of the success criteria that have been set, which are quite strict to begin with. However, if there is content that doesn't require any success criterion to be applied, then we consider the success criterion successful.

In total, there are five requirements that a website and its content must meet in order for that content to be considered as "conforming" to the guidelines:

1. The first requirement for conformance is that at least one of the preceding levels of conformance is met, whether it is A, AA, or AAA. That means at least a few sets of the success criteria need to be applied to the content of the website.

2. The second requirement revolves around the fact that content needs to be accessible throughout a whole web page and not just in a part of a page. There's a loophole in this requirement, however, which has to do with requirement 5.

3. The third requirement for conformance is that when a process is displayed on a web page, if there are any pages that have to do with this process, then all these pages must conform at the specified level of the parent page, or better. A good example of this is an online store, where all the pages that the user is going through until they make their purchase and pay must conform.

4. The fourth and fifth requirements for conformance go together, to a degree. First, any content or functionality that is presented to a user must be presented in an accessible way. What that means is that assistive technologies will be able to display that content to a user with disabilities, no matter

what. The W3C's page gives a great example on this. If you have an image on a web page, a blind person won't be able to see it. However, if text alternatives are provided in a way that assistive technologies can pick that text up and present that information to the user (by the software reading the text out loud), then we can say that the page conforms.

5.   The fifth requirement, though, states that any content or information can be presented on a page, even if it's not accessibility supported, as long as the same information is also presented in an accessible way and as long as the non-accessible content doesn't interfere with that.

Simple, as Figure 3-1 clearly demonstrates.

Figure 3-1. *Graphical representation of my brain and how much it hurt while begging for mercy, after I went through the first web accessibility information. Is this all really necessary?*

Now after reading all this, you might be thinking it's all too complicated or the people who develop all these standards deliberately use long and incomprehensible words to confuse us and make fun of us within their own little obscure gatherings. That's not really the case. In order to achieve accessibility and, consequently, conform to whatever standards have been set, we just have to use our common sense (at least sometimes, since common sense doesn't always agree with facts). We shouldn't include small fonts that will make the users unable to read, we shouldn't include functionalities that cannot be performed, and so on. In a nutshell, we should make things as easy as possible for the user, where "things" means navigating around our website, finding the information the user needs, and completing the goals we have set for them. For the sake of keeping the information digestible and your sanity intact, I am not including the tables with the accessibility criteria.[7]

Nonetheless, common sense can sometimes be an overstatement. More often than not, it can deceive us and make us use the wrong tools or say the wrong thing. We might think it's common sense, when, in reality, we couldn't be more wrong. We shouldn't include small fonts, you say? Well, maybe we should! Maybe the purpose of our website or application calls for smaller fonts to be included, and maybe our audience doesn't care that much because other things might be more important.

Adhering to the guidelines is one thing; however, compromising our specific audience's needs simply to follow some rules that someone, somewhere, at some point, decided are important could be hindering our end goals. In other words, maybe the solution to all this is not to follow the rules blindly but use them when it's acceptable and it helps the goals we have set for our audience. To put it simply, know the rules, use the rules, love the rules, but be prepared to scrap the rules if needed and, please,

---

[7] If, however, you're feeling brave, here's where you can find them: `www.w3.org/WAI/WCAG21/quickref/`. Although this website has an accessibility score of 100 (!), it could use some work UI-wise to make it less intimidating.

don't feel bad about it. Unless you're about to be arrested, since in some countries conforming to web accessibility guidelines is actually required by law. In that case you should feel really bad for breaking the law, you criminal.

Summary

In conclusion, accessibility guidelines are there to ensure that people perceive and understand information regardless of their cognitive or physiological abilities. And in order to be able to understand *how* what we do affects the way people perceive content, ideally, we need to have a generic understanding of how we perceive the world around us. This will give us an insight of the processes involved and maybe help guide some of our design decisions.

CHAPTER 4

How Do People Perceive Content?

Generally speaking, and drawing from our early years of education, we might think that the way we perceive the world around us is as simple as what our senses tell us. We see, hear, taste, or smell something, and then we make sense of it. Even though that's not necessarily wrong, it's not actually right either. Although we do look at the world through our five senses (although we do have more, such as the sense of balance, sense of pain, etc.), what we see and what we understand from different stimuli tends to be a more subjective rather than objective process. In fact, it's so subjective that sometimes what we see is not even real. It's what our brain has decided is real for us at that given time.[1]

Subjective Rather Than Objective

Take Figure 4-1, an example of an optical illusion, for instance. You have probably come across it at some point while procrastinating or while browsing the net for something completely different, but it's a great depiction of the "stupidity" of our brain. The horizontal lines in the following image are perfectly straight and don't slope at all, but somehow,

---

[1] www.sott.net/article/237883-Why-We-Cannot-Perceive-the-World-Objectively

D. Georgakas, *A11Y Unraveled*, https://doi.org/10.1007/978-1-4842-9085-9_4

through all the mess of black squares that try to imitate a vertical line, our brain gets confused and decides that the horizontal lines must slope at the end.

Figure 4-1. *A popular optical illusion where straight lines appear as slanted. This is because your brain tries to focus on both the lines and the black squares, and the end result is a big mess. Don't look at this for too long! (illusion.org)*

Figure 4-2 is even trickier. If you keep looking at the center of the following image, the apparent irregular grid at the sides will somehow fix itself and appear perfect like the rest of the image. Why? Because your brain said so.

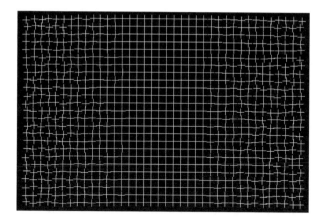

Figure 4-2. *If you look at the center of the image for a while, the seemingly broken edges will start fixing themselves. Apparently, our brain likes regular patterns (kottke.org)*

Still, any two people's brains might not say the same thing when it comes to the same stimulus. A few years back, in 2015, a picture of a dress was circulating the Internet, and people couldn't agree on what color that dress was. Some said it was blue, while others said it was white. In this case, could both be right? Kind of (even though the dress is blue #changemymind). Could it be that what exists is only what we project in the world?

Perception as a Process

Perception is a process that can be described as organizing, identifying, and interpreting information we get through our senses in an effort to understand our environment.[2] Our sight involves light hitting the back of

---

[2]https://archive.org/details/psychology0000scha

our eye and some cells capturing specific information about the light, and after a bit of processing, they send all this to the brain via the optic nerve.[3]

Regarding smell, odor molecules reach our olfactory system and get detected by sensory neurons, which then transmit information about that odor to the brain so the brain can say, "This chocolate smells amazing"[4] (what chocolate doesn't). Vibrations that travel through the air are picked up by our auditory system and transferred to different parts of the brain for processing in order to hear and understand sounds.[5]

Touch involves a process called haptic perception where we understand what we touch by exploring an object's surface; touch receptors on our skin respond to different touch-related stimuli and send this information to our central nervous system.[6] Lastly, sensory organs on the top of our tongue get in touch with a chemical substance, and after a cascade of activation of different nerve cells, this information is passed on to the brain so it can make sense of a particular flavor.[7]

All these seem pretty logical. We receive the signal, and our brain interprets it. We see a green button that says "Buy Now," and we know that if we click it, we will buy that product. Not quite imminently as the wording on the button suggests, since we'd still have to fill in different information like a delivery address and, of course, pay for it, but nonetheless, it's pretty obvious that if we click that button, we will eventually buy that product.

Our brains, though, are not as objective. *How* a person will perceive information (in other words, how the brain will explain to you what's happening) entirely depends on the person's past experiences. Perception, in a way, builds our own objective reality that is based on our previous

---

[3] Goldstein, E. B. (2009), *Sensation and Perception*, Wadsworth Publishing Company.

[4] Rodriguez-Gil, Gloria (Spring 2004), *The Sense of Smell: A Powerful Sense.*

[5] Plack, C. J. (2014), *The Sense of Hearing*, Psychology Press Ltd.

[6] https://askabiologist.asu.edu/understanding-touch

[7] www.ncbi.nlm.nih.gov/books/NBK279408/

experiences, knowledge, and expectations.[8] That only re-enforces the idea of familiarity when designing a website, for example. Based on what has happened in the past, we expect certain elements, like a logo or a navigation, to be placed on certain positions within the page, such as the logo to the left and navigation to the right. A deviation from that could potentially cause a momentary confusion that makes us think, "Wait a minute. This is not supposed to be here," which could make going through a certain process slower than what we would normally expect. In the case of navigating within a website, even a few milliseconds are important in making sense of what we're looking at.

Using the Web

Apart from the weird functions of our brains, not all people use the Web in the same way, even from the same devices. Normally, you'd go online, look into a bunch of websites, read or scan information, make up your mind after looking into endless options, and eventually accept what you read or buy that product that you wanted. The process is pretty straightforward; you'd use a computer to go online or a phone, type in your search query, use a mouse to navigate to a website or just tap different places until you get to where you want to go, and then try to get information from that website by using your mouse or your touch screen. That's not the case for all users.

Some individuals may have limitations that prevent them from using the Internet or any digital product in the "normal way," creating barriers in interactions and access to information. These limitations can be anything from inability to access the Internet in the first place to specific disabilities that prevent users from using our product in an efficient way. That's where

---

[8] A very interesting read about the brain and emotions: *How Emotions Are Made: The Secret Life of the Brain*, by Lisa Feldman Barret.

accessibility comes in, as part of inclusive design, making sure that no one would be excluded from using our products (if they are part of our target audience because if you don't need it, you won't try and use it) and that any barriers in interaction or communication would be effectively reduced. Besides, as the World Health Organization (WHO) puts it, it is the world that should be adapting to the needs of people with disabilities rather than the other way around.

A family resources survey conducted by Scope during 2019–2020 found that in the UK alone, there are about 14.1 million people living with some kind of disability. And this is not necessarily something permanent. There can be many types of disabilities, ranging from blindness to disabilities from injuries. Generally speaking, we can categorize them in four groups: intellectual, physical, sensory, and ones revolving around mental health, with some of them being permanent while others are short-term.

As such, we can also divide disabilities into permanent, temporary, and situational. A permanent disability is one that lasts... well, permanently. Examples include people who might be experiencing, among other disabilities, permanent blindness or loss of hearing, ones that have lost their fine motor skills, as well as individuals with permanent disabilities that are not visible, such as dyslexia or any mental health conditions.

A temporarily disabled person will have lost some of their skills temporarily due to injury or illness, which would cause short-term impairment preventing them from carrying out certain tasks. For example, a user with a broken arm might not be able to use a mouse properly, or someone that has lost their glasses might not be able to distinguish certain elements on a screen.

Certain sources (we are not snitches) refer to other disabilities as situational disabilities, in cases where someone might be temporarily disabled by, for example, holding a baby in their arms or being distracted by loud noises in an office. Ɨ Some people might like to refer to that simply as an inconvenience as Ɨ some people find it hard to digest that being distracted by your baby or your phone as you're walking equates to being blind. The W3C, however, is being a bit more politically correct, referring to these instances as situational limitations, an example being the sun hitting your screen making it harder to navigate a website properly.

Summary

Hopefully, that introduced the point that we are all different and we all use the same things in various ways. Our perception is totally subjective with our past experiences shaping our current and future understanding of the world, consequently shaping the way we use the Web. As no person is entirely the same as the next one, striving to make something that is accessible to as many people as possible, regardless of disabilities or any kind of temporary limitations, is the reason behind the Web Content Accessibility Guidelines.

If what we're looking at is not perceived in the way the content creator meant for us to perceive it, then that specific website or web application might not be as successful as its creator meant it to be, which, eventually, could be detrimental to someone's business. But if people perceive the same things differently, is even the idea of accessibility itself any valid?

Does it make sense to strive to create something that will be perceived and understood in the same way from a variety of people if all these people are fundamentally different? In that case, we basically do what we can. We follow our logic and reasoning to develop a set of standards that shape how content is supposed to be presented to the user. We set the expectations and try to dictate how the different assistive technologies will show that content to a person with disabilities and how will they allow them to use it and, ultimately, set a realistic objective for our content: to be as accessible and inclusive as it can possibly be.

CHAPTER 5

Tell Me What to Do: Designing for People with Disabilities

I can't tell you what to do as, unfortunately, we can't include everybody and we can't design for all. At least, in the literal sense. But we might not even have to, in the majority of cases. In order to design and, consequently, develop a website that can be used by as many people as possible, we need to identify which people are going to use our product in the first place. Not everybody will use what we're offering, and not everybody cares about it to begin with (except for Suzie and Frank, you gossip freaks). However, we need to recognize the ones that will do. One safe assumption to make would be that our digital product will be used by people of different backgrounds and in diverse ways. Our users will be of different ages, different experiences, different educational levels, as well as different abilities and skills. And some of them might be using assistive technologies.

In any case, taking all these into account and designing something that makes the life of people with disabilities easier and enhances user experience supposedly benefits everyone, as everyone, even the people who fall outside the category of "disabled," might experience an inconvenience or a temporary disability at some point in their life, so we

D. Georgakas, *A11Y Unraveled*, https://doi.org/10.1007/978-1-4842-9085-9_5

need to make sure we've accounted for this diversity of users from the beginning of a project up until its release. And that makes more sense; if we have a general idea about our audience and we know it's not for people with, let's say, permanent disabilities, accounting for situational limitations could potentially make their life easier under certain circumstances. Think about the diversity of the people who will be using your product: Who are they, where are they from, what language do they speak, are some of them disabled, and, if so, what kind of disabilities they might have? Is your product going to be used under circumstances that might create situational limitations?

These are a lot of questions. It seems that our designs would need to be adapted in a way that includes elements that help people with current, or potential, disabilities use a digital product with ease. In theory, of course. This is something that doesn't seem hard or tedious if you think about it; clean designs, simple language, making elements distinct enough, and ensuring our content is legible and robust are all small things that actually make sense and could make a difference in whether our users are happy or frustrated (no one wants a frustrated user). Is that difference significant? That is another question.

Designing for Users with Blindness and Other Visual Impairments

"Don't be fancy. Be practical."

First off, we need to define what we mean by *blind*. Like most of disabilities, there is a spectrum in blindness as well. There are those who can't see anything at all, not even light (like Yu in *Rush Hour 3*, not you, Yu – although it's worth mentioning that 100% blindness is relatively very rare[1]), those who are legally blind,[2] and all those in between. There is also my sister who woke up one day – years ago – in the middle of the night and, because it was pitch-black (lights were obviously turned off), thought she was blind for a few seconds. But that's a different story.

According to the UK's National Health Service (NHS), there are at least 2 million people with sight loss in the country, with about 360,000 of them blind or partially sighted. Worldwide, we're looking at about 285 million people who are visually impaired.[3] Color blindness, a vision deficiency that comes with a lower ability to distinguish color or differences in color, affects around 1 of 12 men and 1 of 200 women in the world. This means around 8% of men and 0.5% of women in the planet experience it. In the UK alone, this means about 3 million people, which is around 4.5% of the country's population.[4]

These numbers don't seem at all insignificant and make vision impairments a major factor we need to consider when we're designing our digital products. That is, if we want to be legal, fair, and business minded (as the more people we exclude, the less potential customers, if we're selling something). For example, in Figure 5-1, the colors on the left are as they would look like to a person without color blindness. If someone had protanopia, a type of color blindness where there is insensitivity to red colors, the image on the right is what they would see. Pretty red buttons would mean nothing.

---

[1] www.aoa.org/healthy-eyes/caring-for-your-eyes/low-vision-and-vision-rehab?sso=y

[2] In the USA, to be considered legally blind, you need to have a vision of 20/200 or worse, meaning you would need to be 20 feet away from an object to see it clearly, where people with normal sight could see it from 200 feet away. In addition, you would need to have a vision field of 20 degrees or less in your better-seeing eye.

[3] https://fuzzymath.com/blog/improve-accessibility-for-visually-impaired-users/

[4] www.colourblindawareness.org/colour-blindness/

Normal vision   Colour blind vision

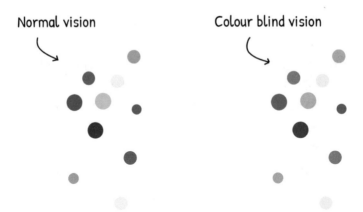

Figure 5-1. *Comparing normal vision with color-blind vision*

Other than being legally blind or color-blind, we could also account for
users who might have lost their glasses (I had to drive with my prescribed
sunglasses once, at night; it wasn't a very enjoyable experience) or users
who might be experiencing any visual impairment, such as cataract,
blurred vision, or light sensitivity. Add the ones that might use their device
under low-light conditions or under the sun or the ones that have their
phone next to them in a low brightness setting when they're trying to fall
asleep at night (because what could be better than stimulating your mind
when trying to get some rest?), and you can clearly see the importance of a
design that addresses those needs.

Users with blindness or other visual impairments face a variety of
barriers when trying to use a website, so the way we design and build that
product could make an enormous impact on their experience. Completely
blind and/or visually impaired users would not be able to use a mouse
to navigate around a website since they would not be able to see the
movement of the cursor and where it points.

Figure 5-2 is an example layout of a page that could be helpful for blind
or visually impaired users, consisting of large headings that organize the
structure of the page, a tool to adjust font size (if needed), and a limited

use of colors to prevent a user from feeling overwhelmed – accompanied by lots of whitespace, short and sweet text, and a proper description for images and icons alongside a color change, in case of an error.

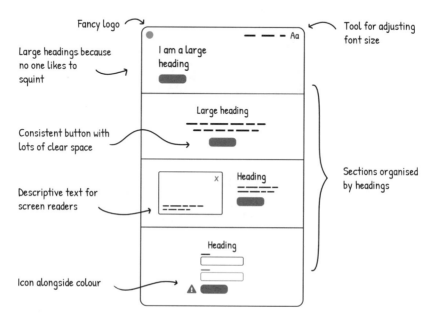

Figure 5-2. *An example layout of an imaginary website, with clearly separated sections and large headings to organize information*

Visually impaired users would benefit from a website that has keyboard navigation for all interactive elements (along with adequate and sufficient focus states – more on that later on) and properly structured markup to allow a screen reader to "translate" the website correctly to them, basically a logical and uncluttered layout with sufficient descriptions for images and links and a well-structured document with proper headings and labels.

They would also need to look at something that has high enough contrast between different elements (provided they are not completely blind). Contrast is essentially the difference between... something – difference between colors, shapes, sizes, and so on. In Figure 5-3 the colors on the left have high contrast, so they're easier to identify as separate. On the other hand, the colors on the right are essentially much the same, but the eagle-eyed among you will be able to tell the difference. Someone who has vision problems probably wouldn't.

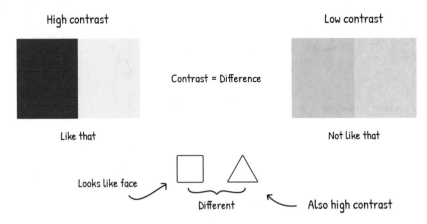

Figure 5-3. *Abstract representation of the power of contrast*

Those who are permanently blind use a combination of assistive technologies trying to overcome those barriers, such as the already mentioned screen reader, which would analyze the layout and the content of a website and then read out what is on the screen. They would most likely use a braille display, which is really an amazing piece of technology, a keyboard-like device able to translate digital text to braille dots, which can be read using the fingers, as well as speech recognition software to interact with a website (or their entire computer system for that matter) using their voice. Users with low vision may also use tools such as a screen magnifier, software that allows them to edit contrast on the screen or various other aspects of their displays.

If a user who is blind or has any other visual impairments goes through such an effort to understand what something means and we don't deliver, it means we haven't done our jobs right. It means we have been trying to be fancy, rather than practical, by using scribbly fonts or monotone colors with no contrast and relying only on color to convey information. If, on the other hand, we *do* do our jobs right, an accessible website for blind or low-vision users would have qualities such as easily distinguishable elements, clear focus states when navigating with a keyboard, and an easy-to-read font, among others.

Designing for Users Who Are Deaf or Hard of Hearing

"Say what now?"

(My dad is pretty deaf; I'm allowed to joke about it.)

Any random day, any random hour (apart from sleeping hours – these are sacred):

Me: Dad?

(Silence)

Me again: Dad?

(Silence)

Also me: DAD?!

Dad: I can hear you. No need to shout.

Me: *Asks any question whatsoever that has all possible answers, apart from Yes.*

Dad: Yes.

This sums up the experience of living with a person who is hard of hearing when wearing his hearing aid and completely and utterly deaf when he's not. Despite the fact that we love our dad more than anything in the world, the reality is that deaf or partially deaf people have a hard time communicating with others, under specific circumstances.

Hearing, according to most people, is the second most important sense, and as such it requires special attention. It can make or break an experience (provided you can see) and really elevates what you're looking at; just imagine watching a film with no sound and compare it with when you are watching it normally. For myself, having a dad who is partially deaf and couldn't hear a nuclear bomb going off next to him without wearing his hearing aid (he'd probably experience it in different ways to be honest, if he were that close) only makes me appreciate more the effect that hearing has in our lives.

Similarly to blindness, there is also a categorization to the degree someone can hear, with different associations identifying different levels of hearing loss.[5] The American Speech-Language-Hearing Association classifies hearing in seven categories, from normal hearing (−10−15 dB) to profound hearing loss (91+ dB), while the British Society of Audiology categorizes hearing loss as mild, moderate, severe, and profound (95+ dB). There is even a writing convention when it comes to how people identify themselves[6] as stated by the US National Association of the Deaf: People who identify as Deaf (with a capital D) are ones that can communicate with sign language and have been deaf for most of their lives. Ones that identify as deaf (with a lowercase d) include people who weren't born deaf but have become deaf later in their life. One that is hard of hearing can be someone that has a certain level of hearing loss, but hasn't completely lost their hearing.

Gov.uk reports that in the UK there are about 11 million people who are hard of hearing or completely deaf, and 151,000 out of those use the British Sign Language (BSL). According to Statista (2015), there are about 328 million people in the whole planet (pretty much around 2.5% of the global population) who experience some form of hearing impairment, with more than one-third of them residing in Europe.

---

[5] Hearing loss refers to how loud something needs to be before you can hear it.

[6] At least within the boundaries of reality, that is, you can't identify as hard of hearing if you're completely deaf. I mean, you can, but most likely you'd be lying to yourself. I'd like to think the categorizations are objectively linked to a medical professional's diagnosis.

So how do we make their lives easier online? Simple. We make sure that any audio or video content is accompanied by appropriate captions. These will help users who cannot hear the sound of a video to feel the pain Alejandro felt after Maria realized he was cheating (Figure 5-4). Don't forget to design these in when necessary (unlike violence, which is never the answer), to help deaf or hard-of-hearing users understand all the audio elements in a video, as, without them, a user with hearing problems might find it difficult to understand what's happening.

Ensure that captions are accurate and no important words are missing as that can be quite frustrating and can lead to the wrong message being communicated. To take it one step further, we wouldn't even rely on automated captions as sometimes they can present a word that sounds like the actual word spoken but it's not quite right, so it might be a better idea to do it manually.

Figure 5-4. *Illustration of a hard ~~slap~~ time in Alejandro's life, after Maria found out about the cheating, inspired by the countless soap operas I have ~~not~~ watched. Without captions it would probably seem like someone is slapping someone else for no reason*

Another great way of improving a deaf user's experience is providing transcripts for audio or video content. The transcripts would be just text that includes everything that's happening on the screen, which would allow users to really digest the content. This doesn't need to be fancy; a simple accessible link to the transcripts would do (Figure 5-5). On top of that, we need to make sure that any audio files or audio within a video has as low background noise as possible, so users who are hard of hearing can identify the different sounds easier and understand your content in a much clearer way.

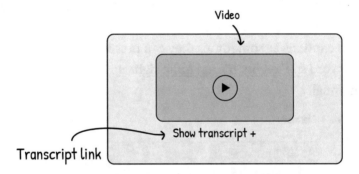

Figure 5-5. *How you can add a simple link to a video's transcript*

Finally, since hard-of-hearing users might find it hard to communicate over the phone, it could be beneficial to them to provide alternative ways of communication, such as an email address or a contact form (i.e., a properly designed one).

Finally_finally_2 (if you are a designer, you know what this means), don't forget that deaf users who use sign language to communicate might not be as proficient in the use of language or as fluent as any other person. Clear-to-understand content, written in plain language with minimum or no fluff, will help users digest it easier and more effectively.

Designing for Users with Physical Disabilities

"Keep it simple."

To put it simply, "keep it simple" always sounds simpler than it actually is, and it's definitely not that simple to be simple (I love a good redundancy). If you are a professional designer, you undoubtedly find yourself constantly trying to fight the urge to go crazy trying to implement that "amazing new idea" or the "make-it-pop/wow factor" in your designs. You probably spent countless hours trying to make it work, only to realize that, in the end, simplicity and practicality were what you were looking for in the first place.

These two are always a winner when it comes to creating something that needs to be used with ease and efficiency (always a bonus if it looks good, but that's a bit subjective). As we have already mentioned, users will use something in a variety of ways. Especially when talking about users with physical limitations, then things become a tiny bit trickier.

I don't think *disability* as a term needs a definition for the readers of this book; however, for the sake of a few more words as well as trying to be as thorough as possible, gov.uk refers to *disability* as "*a physical or mental impairment that has a 'substantial' and 'long-term' negative effect on a person's ability to do normal daily activities.*"[7] In the UK alone, scope.org reports that 14.6 million people have some form of disability (21% of them being working-age adults),[8] and according to the Department of Work and Pensions, 46% of these people have a disability related to mobility issues.[9]

---

[7] Equality Act 2010, `www.legislation.gov.uk/ukpga/2010/15/section/6`

[8] `www.scope.org.uk/media/disability-facts-figures/` (accessed August 23, 2022)

[9] Family Resources Survey: financial year 2020 to 2021, `www.gov.uk/government/statistics/family-resources-survey-financial-year-2020-to-2021`

That number of people is more than 20% of the UK's total population. Simply put, one in five people who visit your website might have some form of physical impairment that could prevent them from using your website the way you want them to. These could include, among others, loss of fine motor skills, muscle atrophy, tremors, lack of coordination, pain from whatever reason that prevents users from moving properly, and lack of limbs.

If someone suffers with a permanent disability and tries to use the Web, there is quite the chance that they will be using assistive technology or any kind of specialized equipment to navigate a website. Users with permanent physical disabilities could be using keyboards specifically designed for their needs and devices such as joysticks, on-screen keyboards and mouth sticks, or even eye-tracking technology in case they can't use their hands. All these require quite a lot of practice and precision, so the more complicated our canvas is, the more difficult they could find to navigate around it.

When designing for people with motor impairments or any physical disability, structure, space, and spacings are very important. Make sure you leave enough space around elements so users with, for example, loss of fine motor skills or ones that use a mouth stick can easily access different parts of your composition, like a checkbox or a call to action (Figure 5-6).

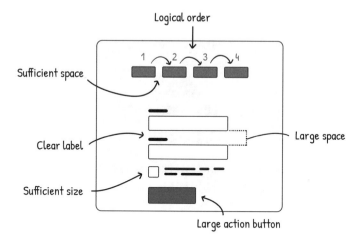

Figure 5-6. *Illustration of a layout with clearly separated elements that hopefully can accommodate for a user's reduced (or lack of) fine motor skills*

That is as far as permanent disabilities go. When it comes to temporary ones, if you lived with me or with my wife, you'd know the struggle of being clumsy as clumsy can get. My wife's hands have more bruises than you can count, and her fingers are constantly swollen because of accidental injuries or fights that have occurred during her netball matches.

My upper thighs ache all the time because for some reason I keep hitting the bed as I walk by, which is strange on its own, since it is probably my favorite piece of furniture in the entire house. It is true what they say: most accidents happen in the house. Figure 5-7 presents different types of disabilities. These can affect people in various ways, as well as how they access and use the Web. On top of all the other problems that someone with one arm or a broken arm would have to face, someone with a newborn would also deal with lack of sleep and a general will to live, so it's our job as web designers to make their online journey as easy and stress-free as possible.

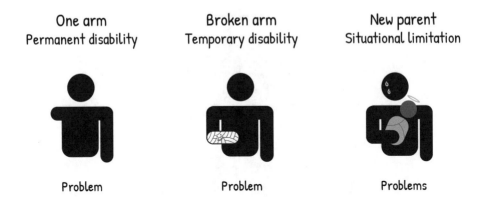

One arm
Permanent disability

Broken arm
Temporary disability

New parent
Situational limitation

Problem

Problem

Problems

Figure 5-7. *Different types of permanent and temporary disabilities*

Temporary physical disabilities can range from something really small (a couple of bruised fingers) to something larger (your whole arm broken or your neck injured in a way that turning your head hurts more than your bruised fingers) and can affect the way we use devices, such as a keyboard or a mouse, or the way we look at a screen. Injuring our thumbs can affect our ability to properly hold a mouse or our mobile device, which could mean we would navigate around a website by hitting the Tab key on the keyboard to get to where we want to go. Whether that's successful or whether we'd find ourselves going through a few dozens of navigation links before we reach the section of interest depends on how accessible said website is.

If keyboard navigation is supported and focus states are visible enough as in Figure 5-8, we would have no problem moving around the different sections and links. This is key if you're navigating a website with a keyboard. No one likes to be lost, so knowing that your actions actually work makes sense. If we were provided with "skip links" so we could navigate from section to section without having to go through all the interactive elements in each one, that would be even better.

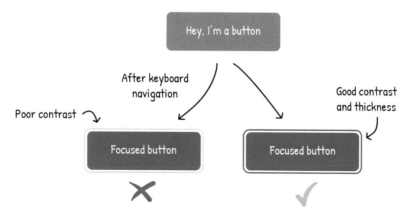

Figure 5-8. *What to do, or not, when it comes to designing a focus state*

Designing for Users with Anxiety

"Don't rush me."

If you're like me and hear that someone gets anxious while browsing the Web, you'd probably be like: "But it's only a website. What can be stressful about that?" If you're also like me, then you'd probably try to know a bit more before forming an opinion and educate yourself on the subject. I kind of did. And I still reached the same conclusion.

There is nothing inherently stressful about a web page; after all, it's just bits and bytes on a screen. However, the way content can be presented can sometimes add to the anxiety a user already feels in general; if you're not stressed to begin with, chances are a website won't suddenly make you jittery.

Think about websites that have flashy graphics, elements moving in all sorts of directions distracting us from what we want to do, and catchy headlines that try to make us buy a product because "The offer will disappear in 15 minutes and 34 seconds, so hurry up!" If you have also found yourself repeatedly feeling frustrated and stressed every time you try to read an article or buy a product online and rude little popups, or any other kind of messages, just randomly appear out of nowhere making your life harder, then you'll know exactly what this is about. Imagine browsing the Web and all of a sudden random blinking words appear, accompanied by invasive popups and text that play on your emotions (Figure 5-9). How stressful is this? Now, imagine you're a generally anxious person and the same thing happens to you. Life is quite taxing as it is. Our websites don't need to be.

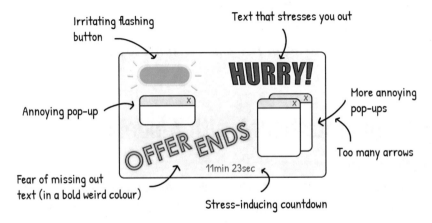

Figure 5-9. *Example of a stressful web page where all sorts of little things happen at once*

We have no way of knowing whether our users suffer with anxiety or any other psychological impairments. For this reason, it would be best if we tried to be a bit mindful and cater for these people by making sure our product works in a way that is as stress-free as possible (however, what if the goal of a product is to increase a user's adrenaline levels?).

Numerous reports throughout the last decade mention a lot of different numbers when it comes to how many people suffer with anxiety in the UK. Mentalhealth.org cites that in 2013, there were over 8 million people dealing with anxiety[10] (that's almost one in ten people in the UK), while the Workplace Health Report of 2022[11] found that almost six out of ten employees experience mild anxiety symptoms. Given the fact that the readers of this book (including you, yes, you) are most likely to be young(ish) professionals, chances are a lot of you ~~need to chill~~ might be experiencing some form of anxiety disorder, whether in your everyday lives (raising my hand) or in the workplace (hand goes back down). Either way you look at it, and whatever number has gotten your attention, that's a lot of people!

Anxiety comes in a variety of types with all of them being characterized by feelings of fear, worry, and uneasiness,[12] and when it's too bad, it turns from a simple nuisance to a, sometimes, debilitating disability. The types of anxiety with the most prevalence are generalized anxiety disorder (or GAD for short), which comes with excessive worry for no apparent reason; obsessive compulsive disorder (the one and only OCD, which many think they have because they like to have things in order), which is characterized by repetitive behaviors or obsessive thoughts and panic disorders that come with episodes of intense fear and agony; social anxiety disorder (SAD for short, quite fitting if you ask me), which makes people feel extremely overwhelmed in social interactions; and, finally, PTSD (or post-traumatic stress disorder), which seems to appear after a traumatic event in someone's life.[13]

---

[10] Fineberg, N., Haddad, P., Carpenter, L., Gannon, B., Sharpe, R., Young, A., Joyce, E., Rowe, J., Wellsted, D., Nutt, D., and Sahakian, B. (2013). The size, burden and cost of disorders of the brain in the UK. *Journal of Psychopharmacology*, 27(9), pp. 761–770.

[11] https://championhealth.co.uk/insights/guides/workplace-health-report/

[12] https://digitalcommunications.wp.st-andrews.ac.uk/2020/02/25/designing-for-users-with-anxiety-or-panic-disorders/

[13] Hss.gov

Apart from the fact that if someone suffers with some form of anxiety, they need to ask for help (although that's easier said than done), there are some things we can do as designers to make their digital journey a bit less stressful and nerve-racking. In my opinion, the most important thing we can give to our users is time – time to go through different options, time to fill in some form, and time to digest our content. It's very important not to rush users through different tasks, as the ones with anxiety are most likely to complete a task slower by being more cautious. Allow enough time for users to fill in a form and perhaps add a little text alongside the heading of an article that says how much time it takes to read it.

Try to always explain what happens on the screen and what *will* happen after the user is finished with a task or transaction. This way you can make sure that users are perfectly informed about what they're getting into and they know what to expect when that's done. In other words, design a "thank you" or a "success" page, similar to Figure 5-10. A heading would introduce the section, and the supporting copy underneath would explain what this is and what the user can get out of it. A clear label above the input field leaves no ambiguity as to what the user needs to input. After the user has clicked a submit button, there is redirection to a confirmation screen explaining that whatever action the user did was successful (or not), restating what has happened and what happens next. If needed, an extra step between these two, where the user has to confirm any choices, can also be used to reduce the possibility of errors.

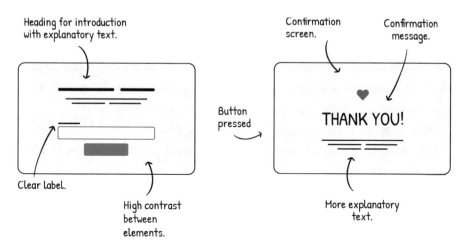

Figure 5-10. *Example of a screen where the user has to fill in some information and submit a form (only one field, I know – it's only for illustrative purposes)*

How many times have you completed something on the Web and you didn't get any kind of success or failure screen? So make sure you design those nice confirmation pages. And, please, leave some white space whenever possible. No anxious user likes cluttered and confusing designs.

Aside from giving users time, we can also give them a variety of ways to communicate. I can't recall how many times I or my wife[14] had to call someone to deal with some situation because our kid is incapable of using the phone (albeit quite capable of venting from a distance, behind the safety of a screen). The reality is that some users might not be as comfortable talking over the phone or they might even be looking for an instant response to an issue, so giving them alternate forms of communication as a live chat or a mailing address could be something to consider.

---

[14] Mostly my wife. I think confrontation is a waste of time.

To sum up and to keep this little section short for the anxious minds out there, give users time to finish tasks and to check any form answers before submitting, present them with clear information, explain to them what will happen if they press that colorful button, and make sure you confirm that they have completed an action.

Now stop reading for a few minutes and go look outside the window. It makes everything better.[15] After you've done that, please come back. We've got loads to talk about.

Designing for Users with Dyslexia

Dlsyexia can be very problematic when it comes to designing a website, but most importantly when trying to lay out and structure your content. For the most of you, the first word of this paragraph would just seem to have a little spelling error, which could make it a bit harder to read; for those who are dyslexic, a little nuisance can be equivalent to climbing a mountain.

Dyslexia is a learning difficulty (not a learning *disability*)[16] with its symptoms becoming apparent at a very young age, around the time a kid starts to read. Common difficulties include confusing the order of letters in a word, inability to spell correctly, confusing some letters because they look similar (e.g., "b" instead of "d"), writing or reading slowly (sometimes letters might seem to jump around and switch places), and finding it hard to follow instructions. Luckily, with it being a learning difficulty,

---

[15] Unless you live in England, and it happened to be one of the 360 gloomy days of the year.

[16] The NHS classifies it as a difficulty because it doesn't affect a person's intelligence levels, although its origins are neurobiological, with some genetic factors affecting a person's working memory and sequencing skills (at least, that's the prevailing theory according to the European Dyslexia Association, but what is this – a book around web design or a biology class?).

when identified at an early age, kids can be helped through educational interventions to help them with reading and writing so when they become adults, the issue is not as noticeable. In some cases though, dyslexia can be a lifelong problem,[17] and as such, we need to do something about it when designing a website.

The NHS states that at least one in ten people in the UK has at least some degree of dyslexia.[18] That's quite common – personally, I'm beginning to think I'm one of them, as lately I find myself increasingly mixing "b" with "d" and sometimes misspelling words by changing the order of letters. To give you an example, this is what part of the preceding paragraph used to look like before I went in and spell-checked it (manually of course, because I like a challenge):

> *Dyslexia is a learning diffuculty (not a learning disability) with its sypmtons becoming apparent at a revy young age, around the time a kid statrs to read. Common difficulties include confusing the otder of letters in a word [...] follow instructions.*

Maybe I am dyslexic, or perhaps I just can't type.

People with dyslexia might often find it difficult to browse a website if it's too cluttered, if the fonts are fancy and not simple enough, or even if the lines within a paragraph are too close together. But have no fear, that is, if we do our jobs correctly, taking the necessary steps to make sure dyslexic users can access our content easily and effortlessly.

---

[17] Science has also revealed that dyslexia can in fact be critical to how humans adapt, since dyslexic brains are more specialized to explore the great unknown, be more creative, and find new solutions to old problems using novel problem-solving strategies. This interesting study can be found here: https://doi.org/10.3389/fpsyg.2022.889245

[18] www.nhs.uk/conditions/dyslexia/

It all starts with good structure. The use of a simple layout with enough white space and a sans-serif font[19] will make your website easier to read, but most importantly to scan, and it won't just help users with dyslexia, as everyone will benefit from such a design decision. I will now assume (although as designers, we should never assume anything) that you already know about serif and sans-serif fonts. If not, the illustration in Figure 5-11 will clear things out. The letter on the right is what dyslexic users would find easier to read.

This is not another one of those random designer claims where people give rules left, right, and center as to how you *must* design something all while trying to look serious and authoritative as if they're solving world hunger. A 2013 study by Luz Rello, from Pompeu Fabra University in Barcelona, and Ricardo Baeza-Yates, from the Yahoo! Labs and Web Research Group, identified just that. Sans-serif fonts significantly improved the readability of a text for the 48 participants of the study, over serif fonts. They even propose which fonts to use to help people with dyslexia: Courier and Helvetica.[20]

---

[19] For those of you who need an extra reminder, a sans-serif font (unlike a serif font) is one that doesn't have those annoying little protrusions at the end of the strokes of each letter.

[20] You can read this very interesting study here: https://doi.org/10.1145/2513383.2513447

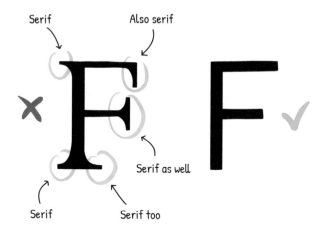

Figure 5-11. *Explanation of a serif font*

Combine that with a large enough font (so maybe something larger than 14 px, or even include a functionality on the page to increase/decrease font size at will) and not too long lines of text, and your users will love you.[21] Ultimately, they might even love your product enough to make a purchase (i.e., if you have an ecommerce site).

Dyslexic users will find it much easier to read and comprehend text if it's presented in a simple and uncluttered way (Figure 5-12). Keep your text justified (left or right, depending on what directions your users read), leave enough space between lines of text so users can easily identify one line from the other, and keep them short (if you can – who am I to judge?).

---

[21] Shorter Lines Facilitate Reading in Those Who Struggle. It's science. Have a look in this link and thank me later: https://journals.plos.org/plosone/article?id=10.1371/journal.pone.0071161

Figure 5-12. *Example of a paragraph layout that could benefit dyslexic users*

You have probably figured out by now that the most important aspect of a website's design for a dyslexic user is visual presentation of text. Letter spacing also helps to make the words easier to read and the individual letters easier to identify. Ideally, italics and underlined words should also be avoided, as they can make a copy look cluttered and harder to understand for dyslexic users (Figure 5-13). Instead, bold text would be easier understood. What color the text is, as well as the background it sits on, could also use some tender loving care. Interestingly enough, black text on light background (maybe an off-white background color) is the answer here.[22]

Figure 5-13. *Representation of what text would be easier for a dyslexic user to understand*

---

[22] A study presented in a 2012 online symposium around text optimization for better readability found just that. Have a look in this link if you're interested in more: www.w3.org/WAI/RD/2012/text-customization/r11

Of course, visual presentation goes beyond how text is presented on the screen. Since dyslexic users might have trouble reading specific words, reinforcing text with icons or illustrations might be a good way to help convey meaning, where some words might be hard to understand. Some users with dyslexia will have issues with light sensitivity, so avoiding bold and bright colors might be a good design choice as well. All in all, if a website allows for customization of how things look (e.g., font size or color attributes), this could help lower the cognitive load[23] needed to understand the information presented.

Designing for Users with Autism

"Keep it even simpler."

Autism is a word used to describe a spectrum of developmental disorders (indeed, the clinical term is autism spectrum disorder, or ASD). Currently, it's not exactly known what causes it, although research points to a combination of different causes, like abnormalities in brain function, genetics, complications at birth, and environmental influences.[24]

It is important to consider that autistic people are not ill, just wired differently. They can still live a perfectly normal life, but they can face challenges along the way, such as trouble communicating and interacting with others and increased sensitivity to light and sounds. In contrast, they

---

[23] Cognitive load has to do with a human's working memory capacity, where working memory is simply the retention of bits of information so you can do different things efficiently. It helps with reasoning and problem-solving, and some users with dyslexia might have trouble retaining information for longer periods of time. So the less they have to deal with, the better. You can find out more about working memory here:
https://doi.org/10.1007/s10648-013-9246-y. But not right now. Now you're reading something else.

[24] www.cdc.gov/ncbddd/autism/facts.html

can also have what others might call superpowers, like remembering more information for longer or excelling in fields such as math or art with a quite disturbing ease.

One challenge they don't necessarily have to face is browsing the Web (this should be made easy for everybody, as mentioned multiple times already; it's not rocket science). Considering autism is not as uncommon as we may like to think (about 1 in 100[25] – on a population level, that's a lot of people), some of your users might be facing online barriers due to autism. Generally, these would be around heightened sensitivity to different elements on a screen, such as movement, light, or sound. Due to this, to cater for autistic users, our canvas would need to be as simple and clear as possible.

Simple layouts are a winner for users with autism. In the example in Figure 5-14, on the left we can see a complicated layout with text overlapping an image making the content harder to read. Complicated shapes can also be overwhelming for autistic users. On the right the design is simplified. The heading doesn't fall on top of an image and has a consistent color. The color of the button has also changed to something less bold, while the navigation has also been simplified. Obviously, take all this with a pinch of salt; what you design will always be dictated by what your audience needs.

---

[25] www.who.int/en/news-room/fact-sheets/detail/autism-spectrum-disorders

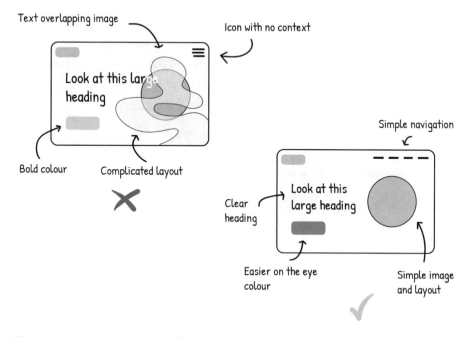

Figure 5-14. *Two example web page layouts that present potential issues for an autistic user (left) and how to overcome them (right)*

Because ASD is quite common, there have been numerous studies around how to design for autistic users, basically telling us what we need to do. To begin with, a simple, consistent, and uncluttered layout is very important for users with autism, as it can reduce overload of information, making autistic users able to process what they're looking at more efficiently.[26] Images and graphics should, ideally, be as simple as possible and not overlaid with text or be used as backgrounds, as this can interfere with content comprehension. It would be even more beneficial if all the images actually served a purpose, like reinforcing what's been said within any copy presented. An example is presented in Figure 5-15, where an

---

[26] Usability Testing with People on the Autism Spectrum: What to Expect, www.uxmatters.com/mt/archives/2015/10/usability-testing-with-people-on-the-autism-spectrum-what-to-expect.php

icon next to a piece of text reinforces what the text is about, which can help autistic users (as well as others) make sense of what's presented to them easier. In the following example, an icon of a car is placed before a paragraph that has to do with cars. Seeing the car icon first enables the user to understand what the text is about just at a glance.

Figure 5-15. *Representation of an icon reinforcing hypothetical content*

Similar to what needs to be done for anxious users, clear-to-read sans-serif fonts are the obvious choice here, as well as lots of whitespace to allow for easier identification of the different sections of a website. Aside from the use of font, what's actually within the copy can make tons of difference between a happy and a frustrated autistic user. Easy-to-understand copy with no complicated language, simple sentences, and descriptive buttons that remove ambiguity would be preferable. Reducing wordiness and creating simple chunks of text would actually benefit everybody as there is this thing called TL;DR (Internet slang for too long; didn't read – basically ignoring long paragraphs of text because they are... long).

Summary

I didn't tell you what to do.

All this is in no way an exhaustive list of what needs to be done in order to design and develop a website that is accessible to as many as possible. In the following chapters, the WCAG 2.1 and 2.2 criteria for web accessibility conformance will be laid out thoroughly (debatable) along with practical examples of how elements should look according to the guidelines and what that means for specific users. You got, however, a good idea of what problems some users might be facing and some quick things you can do to help them. Hopefully, you will have already thought of (and be implementing) the majority of these. Now, you might be wondering, "Did I need to know about all that to design a website or any kind of digital product? I'm doing my job just fine." Well, yes and no. This brings me to my original question of: "Does it matter?"

Yes, because you can't have a solution to a problem unless you know what the problem is. In this case, the problem is the diversity of users who will use your product. Since many of them will be facing specific challenges, you need to know what these challenges are in order to overcome them. You don't necessarily need to know the types of deafness, but you need to be aware of deaf users' issues in order to design and develop something that eliminates, to a possible degree, those barriers.

No, because you don't really need to know how many color-blind people there are in the UK (especially if you live in a different country) or any other kind of statistic in order to be a more thoughtful designer. You will probably never design something that has such low contrast that you can't read content, and you will probably never design something that's cluttered, monotone, and unstructured. You don't need to know what deafness is (or any other type of disability) to design something that looks good and works at the same time, as long as you know your audience. More on that later down the pages.

Look at you. You're already designing accessible websites. Who would've thought? Are they accessible enough, though?

## CHAPTER 6

How Do I Know I'm Doing It Right?

There are various ways to "measure" web accessibility (Figure 6-1). I've put the word "measure" in quotes (I've done it again) to indicate that even though it's something kind of measurable, it's not exactly a straightforward process, especially if you don't do a thorough job since there are a lot of components to think about. A more appropriate phrase could potentially be "testing for a degree of web accessibility or to see how accessible a website is for different users."

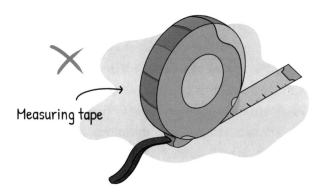

Measuring tape

Figure 6-1. *No, a measuring tape is not the right way to measure web accessibility. This is used to measure other stuff, like furniture or how big a room is*

D. Georgakas, *A11Y Unraveled*, https://doi.org/10.1007/978-1-4842-9085-9_6

Automated Web Accessibility Testing

The first approach to give you an indication if you're on the right path would be to conduct a web accessibility audit by using automated software. There are a lot of tools out there, and some of them are installed as a browser extension that returns the results of the audit on a page that shows specifically which elements have failed accessibility checks, such as color contrast or page structure.

These tools will scan your website looking for something that's not in line with the web accessibility guidelines. They will give you an idea of what's wrong and even give you suggestions on what to change and where. Automated tools like that can be quite handy, especially if you need to go through a lot of pages; checking for a specific issue over potentially hundreds of documents can be quite tedious and mentally tiring (if you're a weirdo like me, though, you'll probably go through all the pages and do it manually trying to have some kind of control over the process).

Be that as it may, nothing comes without drawbacks. As practical and easy to use these tools are, they will never give you a complete overview of all the things that might be wrong with your product in terms of accessibility, and they will always lack the context that comes with a human user's experience. They will never check for things that only a user can look for and determine if they're accessible, such as image descriptions, keyboard traps, caption links, or how easy the content is to understand. These are important limitations, so a thorough web accessibility audit can only be done if it also includes manual checking – most importantly, manual checking from people with actual disabilities (if possible), so they can check if the barriers they are facing can be overcome. Regardless, these tools are a great start.

My personal preference when it comes to an automated tool is Google's Lighthouse, which, unlike others, gives you an actual score so you can have at least some quantitative information that makes sense. It's open source, and its main purpose is to help toward better-quality websites.

I'm sure that most of you probably know of it, but for the sake of revising information, you can access it on Google Chrome by right-clicking anywhere on a page, selecting Inspect, and then clicking Lighthouse, it's one of the last menu items on the right, as depicted in Figure 6-2. From there you can select a number of audits, like performance, SEO, and so on.[1]

Figure 6-2. *Graphical representation of how to access the Lighthouse tool on the Chrome browser*

Yes, it would be easier, and probably clearer, to have actually screenshots, but what's the fun in that? This is far more entertaining and will (maybe) make you think a bit more, adding to your decision-making skills (last sentence courtesy of the blagging designers have to do sometimes to make a point; you know you're doing it).

What this accessibility check does is making sure that a page can be navigated with a keyboard or a screen reader (whether that navigation is logical or not would require manual testing, so decision making is another

---

[1]Lighthouse tool information, https://developers.google.com/web/tools/lighthouse

skill that is good to have) and that all the page's elements are correctly marked up. After that, it determines if the text elements on a page have sufficient contrast ratio, which the W3C has set in order for a web page to be considered accessible.

That's what the AA and AAA levels are essentially, a grade on a set of techniques and how well these techniques are incorporated. So, for example, to get an AA level, you need a contrast ratio of 4.5:1 between text and its background, according to WCAG 2.[2] That was later revised with WCAG 2.1, which also requires a contrast ratio of 3:1 for UI components.[3] That's obviously because text needs to be read, so we need a higher contrast ratio, while UI components don't need to be; however, they do need to be designed in a way that they're easily identifiable. Google uses a set of factors,[4] whose number has changed throughout different versions of the tool, to determine the accessibility score. These factors span from button labeling and color contrast to video captions and ARIA attributes.

Those factors also have weights assigned to them, depending on how important or not they are in a website's accessibility score, so the larger the weight, the more it contributes to the overall score. As mentioned on Google's website, this score can fluctuate due to a variety of factors, such as Internet speed, any A/B testing[5] that might change attributes on a page, testing on different devices that might show different performances, browser extensions, and even antivirus software. For the record,

---

[2] Some additional information about the WCAG can be found here: www.w3.org/WAI/WCAG21/quickref

[3] Understanding Success Criterion 1.4.11: Non-text Contrast, www.w3.org/WAI/WCAG21/Understanding/non-text-contrast.html

[4] A bit more reading for you about Google's scoring system: https://web.dev/accessibility-scoring/

[5] An A/B testing is basically a randomized experiment using two versions of a page (the A and the B), trying to see which performs better and then figuring out what helped one page perform better than the other, based on the characteristics of each page and what was different on each one.

Wikipedia's homepage has an accessibility score of 91 (at the moment these lines were written), which is not bad (it fails on ARIA attributes; isn't that a coincidence?). For random internal pages, the accessibility score spans from 90 to 95. Perhaps that's expected to be a bit higher since these pages are far more important because that's where all the information lies. Personally, I've only gone to Wikipedia's homepage to check its accessibility score. Usually, you'd land on an internal page after you've done an online search and clicked the appropriate result. Plus, it's quite ugly, although quite accessible.

As a quiz and before you go forward, can you guess which is number one in the list of important accessibility factors? Or the first three? I bet the answer will surprise you! It did surprise *me*, but then again, I get excited very easily from the tiniest things, so I might not be the perfect audience. If you can't guess at what position the supreme and paramount color contrast is, I'll give you a hint: it's not even in the top five.

Web Accessibility Factors That Google Uses in Their Lighthouse Tool

Some say color is the most important aspect of web accessibility, but is it, really?

Well, yes, it is. But maybe it's not.

As always, it depends.

There are 42 factors that the Lighthouse accessibility tool considers (updated September 7, 2022), ranging from button names to the alt text of an image.[6] Let's see which ones they are and what designers can or cannot

---

[6] Alt text, or alt description, refers to a written text that appears instead of the image, whenever the image fails to load on a user's screen. This is actually really useful, since this text will be read by screen readers, which will help users who are visually impaired to know what the image is about, and also, search engines use it to better rank and crawl a website.

do about them. Right at this moment, you might be wishing for a skip link on a printed book since this is an extensive list with even more extensive definitions. The existence of a skip link is also one of these accessibility factors, so if you're interested in knowing more, bear with me and keep on reading. Otherwise, to return back to sanity, please use this manual skip link and go to section "Manual Web Accessibility Testing".

Table 6-1 lists some of the chaos we'll be trying to sort out, spanning on a few pages.

Table 6-1. *Factors that Google's Lighthouse tool uses to determine a web accessibility score*

Audit	Weight
[accesskey] values are not unique.	3
The page does not contain a heading, skip link, or landmark region.	3
Headings skip levels.	3
Some elements have a [tabindex] value greater than 0.	3
Document doesn't have a <title> element.	3
Form fields have multiple labels.	3
<frame> or <iframe> elements do not have a title.	3
Links do not have a discernible name.	3
<object> elements do not have [alt] text.	3
Background and foreground colors do not have a sufficient contrast ratio.	3
<dl>s do not contain only properly ordered <dt> and <dd> groups, <script>, or <template> elements.	3
Definition list items are not wrapped in <dl> elements.	3
Lists do not contain only <li> elements and script-supporting elements (<script> and <template>).	3

(continued)

Table 6-1. (*continued*)

Audit	Weight
List items (<li>) are not contained within <ul> or <ol> parent elements.	3
Presentational <table> elements do not avoid using <th>, <caption>, or the [summary] attribute.	3
Cells in a <table> element that use the [headers] attribute refer to an element ID not found within the same table.	3
<th> elements and elements with [role="columnheader"/"rowheader"] do not have data cells they describe.	3
<html> element does not have a [lang] attribute.	3
<html> element does not have a valid value for its [lang] attribute.	3
[lang] attributes do not have a valid value.	3
[id] attributes on active, focusable elements are not unique.	10
[aria-*] attributes do not match their roles.	10
[aria-hidden="true"] is present on the document <body>.	10
[aria-hidden="true"] elements contain focusable descendants.	10
Not all ARIA input fields have accessible names.	10
[role]s do not have all required [aria-*] attributes.	10
Elements with an ARIA [role] that require children to contain a specific [role] are missing some or all of those required children.	10
[role]s are not contained by their required parent element.	10
[role] values are not valid.	10
Not all ARIA toggle fields have accessible names.	10
[aria-*] attributes do not have valid values.	10

(*continued*)

Table 6-1. (*continued*)

Audit	Weight
[aria-*] attributes are not valid or misspelled.	10
ARIA IDs are not all unique.	10
Buttons do not have an accessible name.	10
Image elements do not have [alt] attributes.	10
<input type="image"> elements do not have [alt] text.	10
Form elements do not have associated labels.	10
The document uses <meta http-equiv="refresh">.	10
[user-scalable="no"] is used in the <meta name="viewport"> element, or the [maximum-scale] attribute is less than 5.	10
<audio> elements are missing a <track> element with [kind="captions"].	10
<video> elements do not contain a <track> element with [kind="captions"].	10
<video> elements do not contain a <track> element with [kind="description"].	10

That was a long one. If you're confused or don't recognize some of the terms in the preceding table, do not be afraid; you are not alone. In fact, most of these audits are requirements that need to be implemented at a web development level. The first one, for example, the "[accesskey] values are not unique" audit, checks if the accesskey attribute is present. The HTML code would be something like

```
<element accesskey="character">
```

or, for example, `<button accesskey="b">Call to action</button>`

In simple terms, the accesskey attribute is added to an element to specify a keyboard shortcut that can be used to focus on that element. The value of the attribute needs to be only one letter, and it can be accessed by not pressing that specific character but rather a combination of keys on the keyboard, such as Alt + attribute value, for example, Alt + B.

If you are one of the lucky, or unlucky, ones to have a Mac device and use Safari to access the Web, then this keyboard combination becomes the amazingly easy control + option + shift + attribute value. At this point I would like you to take a moment to consider how this is making your life easier (Mac's superlong and complicated shortcuts are also something that could use a book on its own).

There are also a few more concerns surrounding the accesskey attribute, which of course show why its presence has such small weight in the overall accessibility scoring.[7] One concern is that the value of the attribute can easily be similar to a system, browser, or assistive technology shortcut, which would probably create even more confusion. Another concern is that specific values might not be present in specific keyboards. However, the most important issue in this case is how you actually inform a user that accesskeys are present and that they can use this functionality.

This leads us to ask the question again: does this accessibility practice matter? As always, it depends on the case and your users. Obviously, it was developed for a reason. Many web developers choose to ignore this functionality completely, mainly for reasons of browser compatibility; however, in some cases, for example, where a repeated process might be needed, it can be quite beneficial since all you have to do is press a key. Or two keys. Or three or four keys if you're on a Mac.

Other items from the table might be as unknown to you as to many other designers out there. Another one that catches our attention is the tabindex attribute. This one also needs to be implemented by developers

---

[7] Learn more about the accesskey attribute in this link: https://webaim.org/techniques/keyboard/accesskey

as it is used to manage focus on interactive elements, and that might seem like a good thing, but if this attribute is used improperly, it can actually have detrimental effects to usability when a user is navigating with a keyboard.

A focus state is how an element will appear when a user navigates on a web page with their keyboard by pressing the *"Tab"* key. For example, you might have noticed that when you're on a web page and you press that button on your keyboard, an element appears highlighted and, as you keep pressing *"Tab,"* more elements get highlighted, indicating that they are selected and that they can be interacted with.

The way the highlight appears is the focus state and browsers by default have a specific styling for it. When using the tabindex attribute, you can manage how that focus state is handled. It can have a negative value, a value of zero, or a positive value.

A tabindex value of 0 just inserts the element in the tab order based on where it is in the website's code. The syntax is like this:

```
<span role="button" tabindex="0">
  Lorem Ipsum
</span>
```

That's not always necessary as elements that need to be interacted with, such as a button, a link, or form controls, receive focus by default. When a custom element or a custom widget is created, though, then it might be more appropriate to use it.

As mentioned, the tabindex attribute can also receive a value of "-1", which basically removes it from the tab order (meaning you can't focus on it by tabbing). The most dangerous thing you could do, on the other hand, is give the tabindex a positive value. That is because elements already have a sequential order depending on where they are in the source code and users who navigate with a keyboard expect these elements to be focused on a specific order. By giving an element a tabindex value of 1, you're essentially telling the keyboard to skip all the other focusable elements and go straight to that one. Not very handy, if you ask me. Again, there might be some value to it in custom widgets.

So what is the benefit of using tabindex? Well, it depends on the application (let me know when you'll get tired of reading "it depends"). If it's not there, most websites shouldn't be affected negatively as calls to action that need to be interacted with already are focusable elements by default.

Generally, though, consider this: if something doesn't affect something else negatively, does it then need to be removed? Maybe not, since it probably doesn't do any harm. But if something doesn't affect something else negatively, it doesn't mean it affects it positively, which brings up the question: if its presence is insignificant, does it really need to be there?

Automated tools are such a delight. They do the work for you, point out any errors or things you might need to check, and make your lives easier. But they're not perfect. According to an article from essentialaccessibility. com, automated scans can only pick up about 20–25% of accessibility issues (when checking for AA criteria), leaving the remaining 80% undetected.[8] KMA Global takes this even further by stating that automated tools can test about 30% of the WCAG 2.0 criteria and 0% (!) of WCAG 2.1.[9] Hope is on the horizon though, as Deque Systems,[10] a US company that deals with compliance issues, claims their automated tools can identify 57% of any accessibility issues, much more than 25–30% and much more than 0%.

Whatever the percentage, this goes to show that automated checks are not enough. They're a good start to identify issues such as color contrast, improper code, and document structure but fail to account for things such as keyboard navigation, logical order, or even how exactly a document might be presented to a screen reader user.

---

[8] www.essentialaccessibility.com/blog/automated-accessibility-testing-tools-how-much-do-scans-catch

[9] https://kma.global/wp-content/uploads/2019/07/WCAG_2.1_Checklist.pdf

[10] www.deque.com/

Manual Web Accessibility Testing

Imagine a scenario where you have to decide if an image's alt text is good enough. If the image shows a person holding a candle and the alt text reads "candle holding a person," when checked with an accessibility tool, it will get a pass mark, because the alt text is there. However, the tool doesn't know if this image is decorative, in which case, an empty alt attribute would be enough (so *alt=""*), or if the description is actually accurate. That's where a human checker needs to intervene and decide if this is a failure or a pass of web accessibility guidelines (you will never beat us, robots!).

Figure 6-3. *Random hypothetical website with a picture of a stickman holding a birthday cake*

If the alt description for Figure 6-3 stated "Lonely birthday cake holding a person while singing happy birthday," this would be totally correct in the "eyes" of an automated tool that checks for web accessibility issues.

In the case of an accessibility audit from an actual person, this would have to be put down as a failure, because even though there is an alt description for this image, it is inaccurate and would create confusion to a user relying on this.

Catching very specific issues that might burden users can only be achieved by someone going through processes such as browsing a website by using a screen reader and making sure everything is picked up properly and read aloud correctly; even lowering a screen's brightness, muting the speakers, and seeing how content is understood all allow for a chance to review a website from an actual user's perspective.

Test Keyboard Navigation

WCAG 2.2 brings nine more criteria compared with WCAG 2.1. It's not a massive change, so basic principles of testing for web accessibility remain. Pressing the Tab key on a keyboard and seeing what happens ensures a website can be navigated using a keyboard. Using keyboard navigation, you can also see if there are any keyboard traps, cases where you use the keyboard to open, for example, a hidden menu and you can't get out of it. This will also allow you to check for the existence of a "skip link" that would allow users to go directly into the main content or different sections of a web page without having to press Tab on their keyboard 124 times, trying to move through a really long navigation list. Testing keyboard navigation will also reveal if focus states are there and if they are visible enough for a user to distinguish.

If you can't Tab through a website, go back to the drawing board, make sure keyboard navigation is supported and works correctly, and then check for everything else.

Use a Screen Reader

If you are a bit more advanced, you can always use a screen reader software. This will enable you to get a better understanding of how accessible a website is for users who are blind or visually impaired (you can lower your screen's brightness for an even more accurate experience). Successfully completing a task using a keyboard and a screen reader only can be a major task for disabled users, so if you're manually auditing a web page or whole website, it is a chance to see if everything is working as it should be. Assign yourself a certain task and see how easily or not you can complete it. Hats off to people using a screen reader. The first time I tried it, it took me over 45 minutes just to click a specific button, using screen reader software on a Mac. That experience was definitely an eye-opener.

Check for the Basics

Remember to always stick to the basics when it comes to testing how accessible a design is. Look for any forms and see if they have clear and explicit labels in their fields (and if they don't, look for ARIA labels; they might be there). Test the form to see if it works correctly and if any errors are clearly identified and easily understood. Keyboard navigation must also be supported so a user must be able to use a form from beginning to end by using a keyboard only.

Check your color contrast. The WCAG have very specific requirements when it comes to contrast ratios between text and its background, user interface elements and their background, and so on. To be fair, if you've done that already during designing that thing, you shouldn't even have to check for that. But if you're checking someone else's work, then it would be a great idea to start looking for those nasty pale-gray texts that ~~I like to~~ some ~~awful~~ inexperienced designers like to put in their canvas.

Check the Content

- Are all links descriptive? A visually impaired user navigating with a keyboard would much rather have their software say, "See all jobs available in Kentucky" than "Read more." Can you see any generic "Click here" or "Read more" links? If yes, flag them, as ideally these would need to be descriptive and understood regardless of context around them.

- Do all images have (at least the ones that need it) a descriptive alternative text that makes sense? You can even disable all images to get a better idea of their role in understanding the content.

- Are headings descriptive and in order (if needed), and does the structure make sense? If a heading is there and reads "How to bake a cake with no ingredients" and the copy below it reads about space exploration, then that's clearly a failure.

- Can you understand what's written, and is the language plain enough (unless that's not the purpose of the website) so all users can understand what is in front of them?

- Do all pages have unique and descriptive titles? If someone uses a screen reader and every page they go to is announced as a company's name, it would be a bit more difficult for them to understand where they're at.

- Check that videos have descriptions and captions. You can also watch/listen to them, making sure the audio is clear enough.

- Zoom in to 200% and see if the content remains clear and distinguishable. Is the navigation still there and easy to access? Does any content overlap, and do you have to scroll horizontally to see content? If yes, that's a failure, once more.

- Disable all CSS and see what happens. If you can still understand and use the page in front of you, great! If not, not so good.

- Is the content still the same, does it work the same, and is it understood the same if you try and view it on different devices?

Testing with the Help of Real Users

No tool and no single person can test a website like users would. We often forget that we are not the typical users nor the experts. Looking into a web page way too often usually will cloud our judgement and could make us miss obvious problems. That's where real users with no bias need to come in to ensure that what we have made serves its purpose. In the case of web accessibility, the help of impaired users is definitely key toward the right direction. Create tasks for them and see how easy it is to complete them. They'll be able to give you all the feedback you need and reveal pain points you didn't even know existed.

These manual tests are in no way an exhaustive list of what you could be doing. But it would be enough to get you started in testing (and ultimately understanding) if a page has the basics that are needed for a good level of web accessibility. The more you do it, the more you'll be able to spot the problem straight away. It took me about 2 weeks doing my first accessibility audit, and I must have filled about 50 pages full of issues. It's a learning process that sometimes can seem daunting, but remember to think of the end goal: the benefit of your users.

"Oh, Wait. Who Is This ARIA You Spoke Of?"

Only a few pages in and we're already overwhelmed by acronyms; isn't the Web great? I'm not a developer, and this will be my puny attempt to present a few generic information about what ARIA is and how it's used. It's an integral part of web accessibility, and there is a ton of information out there should you need to read more on the subject. ARIA stands for Accessible Rich Internet Applications, and it is part of the Web Accessibility Initiative, which features strategies that have been developed by the W3C in order to make the Web more accessible.[11] The first concept came to be around 2008, and by 2014 it was published as a recommendation by the W3C, at which point it became a web standard.[12]

They are primarily, again, for web developers (that does not mean that web accessibility is only a developer's job, as it's a bit of everything: UX, design, code, testing, etc.) who need to make sure elements have the proper ARIA labels, as they're called. Think of it as add-on code on top of standard HTML that helps identify different elements so that assistive technologies can pick these up and help the user browse and navigate the web page they're on. It's not magic, and it definitely doesn't change the appearance of different elements on a web page. Instead, it's a way for different elements to appear as… something else for users who need assistive technologies. For example, think about the close button in a modal window, as shown in Figure 6-4.

A modal window sits on top of every other element, and you can't use any of them unless you get rid of the modal, which can get quite tricky if you're trying to be fully accessible. Modals do provide focus on something

---

[11] Michael Cooper, WAI-ARIA Overview, `www.w3.org/WAI/standards-guidelines/aria/`, accessed November 5, 2020

[12] `www.lullabot.com/articles/what-heck-aria-beginners-guide-aria-accessibility`

specific, but think carefully about whether you really need them (also, adding the word "close" next to the close icon can help give even more context to what that button does).

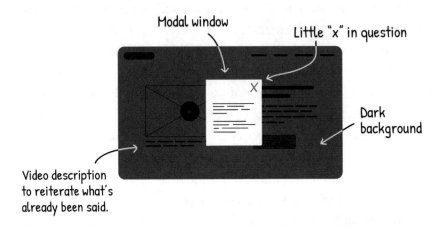

Figure 6-4. *Illustrative example of a modal on a random website*

There's nothing to indicate to a screen reader that the round circle with that little X in the middle is used to close that dialog, so an aria-label attribute needs to be added to the X, which effectively names the button, which is one of the requirements in a Google audit. This is basically hidden text that doesn't appear on the screen but lets the screen reader know what that element does, for instance:

```
<div id="box">
    This is a modal box.
    <button aria-label="Close" onclick="document.
    getElementById('box').style.display='none';"
        class="close-button">X</button>
</div>
```

ARIA uses three main components: roles, states, and properties. Roles refer to defining an element on a user interface (UI) by giving it an appropriate name with

`role="name_of_role"`

ARIA Roles

Document structure roles are a category of roles that assistive technologies will use to recognize what content the user is going through, so they can provide them with some context as to what they're actually doing and what content they're looking at.[13] In some cases, this technology can already be integrated within a browser, so in that case, ARIA labeling is not needed. However, just to make sure we cover all of our bases, it might be a good idea to use both.

Landmark roles, another category of this component, are mainly used for easier navigation. Each section of a web page (e.g., the header, main content, footer, etc.) is being specifically defined as such by assigning a role to it. Aside from the five roles depicted in Figure 6-5, there are also a "search," "form," and "application" role. A screen reader will pick up these roles and will announce for the user the start and end of each one on a page, as the user navigates through it.[14]

---

[13] www.w3.org/TR/wai-aria/#document_structure_roles
[14] www.w3.org/TR/wai-aria/#landmark_roles

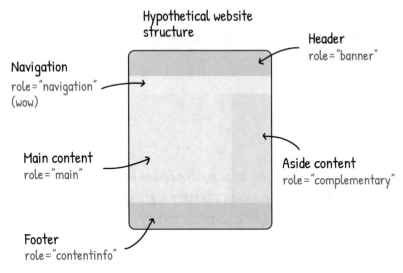

Figure 6-5. *Landmarks on a hypothetical, beautifully designed, website structure*

ARIA States and Properties

States and properties usually go together and support any other ARIA roles that might already exist on a web page. There are four categories of states and properties:

1. Drag-and-drop attributes[15] (you guessed it) are used for drag-and-drop elements, for example:

    aria-grabbed="true"

2. Live regions attributes[16] are used by assistive technologies to inform a user about what's happening on a page by announcing any changes. If you have ever used a screen reader and after

---

[15] www.w3.org/TR/wai-aria/#attrs_dragdrop
[16] www.w3.org/TR/wai-aria/#attrs_liveregions

submitting a form you got an out-loud notification message saying something like "Your message has been sent," this is because of a proper use of a live regions attribute.

3.   Relationship attributes add a relationship between different elements so the user can understand when information on a page is related.

4.   Widget attributes are used on user interface elements that require some sort of input and processing of user actions.[17]

That's all nice and pretty, but do we really need to use all that? Well, *designers* don't, but developers, ideally, need to be aware and able to implement ARIA labels where necessary. Still, the truth is that most browsers (except for ~~the one that shall not be named~~ Internet Explorer) have a native support for HTML5 accessibility features. In fact, according to html5accessibility.com (Figure 6-6), Edge (who would've thought?) has 100% support for any accessibility-related features (as of June 24, 2021).[18] Chrome wins the silver medal by a very small margin (98.5%), followed by Safari (97%). Firefox completes the team of the four major browsers with 94% support. So when and why do we need to use ARIA labels? Does this amazingly high percentage of native support for accessibility features mean that ARIA is something we need to know about but never use? Not exactly.

---

[17] www.w3.org/TR/wai-aria/#attrs_widgets
[18] www.html5accessibility.com/

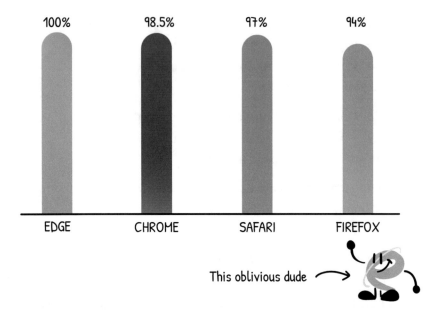

Figure 6-6. *HTML5 accessibility features browser compatibility. For some reason Microsoft Edge is in the lead, and for another equally mysterious reason, Internet Explorer is not even in the list*

There are a few things that need to be considered before an HTML feature is regarded as accessible. Accessibility supported means that a given browser must support that feature, recognize it, and render it properly as expected. And even though there is accessibility support for a lot of features in HTML5, there are still too many ARIA roles and properties not supported (as in, there are no native elements in HTML5 that are accessible by default). These include roles such as "alert," "marquee," "scrollbar," "menubar," "region," and "search", to name a few. On the other hand, we don't always have to use ARIA. The W3C was kind enough to have created a list of five rules for when to use it, but more specifically, when *not* to use ARIA.

The First Rule of ARIA

Similarly to the first rule of *Fight Club*, the first rule of ARIA use is we don't have to use it all the time. If we can use native HTML elements, then we should do so. When in doubt, ~~C4~~[19] HTML, as they say. Of course, if a feature is not available, we cannot use it by default. On top of that, this doesn't apply to circumstances when the design is such that rules out a specific native element that can't be styled the way we want to. In that case, design the masterpiece you have in mind and then give it a proper ARIA label so it can be recognized as one.

With that being said, there is one case where an ARIA label might be more beneficial than native HTML. A UX engineer named Sandrina Pereira identified an issue when it comes to using native HTML with disabled buttons.[20] Normally, a disabled button would be coded like this:

```
<button type="submit" disabled="disabled">
  Pretty text label on button
</button>
```

(You can also have just disabled as an attribute, since it's a Boolean attribute, meaning it can be one or the other).

When someone that uses a keyboard to navigate tries to focus on that button, that would be impossible as because of the "disabled" attribute, the button will be skipped. But what's the harm in that if it's disabled? The problem comes from the fact that even disabled buttons might have some information associated with them, as they are disabled for a reason. For example, a "Submit" button might be disabled until all form fields are completed, or an "Add to cart" button might be disabled until the

---

[19] I need to stop the *MythBusters* references. If you don't know about that show, please put the book down and educate yourself (kindly requested). After that, please pick this book back up.

[20] https://css-tricks.com/making-disabled-buttons-more-inclusive/

quantity of a product is selected. By skipping the button, users might not understand why that element can't be clicked, as an interaction with it would provide feedback, perhaps in the form of a tooltip along the lines of "You need to complete all fields to submit" or "You need to select quantity to continue." If you're using the keyboard, you will never see that extra information that will clarify what's happening.

The disabled attribute *aria-disabled="true"* will solve this problem, as the button would now be focusable, and the little tooltip would appear. In addition, the actual click on that button would need to be prevented by using JavaScript until all requirements are met. All in all, this could potentially make the life of a keyboard user easier with less friction in their experience. Thank you, Sandrina!

The Second Rule of ARIA

The second rule of ARIA states that we should not change native HTML unless absolutely necessary. For example, we wouldn't assign a tab role directly to a, let's say, H3, as this would change the tag. Instead, we should add role=tab to a div that surrounds the H3 tag. Something like this:

No no no.

<h3 role=tab>I am a marvellous heading</h3>

Yes yes yes.

<div role=tab><h3>I am a marvellous heading</h3></div>

The Third Rule of ARIA

The third rule of ARIA is about how a user uses a keyboard for interactive elements. If something is interactive, all the controls associated with the functionality must be usable with a keyboard as well. If there is a slider on a web page that slides left to right by scrolling, tapping, holding, sliding, or in any way possible, this kind of action must also be done with a keyboard.

The Fourth Rule of ARIA

The fourth rule of ARIA states that any elements that receive focus must *not* have *role="presentation" or aria-hidden="true"* as this might result in users ultimately focusing on nothing, which of course might create confusion.

The Fifth Rule of ARIA

The fifth and last rule of ARIA says that all interactive elements need to have an accessible name, which is pretty much the name of that element on a user interface. If there is a button on a page and that button has the name "Fred" assigned to it, when the element becomes focusable, the assistive technologies will pick that name up, and a screen reader will say something along the lines of "Push button Fred."

Are Designers Involved Anywhere in This?

We can assume that all the preceding factors and the weights assigned to them show some kind of hierarchy as to which ones are more important than others. Out of the preceding accessibility audits, only a handful of them are associated with something that a web designer can help with (as in, if they're not doing any coding, strictly visual design speaking). That doesn't mean there aren't any other areas that designers are involved in. This is specifically about the audits Google uses to rank a website's accessibility level. The first audit that web designs can have an input in is the headings skip levels.

You might have heard or read that every website, or digital document for that matter, should follow a hierarchy when it comes to heading levels. This means that we start with the most important heading, the H1, and continue down to H2, H3, and so on (Figure 6-7). Skipping a level in this case would mean a H2 is followed by a H4. In other words, headings don't follow a logical order. Practically, and with the W3C's blessings, if the overall document structure makes logical sense, skip away and mix them up.

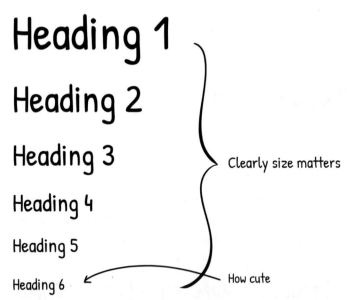

Figure 6-7. *Order of headings that should, ideally, be followed within a design*

Headings help organize your content. In this sense, a well-placed heading structure will make it easier for the users to scan your content and understand it without putting in too much effort, in theory. On the other hand, when we talk about accessibility, properly structured headings mean that a user using assistive technology to browse around your website will do so in an easy way. Headings from H1 to H6 show where a section on a web page starts, and they have been around pretty much since the birth of HTML. Despite that, though, there is still some confusion as to what exactly constitutes an accessibility failure and what doesn't.

Unless you're going for an AAA level of WCAG conformance, even a complete lack of headings doesn't mean that your content won't be accessible. Success Criterion 2.4.6: Headings and Labels states: "This Success Criterion does not require headings or labels. This Success Criterion requires that *if* headings or labels *are* provided, they should be descriptive."[21] Similarly, Success Criterion 2.4.10: Section Headings doesn't even require the use of headings to organize content,[22] which does make this feel wrong. However, the experts have spoken, and this is not a failure of the WCAG.

Even the absence of a H1, which most designers, developers, and people in marketing would argue that not having one is a big mistake (and it probably is, but that's for another entire book on its own again), doesn't constitute a failure of the WCAG. The opposite is also true. Having more than one H1 still doesn't represent a failure of the WCAG. Skipping heading levels, therefore, does not mean that our content is not accessible. It might mean though that you probably won't be able to convey the information you want in the most usable way (please avoid that whenever you can). The key word here is "might," since unless we test it, we cannot be sure of it.

---

[21] www.w3.org/WAI/WCAG21/Understanding/headings-and-labels.html
[22] www.w3.org/TR/WCAG21/#section-headings

What *will* make you fail accessibility guidelines is the absence of properly marked-up content, for example, heading-like content that isn't marked up as a heading. If a piece of text is used to indicate the start of a section and it looks like a heading, as in it's big and bold, then it needs to be marked up as one.[23]

In addition, you will also fail the WCAG if your headings don't have a logical order. When you first read that, you might think, "Wait a minute. You just told me I can skip heading levels, and now you're telling me I can't." Not exactly. You can skip heading levels, as in a H3 can be followed by a H5. That won't make you fail the WCAG. If, however, the heading levels don't reflect the content's hierarchy, you will have failed the guidelines.

If this seems confusing, here's another way to think about it. You can skip heading levels, but you can't reverse the heading order in content that is grouped together and has a clear hierarchy. A heading in the content that's visually of less importance must also be assigned a heading tag that's lower in the heading hierarchy. In completely simple terms, what that means is you can skip the heading when changing sections. For example, you have a *<h2>* followed by a *<h3>* and then a *<h4>*. That *<h4>* followed by some copy signifies the end of that section, so the next one will start again with a *<h2>*. You're going from heading 4 to heading 2, but that doesn't matter since you are in the beginning of a new section.

If you're lost, you can join the ever-growing group of professionals in the web and digital sector who are lost about these things every single day. The issue with this is that there is no such thing as a "normal" user. The way each and every one of us uses the Web has to do with personal experiences of the past, knowledge, and abilities; our perspective is quite narrow to begin with. I might like red buttons, and you might like green buttons, and that's okay either way. There's no harm in using either. Whether one will be more successful than the other can be proven over an experiment, where we could decide which is the one that works better for

---

[23] www.w3.org/WAI/WCAG21/Understanding/info-and-relationships.html

our purposes. However, when it comes to users with disabilities, people often will navigate from heading to heading, and if the structure isn't hierarchical with no logical order, we might create confusion, and the users might not understand the content.

Despite the fact that headings, ideally, need to follow a specific structure in order for the content to be easier to digest, I decided to put it to the test, for users with no disabilities, in an attempt to strengthen the argument that if your audience doesn't require full accessibility conformance, a few "mishaps" in how content is presented wouldn't make a difference.

A small comprehension experiment was carried out where a couple of brief paragraphs were presented to users and, after a short period of time, they had to answer a few questions about the text to see how well they understood it. According to Nielsen Norman Group (2015), comprehension "measures whether a user can understand the intended meaning of a text and can draw the correct conclusions from the text." So the aim for this was to test whether there was any difference in comprehension based on how the content was presented.

The actual text used was referenced from various online sources, more specifically already credible news websites written by people who know how to present a text in a way that has meaning (unlike the author of this book), so it was assumed that it was written in a way that it was easy to understand anyway. The difference was in how the text was introduced visually.

The users landed on a page with a set of instructions that prepared them for what they had to do. They had to select a category of content based on their familiarity level. No need to mention them, but in the effort of putting even more words in this book, they were art, entertainment, history, economy, and politics. Upon selecting their favorite category, they'd land on the page with the text where everything was set out as a normal website, with an image accompanying the text, a logo of the "company," and a traditional navigation (albeit none of the menu items was usable – it was just there to give the impression of an actual website and to provide a possible distraction).

All elements of the text, such as line height or font size, were displayed according to W3C accessibility guidelines for an AA conformance level. After 10 seconds the user was redirected to a page where they had to answer four questions related to each part of the text – heading, subheading, and main paragraph. Each user would then have a score assigned to them, depending on how many out of the four questions they got right. The minimum they could get was two (zero questions right), and the maximum was ten (all questions answered correctly).

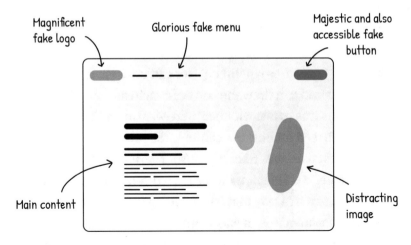

Figure 6-8. *Illustration of the web page given to the control group of the experiment*

As the illustration in Figure 6-8 shows, everything is as one would expect on a typical web page; logo, menu, buttons, and images are all there to "distract" from the main content of the page. In this instance, the content was fully presented according to the WCAG. On that page, a H1 heading is at the top, and the H3 sits below it. Yes, I know. I didn't mention before that a H1 was followed by a H3, which technically skips the H2. But that's fine; it's allowed.

Users were randomly split into four groups, depending on how the text was presented to them. In the control group, the text was presented as someone would expect, starting with a H1 heading, followed by a subheading and then a small paragraph. The second group was the "skip heading" group (catchy and self-explanatory) where the order of the heading and the subheading were reversed (Figure 6-9).

The third group was the "no formatting" (Figure 6-10), where the text was presented as an entire paragraph with, you guessed it, no formatting whatsoever (who would have thought?), so there was no different styling for the heading or the subheading, no bold font weights, or anything similar that would make a particular piece of text to stand out from the rest. All the content was one block of text, following the W3C's guidelines on presentation of text for an AA conformance.

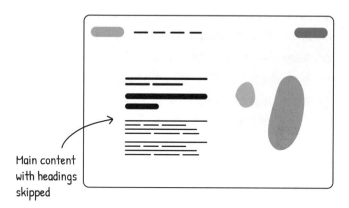

Main content
with headings
skipped

Figure 6-9. *Illustration of the web page given to the skip heading group*

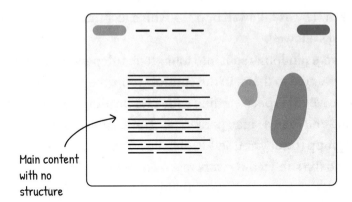

Figure 6-10. *Illustration of the web page that was shown to users of the no formatting group*

The fourth and last group was the "contrast" group (Figure 6-11). This is a bit different than the rest. The text followed the structure of the control group, but the contrast of the content was lowered to something below conformance level. The change wasn't dramatic. Just enough to justify failure. And maybe a little bit more. And a bit more after that.

This was a desperate attempt from myself to finally have some data to justify my design choices, as I love having elements on the canvas slightly less prominent sometimes to achieve the desired aesthetically pleasing result (most of the time, it's only pleasing to me, but please don't judge me).

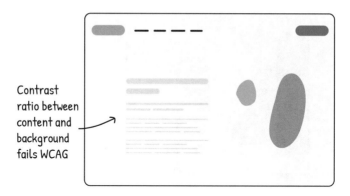

Contrast ratio between content and background fails WCAG

Figure 6-11. *Illustration of a web page that was given to the users of the contrast group*

When it came to skipping headings, the test didn't prove the theory very wrong. Users in the control group averaged a score of 8.1 (±2.68), and the participants in the skip heading group averaged a score of 6.3 (±2.6) (Figure 6-12). This difference might seem a lot; however, following a simple statistical test, it turned out that there isn't a statistically significant difference in the scoring between these two groups, and the hypothesis that the users in the control group would score higher on average than the users in the skip heading group was rejected,[24] meaning that, in this case, heading levels didn't matter when it came to how users understood the content.

---

[24] Data were analyzed using a Mann-Whitney U test.

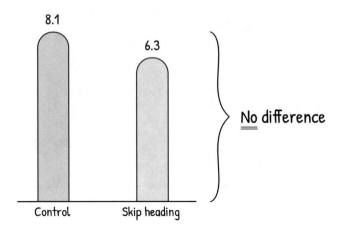

Figure 6-12. *Average comprehension score for the control and the skip heading group for all users*

But, when checking for any differences between age groups in the control group, the results were more than conclusive. Users above 45 years old scored lower (on average) than users below that age, and *that* difference was statistically significant. The control group with the older users had an average score of 5.8 (±3.7), while the younglings scored 9.4 (±2.71) on average. This was replicated in the other groups, with the biggest difference observed between the groups that had the pages with lowered contrast. Older users only scored 4 (±1.7) on average, which was the lowest scoring in the whole experiment, while the younger ones scored 8 (±1.88).

The interesting thing though is that when looking into the results between age groups in the "skip heading" group, no significance difference was observed. In fact, their results were pretty similar (average score of 6.6 (±3.2) for the youths and average score of 6 (±1.7) for the retirees). Skipping headings? Not a big deal. At least for the few people participating in my experiment. Checking web accessibility? A very big deal.

Summary

Knowing if what you're doing works is essential in any field, and not just in web design or when incorporating web accessibility practices. We have seen two ways of checking the level of accessibility of a digital product: an automated testing, using different tools and plugins, which are widely available online, and a manual testing, where a user takes control and checks to see if the practices implemented actually make sense, logically speaking.

Various approaches can be followed to manually test for accessibility issues, such as testing keyboard navigation and making sure that any alternative text makes logical sense and that ARIA labels have been correctly included, following the ARIA rules mentioned.

As designers, we address accessibility issues from the get-go by making sure we follow best practices, such as having a logical structure in our document and a simple and (hopefully) effective layout. Ensuring our designs reflect the needs of our audiences, some of the accessibility practices might not be needed to the highest degree (e.g., contrast requirements). All in all though, it's best to be on the safe side until we can be proven correct. Or not.

CHAPTER 7

Do I Have to Do All These Things?

This is it. This is where the criminals separate from law-abiding citizens.

I'm only joking. It's not that bad. Even though if you were one of the about 2,000 companies that were sued in the USA in 2020 because their websites weren't accessible and because users were finding them frustrating, you'd probably feel differently. Especially if you had to put your hand in your pocket and take some cash out. Target, a retailer company originating from the USA, was sued in 2005 by the US National Federation of the Blind (NFB), over the fact that its website was inaccessible to visually impaired users. Based on whatever we've discussed in the previous chapters, you'd think the little things like an accessible alternative text for images, headings, and keyboard navigation would all be there and working correctly. Alas, Target failed to do even the basics and eventually had to pay 6 million dollars in class damages.[1]

Who's Affected?

Web accessibility lawsuits don't just affect big companies. Considering the great number of users with some form of disability, every business's website could potentially be hindering users from completing a task that

---

[1] www.accessi.org/blog/famous-web-accessibility-lawsuits/

© Dimitris Georgakas 2023
D. Georgakas, *A11Y Unraveled*, https://doi.org/10.1007/978-1-4842-9085-9_7

might affect their everyday lives. Over the past decade, legal cases around web accessibility have increased around the globe, for the most part in the USA. At the end of 2020, there was a 25% increase in web accessibility cases compared with 2019, with over 3,500 companies being sued on simple things such color contrast, proper structure, and alternative text. In 2021, about 75% of these companies were in ecommerce,[2] and that makes sense since it's a way for people to access services and goods. What's even more disturbing is the fact that about a fifth of these companies had been sued in the past about web accessibility issues.[3] You'd think they'd learn.

Different countries have a different legislation that governs the Web and the issue of web accessibility. Most of the legislation focuses on public bodies and private companies implementing the WCAG on their websites.

UK

In the UK, things are simple: whether you are a public or private sector organization, you should follow certain laws around web accessibility, and it is your ethical responsibility to make sure your users' lives are as easy as possible.

For public bodies this is a legal requirement, under accessibility regulations that came into effect in 2018, which state that your website or mobile app needs to conform (to the possible degree) to WCAG 2.1 requirements.[4] These regulations (their official name is The Public Sector Bodies (Websites and Mobile Applications) Accessibility Regulations 2018) are built on requirements under the Equality Act 2010 (or the Disability Discrimination Act 1995 if you're in Northern Ireland).

---

[2] https://info.usablenet.com/

[3] https://littleforest.co.uk/a-summary-of-2020s-web-accessibility-lawsuits/

[4] Go on and have some fun: www.legislation.gov.uk/uksi/2018/852/contents/made

It's worth noting that private businesses don't have a *legal* requirement to make any adjustments to their websites so they can be accessible by people with disabilities. However, given the potentially great number of users who could need your services, it would make sense to design and build accessible content. But, under the Equality Act 2010 or the Disability Discrimination Act 1995, you still have to make "reasonable adjustments"[5] for disabled users if they are required. For example, if you have a company that sells products for disabled people, you are legally expected to have a website that conforms to the WCAG 2.1 AA level.

If your audience does not include disabled users (congratulations if you've managed to pinpoint your exact audience down to the individual, which doesn't include the one in five people who might have a long-term disability in the UK or *all* the people who might face a situational limitation at some point), you should also do something about it, since practices like a readable font or appropriate contrast go a long way to help everybody. If you don't even do the basics, then hell awaits you.

You don't even have to do the basics if there is going to be a disproportionate burden to you by applying these guidelines. This means you don't have to do anything if it's going to be a massive burden for your organization (as long as you can prove it). To be perfectly honest, even if you're a one-man band, there isn't any additional cost to design or develop something the right way. There isn't even any significant extra time required. And if you find that there is, it would definitely be helpful for your users and beneficial for you in any case.

If you're a private business, you can show off your commitment to your users by adhering to the BSI 8878 Web Accessibility Standard, a voluntary standard that separates the ones we point our fingers at from the ones we pat on the back.[6]

---

[5] www.gov.uk/guidance/accessibility-requirements-for-public-sector-websites-and-apps

[6] www.bsigroup.com/LocalFiles/en-GB/consumer-guides/resources/BSI-Consumer-Brochure-Web-Accessibility-UK-EN.pdf

USA

The land of the free has a number of acts around discrimination and web accessibility, but compliance mainly revolves around two acts. The Rehabilitation Act is the first one. Started in 1973,[7] it was the first piece of law that prohibited discrimination against people with disabilities. In 1998, there was a very important amendment that added the right to access to electronic information for people with disabilities. This section (508) was again amended in 2018 to add even more information and bring it in line with technological advancements, which included adding the WCAG as the international recognized standard for website accessibility.[8] However, that section only applies to government bodies, so private organizations wouldn't have to follow it, unless they (you) receive government funds.

If private companies in the USA don't have to follow the preceding legislation, then where would their responsibility of catering for disabled users come from (aside from being ethical)? The Americans with Disabilities Act (ADA)[9] dates back to 1990 and states that no person with disabilities should be discriminated against in "places of public accommodation." Most courts in the country, as well as the US Department of Justice, recognize websites as such.

The problem comes from the fact that this act dates back to 1990 and there is no mention of the WCAG or any other kind of standard that sets out web accessibility guidelines. In this sense, websites need to be accessible, but they're not required to follow any specific standard to do it. Kind of like you need to follow the law, but you know, do whatever (you'd think there would be an amendment for this as well).

---

[7] www.access-board.gov/law/ra.html

[8] www.section508.gov/manage/laws-and-policies/

[9] www.ada.gov/pubs/adastatute08.htm

Despite that, during legal cases WCAG 2.0 and 2.1 are being recognized as the standards for web accessibility, and the companies being sued are required to make necessary adjustments in order to become compliant with these guidelines. If they were going to fine me 6 million dollars, I'd probably comply too.

Greece

What is this legislation thing you're talking about?

Rest of the European Union

(Not a country and doesn't include the whole continent of Europe, for the non-geographically fit of you out there.)

The European Union (EU), thinking it's better than everybody else, has a whole directive dedicated to web accessibility. This came about in 2016 complimenting the European Accessibility Act and clearly lays out the rules for member states to follow, toward accessible websites as well as mobile apps. The directive pretty much follows everything within WCAG 2.1, so if your products conform to that, then it's all good and no prison for you. In addition to the guidelines, a few things are also required, both from public bodies and private companies: to have an accessibility statement for each product and some kind of feedback tool for users to report accessibility issues or to request content that might not be accessible in another way. Constant and regular monitoring is also required (they've covered all their bases), so there's no way you can get away with it. Might as well comply (once more think of the 6 million *dineros* we were talking about before).

Ethics, laws, and all kinds of legislation aside, there really is one reason only as to why you should start making your websites accessible now rather than later. And that's no other than a massive improvement in usability, as in the way your product is used.

Accessibility and usability have the most romantic love affair with one completing the other, one washing away the other's troubles, and one being the reason the other one wakes up every morning.

Summary

Having had a quick glance at legislation around Web Content Accessibility Guidelines, it's clear that if you have an online business, or any kind of website really, chances are you'd have to comply with these guidelines, if you want to be ethical but also out of jail, as well as out of what could be hundreds of pounds in fines. Considering the vast number of users with potential disabilities, it goes without saying that in order to be successful, you need to make the lives of your users easier.

Different countries might have somewhat different requirements when it comes to what you need to do exactly. Generally speaking, complying to the degree that you can with WCAG 2.1 (at least at the moment of writing) would be enough to avoid potential lawsuits and to also get that much needed satisfaction that you've done a good job.

CHAPTER 8

What Is Usability?

Okay, I admit it. This is a subject that with a little bit of Google search (or any search with any search engine as this is a very inclusive book), you can learn a good deal about. You can Google search accessibility as well, or anything really, but then a book is better as you get to focus more, improve your attention span, stimulate your imagination, and have everything in one place, which you can refer back to multiple times, unlike going through a messy search history on your device.

So if you're familiar with the term and what it entails, please use this additional fictional "skip link" to the next chapter. If you're not, this chapter will give you some of the basics of usability, what it is, and how it connects with web accessibility toward an overall great user experience.

Overview

During my professional experience, I've often found that digital designers of any kind, or just web professionals really, like to sound pompous and important, using terms and definitions with long words such as

> *Usability is a measure of how well a specific user in a specific context can use a product/design to achieve a defined goal effectively, efficiently and satisfactorily.*

> —Interaction Design

D. Georgakas, *A11Y Unraveled*, https://doi.org/10.1007/978-1-4842-9085-9_8

or

...usability can only be quantified through indirect measures and is therefore a non-functional requirement...

—Techopedia

That last word (*satisfactorily*) really got me.

To put it in more plain words, usability has to do with how easy it is to use... something. That something is hard to use? Low usability. Is that something easy to use and complete a task? High usability. This high degree of usability doesn't necessarily need to be satisfying to begin with (using this book is fairly easy but might not be as satisfying). If you can get to a point where ease of use is accompanied by pleasant emotions while doing something (like easily buying takeaway for some people), then the overall usability and consequently user experience is pretty good.

When it comes to using a website, the easier it is to use it to complete a task, the higher the usability of this product. But how do you do that? Performing a quick (Google) search returned results such as "*9 guidelines for exceptional web design and usability*," "*a 7-step guide to website usability*," or "*18 usability guidelines and website design standards*" (if that number is not constant, is it really accurate?). Pfff, more rules man.

If you were expecting to see fancy but complicated graphics and diagrams that make this subject look like nuclear physics by breaking down into different sub-subjects and processes, I'm afraid you're in the wrong book! Instead, here's something easy to think about. Apparently, usability revolves around a few components:

- The first one is called **"learnability,"** or how easy it is to learn to use something and complete a task if you see a website for the first time. For example, let's say that you want users to click those nice big buttons on your design and be directed to the appropriate paths.

If you hide those nice big buttons within complicated content, you make it harder for a user to "learn" your canvas the moment they land on your web page. You can be sure that no one will click your buttons and that they will try their luck somewhere else.

- Another component of usability is **"efficiency,"** or how quickly a user can perform a task. For example, let's imagine you've just added something to your shopping cart while on your favorite ecommerce website. You click the checkout button, and you are now presented with a multitude of options before you actually purchase the product. How much easier would it be if you weren't forced to make an account and fill in all sorts of unnecessary details before actually buying something? Especially if all the fields you have to fill in are presented in a nonintuitive and complicated way.

- **"Memorability"** has to do with how easy a user can perform a task on your website when they return to it after some time. Chances are if they find completing a goal easy the first time, this will be repeated in their other visits as well, provided you've not changed your product into something totally incomprehensible.

- The amount of **"errors,"** their frequency as well as their impact on a user's journey, is another component of usability. If you're trying to use something and errors come up, this is probably poor design and overall usability to begin with, but we are humans and we make mistakes, especially when we're trying to type in while doing other things.

- After that, we have **"satisfaction."** Personally, I don't need to find something satisfying in order to use it, but I guess it depends on how it's defined. If we are talking about satisfaction meaning how easily a user is completing a task, then, yes, finishing what you started on the Web is always a bonus (considering everything is full of distractions nowadays). If satisfaction means it makes a user feel good *while* using something (maybe because the design is pretty, touching their inner soul), then that's another thing. The latter doesn't apply to me, as I find utility more important than looks (without saying looks are not important – because they are).

- Lastly, Mohamed Benaida, from the Islamic University of Madinah, adds another component to usability, that of **"culture."**[1] As some cultures might find online content not aligned with their own values and customs, that could potentially affect usability and overall satisfaction. I guess it's a way of saying our designs and content could benefit from trying to be more inclusive.[2]

---

[1] Benaida, M., 2022. Significance of culture toward the usability of web design and its relationship with satisfaction. Universal Access in the Information Society 21, 625–638. doi:10.1007/s10209-021-00799-y

[2] That is, if it's needed. A tavern selling meat products that doesn't look into expanding its customer base or profits, wouldn't have to include vegan options in its menu.

Think back to the times where you had to use a website (you won't have to think back too much, probably a few minutes). How often have you abandoned a website you were on and gone somewhere else because it was too cluttered? Or because it was filled with incomprehensible lingo and you didn't know if that website was the one you wanted? Or even after beginning to perform a task, how many times have you abandoned the process because it became too complicated?

The reality with usability and user experience is that people don't put up with a bad user experience. If they don't like how a website performs or the way they have to use it and they can't figure it out (in more complex designs), then they will simply leave, go back to Google or any other search engine, and find another website to meet their needs. In fact, this has been researched, and 88% of users are pretty much unlikely to come back to a website they've had a bad experience with.[3] However, if a website is user-friendly, then users will keep coming back to it. Simple as that.

Regardless of how many rules you have to follow, there is a general pattern that can be recognized, and followed, and will most likely lead to high usability: simplicity and clarity in design, avoiding overly complicated interfaces filled with a thousand distracting choices that might lead to an error and providing an easy-to-understand way for someone to complete a task without having to know how a computer or web browser works. This simplicity will benefit everybody. It will most definitely benefit users with disabilities (Figure 8-1).

---

[3] www.sweor.com/firstimpressions

Complicated

Easy

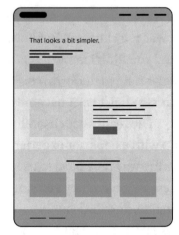

Low usability

High usability

Figure 8-1. *Example of two user interfaces*

Generally speaking, something that is simpler and doesn't require a lot of thinking should be easier to use as well. The design on the left is filled with content, close space between sections, and an array of buttons with different, unrelated, colors. At a first glance, it seems quite intimidating, so I don't know about you, but I'd probably move away to something else. Imagine if the images behind the content had text on them as well. The horror. The interface on the right seems a bit cleaner, with lots of white space and less content to make sense of what you're looking at. Definitely it doesn't require as much thinking to move around and do whatever you came there to do.

Accessibility and Usability: A Love Affair

Usability focuses on making a website easy to use. Web accessibility guidelines focus on making the lives of users with disabilities easier when using the Web, reducing access barriers. While doing that, it turns out that when accessibility requirements are put into place, there is an additional benefit on general usability of the product. For everybody. Might be a bit unintentional, but still.

The Interaction Design Foundation, a leading online design school, lists out 25 different things you could be doing to make your website more usable, from keeping your content consistent to having easy-to-use forms and simple typography.[4] Eighty percent of those 25 guidelines (rules? Proposals? Not sure how to call them) also have to do with accessibility guidelines, ranging from having alt descriptions to images to prioritizing structure and making sure errors are easy to identify. The simplicity pattern is obvious here as well.

Using plain and easy-to-understand language makes completing a task easier by ensuring instructions are easy to follow. At the same time, a simple and clear layout is easier to understand by people with cognitive disabilities but also much more efficient for everybody, when trying to complete a task. Users won't come on your website to be awed; they will come to either buy a product, hire you for a service, or find any kind of information. Unnecessary clutter, complicated designs, and fancy fonts belong to award competitions, not a real-world, usable product.

The use of color (or not, if you like being a bit minimal) is an essential part in the overall usability of a website. Just think back to the endless hours you might have spent trying to find the correct hue that fit with your design, trying to find a color that matched another one or one that conveyed a very specific message.

Then stop and think back to all the times you designed something where different elements didn't have enough contrast between them or where you used a light-gray text on a white background because you thought it looked nice, which it does, but then again, if you can't see

---

[4] www.interaction-design.org/literature/topics/usability

it, what's the point of it being there? Hubert Florin, a product designer working at Slack, probably said it best: "*If it's okay for some people to not see a part of your site, then why is that design element there in the first place?*", which makes total sense.

Having high enough color contrasts ensures a website can be used by people who might have visual impairments but also ones that might find themselves using a device in different light conditions, under the bright sun, or in a dark room. There is an abundance of tools out there to help you achieve that, online or offline, such as the WAVE plugin, a contrast checker called WebAIM, or even Adobe Photoshop (just go into View and then Proof Setup and from the menu choose Color Blindness – who knew?).

Figure 8-2. *Using a mobile device while lying on the beach*

Let's pretend for a moment that it's summer and you're lying on the beach, much like the guy in Figure 8-2. If it is actually summer when you're reading this, even better. If you are reading this, it's summer, and you're on a beach, please teach me your ways. If the sun is too hot and it's right in your eyes, it would be harder to see the screen of your device, and if the colors are too pale or the layout is a bit complicated, you will have a hard time understanding what you're looking at. Now, you might say, "I have a new phone. I'll turn the brightness up. It's all good." Let me remind you we're trying to design for all, not just for the people who go to the beach and, instead of jumping in the water or having a conversation with their friends, prefer to look at a screen and scroll for no reason.

Apart from users with hearing issues or ones with learning disabilities, captions on videos will benefit users who might find themselves in a noisy or a quiet environment, even the ones that might not be as proficient with the video language or ones that like to watch videos online when others are asleep. One thing to notice here is that auto-generated captions can sometimes be inaccurate, so a manual edit would probably be the best approach.

Figure 8-3. *Captions are great for people who are deaf or hard of hearing*

Captions also great if you find yourself in a quiet environment, a library, for example (Figure 8-3), and instead of reading a book decide to go on your phone or laptop and watch the latest online videos. Of course it's not your fault that no one else close to you can't do their job because of your noise. It's the web designer's and web developer's fault for not including captions in their videos.

Large enough buttons will be beneficial to people who might have fine motor skills limitations or perhaps vision impairments, but also to users who might, for example, be on a bumpy plane ride (Figure 8-4), using any type of device. Especially on mobile phones where touch is the main form of interacting with content, a large target will ensure you accurately press what you need to press, regardless of finger size or whether you're using the device with one hand, because your other hand is occupied holding a baby or a snack.

Figure 8-4. *Trying to use a mobile device on a bumpy plane*

To check if your design is usable, you can start from the point of deciding on or applying the basic elements on the canvas, such as colors, font, or layout. Following a nonlinear iterative process (designers have even labeled it "iteration design"; we love our labels), you can optimize your design from the beginning without having to wait until you have a fully functional, high-fidelity prototype. Early evaluation from other designers, developers, and obviously (and most importantly) users will give you the necessary feedback to reach the desired level of usability (Figure 8-5).

Generally, you'd start by identifying an issue that you will have come across based on user research. You'd think to yourself, "Who is most likely to use my product, and what would some potential issues for them be?" Once you've actually figured out what that possible problems could be, you'd put your ideas on paper trying to solve them. A "problem" doesn't necessarily have to be something complicated or something that will prevent users from using your website in the first place. A problem can just as easily be: How do I make the experience of paying for a product on my website as efficient as possible?

After this is done, you'd make a very loose prototype, which you can then test with your clients and/or actual users. And this doesn't need to be fancy. Fancy comes later. At the moment, you're still trying to figure out how to solve a particular issue. Then, once you've analyzed the results from whatever feedback you got, you have the options of either polishing up your designs, making something pretty out of your scribbles, or, if you discover more issues or barriers that prevent your users from completing their tasks, going back to the drawing board. Rinse, and repeat.

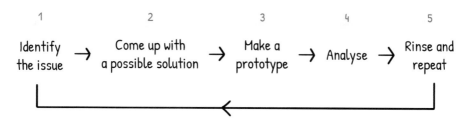

Figure 8-5. *Stages of iterative design[5]*

There are a few specific techniques designers can use in their deliverables to aid both usability and accessibility at the same time. The following list is not extensive. There are a ton of things that need to be

---

[5] Heavily influenced by this great article on iterative design: www.editorx.com/shaping-design/article/iterative-design

taken into consideration. This is just a taste of probably best accessibility and usability practices. Note that the individual WCAG are not yet mentioned, as this will come later on.

User Interface (UI) Components Contrast

When we say about UI elements contrast, we basically mean that each section of the web page needs to be clearly defined from one another in order to help users with visual difficulties see where everything is and how all the different parts of the page are separated. After that, individual elements inside each section need to be distinct and have enough contrast with each other in order to be easily identifiable. Areas of interaction, like a button, need to be clear that they are just that.

One of the big issues I see sometimes in designs is a canvas with different elements, all of them looking like one big thing lacking the contrast needed, with no separation whatsoever. A clear and logical design with no clutter as well as a consistent navigation is key.[6]

If you look at Figure 8-6, the image on the left side has clear separation between each section, and you can easily tell where one subject ends and another one begins. The text is clearly visible as well as the button with its label, and there is no ambiguity on what to do and where to click. The example on the right is a bit of a mess. Too light text and no clear structure would make this thing unusable, and once you landed on it, you'd probably not even attempt to read what it's about. However, I'm not saying don't do the example on the right. Any answer to any design problem would always be "it depends." Perhaps you've done your research, and you've found out that actually your audience would be fine with this type of design and it serves your purpose. In that case, well done and Godspeed.

---

[6] www.nngroup.com/articles/consistency-and-standards/

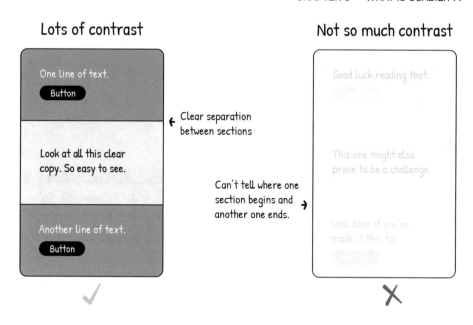

Figure 8-6. *Illustration of two web pages, with high contrast between sections and content (left) and low contrast (right)*

Page Layout and Structure

This is somewhat connected to the previous one. For best accessibility the layout of the page should be clear, allowing for a comprehensive flow of information that might potentially come from a screen reader. At this point, typographic structure is also included, meaning a clear heading followed by a supporting copy followed by a call to action.

The first example at the top left in Figure 8-7 seems to be a bit clearer; the heading, its supporting copy, and the button related to them are clearly separated and can be easily understood. The bottom right example follows a more "in-your-face" approach, where all the elements are close together and the subheading or supporting text is slightly smaller than the heading itself, making it a bit harder to even begin trying to understand what is being written. Why would you want to make the lives of your users hard?

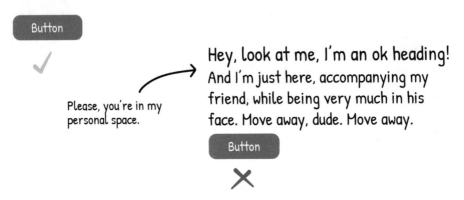

Figure 8-7. *Example of different types of typographic structure*

Color, Color Contrast, and Noncolor Elements

This is really self-explanatory and directly connected to usability as well as accessibility. There are a lot of tools out there that check color contrast between a background and a foreground, which most of the time is probably text that sits there. Research suggests that color seems to be a bit more important for usability rather than accessibility and, sometimes, depending on who the users are, it doesn't even matter (obviously, within reason).

A web accessibility requirement is that we shouldn't really rely on color alone to convey information (with a catch, of course, as it only applies to specific situations). Users who can't tell the difference between colors or have a monochrome display might find information received only by color a bit useless. So we need to make sure that information conveyed with color is also available without color, for example, from context or markup (Figure 8-8).

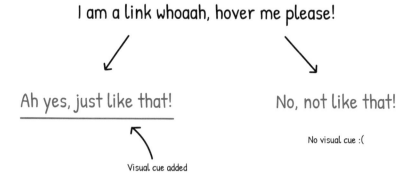

Figure 8-8. *Hover examples with (left) and without a visual cue (right)*

Adding a visual cue is beneficial to users who might not be able to distinguish the change in color. The visual cue doesn't have to be an underline either. A dot, icon, or bold text (although it doesn't look very smooth in real life), all can be used alongside the color change.

There are not a lot of black-and-white displays around lately, you might think. There is also the argument that as long as the different information is presented with different colors, as in there is enough contrast between them, then there is no need for supporting information or specific colors to be used. As long as there is high contrast, then the actual colors don't matter.

A good example to see that color contrast is really important for usability but not equally important for accessibility (*sometimes* – it is interesting to see that it doesn't weigh the same for accessibility as proper markup does in some cases and that semantics matter when we talk about these things) is the CV-Library website. CV-Library has an accessibility score of 98. 98! This is almost perfect. However, if you look at where it fails, it's contrast and legibility of content. I don't know about you, but to me that's really interesting.

Focus States

This is definitely something designers should be considering and implementing in their design process. A focus indicator comes up when an element is selected, like a button or a link, and it could be something as simple as an outline around the element. There is a default style that browsers adapt to show those indicators, but it's really not very nice, and in most cases it won't fit the overall style or brand of the page. Focus indicators can be extremely important for keyboard users as they allow them to know where they are on a page and that the element that is focused can be interacted with.

So ideally we'd need to create one that has high visibility and a good contrast and one that stands out from the rest of the surrounding content.

Hover States

So do hover states matter for accessibility? Or usability for that matter? Yes, they do, especially for accessibility. One might argue that for usability it's not really that important or doesn't need to apply everywhere, since a hover state on a button, for example, will only appear for a third of a second. Once the user has already made the decision to click that button, they're already engaged.

However, in order to identify something as clickable, whether it's a link or a tab, you'll still have to make an effort to target that link. You will need to move your mouse cursor and check if it's on top of the link. A hover effect will happen when the mouse is on the target and it needs to be clear enough and easily identifiable so the user won't have to focus on the cursor but rather on the content itself.

What matters most is the ability to find that point of interaction, and we can help with that by making sure it stands out from surrounding elements and that the text on it makes the action that we're about to perform clear, clear enough that can be understood out of context. That will make the goal that we have set for our users easier to be reached, and, of course, it goes without saying that common sense needs to be followed, so green text on a green button is not really acceptable.

Forms: Input and Labels

From a design perspective, this is probably closer to usability issues. When designing forms we (ideally) need to make sure that we have enough contrast between the form input fields and the surrounding background (Figure 8-9). That could be done with, for example, a slight border around the input field or the use of a different color.

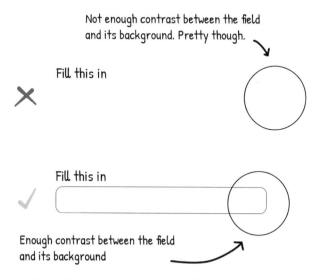

Figure 8-9. *A form field with a border (bottom) is more distinct when it's against a low-contrast background*

And it doesn't even have to be black. Any color would do, as long as the contrast is sufficient. Now, someone might say, "But I can see the label and maybe some text above it that indicates that there is a form field there that needs to be filled in." You can; others might not.

On top of that, one thing that we usually do is an improper use of form labels, that is, putting the label inside the input field where a placeholder text (which is basically a helpful piece of text making it even clearer for the user what needs to be done) should be. Following best practice, all form labels should sit *outside* the form while accompanied by a placeholder text, if you need to.

The intention here is to have something that works both ways to (in theory) save time for the user and some space for the designer. However, when users scan, the layout in Figure 8-10 (right side) would be easier for them to identify and use, as we usually scan from top to button.

In the example on the left, that label will probably go away when the user starts typing in the field, making it unclear as to what information was required, especially nowadays when we're moving faster than ever. While this *might* prove to be okay in smaller forms or something that doesn't require much effort, having to fill a larger, complex form with lots of information might prove to be a bit challenging for some users. In addition, if the field is already populated, it would be easier to understand the data or check that it's actually correct, since you'd read the label first.

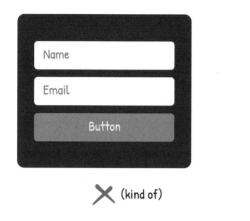
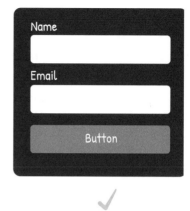

Figure 8-10. *Two examples with different placements of form labels*

Video and Audio Transcripts and Captions

The importance of captions and transcripts has already been mentioned. When images are not accessible for people who have vision problems, we use alt tags so they can easily identify them and get access to that content. In the same way, when audio is not available to people who can't hear or are hard of hearing, we need to provide them with an alternative method of getting access to that content. When video is not available to users who can't see, they need to have a different way to get access to that information by having a transcript read out to them by a screen reader. On top of that, when someone has a video playing in the background, such as a driver, they obviously have to look at the road. An audio description will ensure the driver gets access to the video information while not having to look at it.[7]

---

[7] This is clearly sarcasm. Don't do other things while driving.

In addition, search engines will also pick up the transcript content, so there is a link to a potential SEO benefit as well, since it is more relevant content. So, from a designer's perspective, all we should do is include a text link that will link through to a transcript page or a transcript modal with the content of the video or audio file.

Visual Presentation of Text

There is evidence that people with cognitive disabilities will find it hard to track text if lines are too close together, so providing extra space allows for easier reading as it's clearer where the next line of text is. These users might also experience problems when the text is fully justified. That's because a justified text leaves either big gaps between words, which make reading impossible for them, or really small gaps. In this case, users with disabilities might not be able to locate word boundaries, as they can't tell where one word ends and another one begins.

Hidden Content

This might not have much to do with accessibility, since if the content is there and it's accessible by a screen reader (so properly marked up), the screen reader will ignore the code that hides the content in a slider or a tab and it will go ahead and read it. Assuming that tab links are also properly marked up and keyboard navigation works correctly, that shouldn't be an issue.

For usability purposes though, hidden content is generally thought of as bad user experience. It's like breaking a user's expectation, like having a newspaper with no titles. Research has shown that hidden content, for example, in sliders, is not really used. Carousels might get interacted with about 1% at a time, meaning if you put important information in slide number 2, it will probably be missed. Also search engines value hidden content lower than visible content. On the other hand, of course, low-value hidden content is always better than no content. Unless the flow and the goal of the page require hidden content, there is really no point in hiding information.

General Usability Standards
Easy and Consistent Navigation

Generally, a traditional navigation with a list of links works better than a burger menu, mostly because a burger menu implies hidden content and some of the menu items can easily be missed. Besides, if you want to put numbers on it, according to a study by Nielsen Norman Group, a visible navigation is likely to be used almost twice as much as a hidden one (and faster).[8] Ideally, if you need something aesthetically pleasing, a combination of a visible menu with the most important links always there at a glance and a hidden menu should be fine. Consistency in navigation is also really important, so make sure it remains the same throughout the whole website.

In Figure 8-11 the first navigation at the top follows a standard practice, easily recognizable by pretty much every user. Links are visible at all times, and there's no confusion whatsoever. In the second case, this could also work for certain cases as you'll have important links that you don't want a user to miss visible at all times and everything else inside a hidden menu, nicely organized and prioritized (hopefully!). The third option only uses an icon for the navigation (without even a label to go with it, so go figure), effectively hiding every link out there, making it harder, and slower, for

---

[8] www.nngroup.com/articles/hamburger-menus

users to interact with it. Accompany that with the potential of a developer not building this thing correctly, which could lead to keyboard traps when using keyboard navigation, and you've got yourself a ~~winner~~ loser.

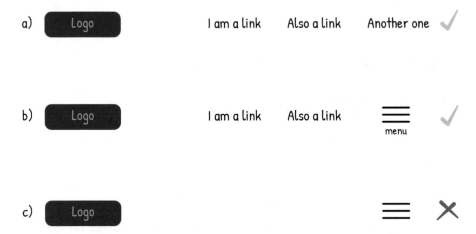

Figure 8-11. *Different types of a website's main navigation*

Going Back Home

There are typically two ways to go back to the homepage, either by clicking a logo or a link that says Home or something that exists somewhere within the content. It's safe to say that because we use search engines, more often than not we will bypass the homepage and land somewhere else. So providing users with a way to go back to the homepage to find information or go through a different journey is essential, and we can do it through logos, but we can also do it through breadcrumbs, mini navigations that tell you where you are and where you can go from there (Figure 8-12).

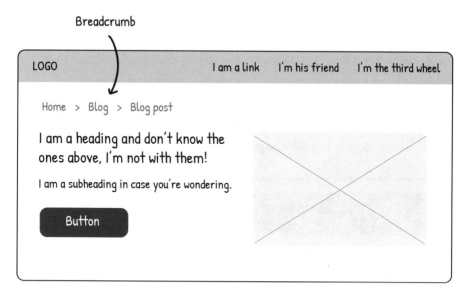

Figure 8-12. *Example of a breadcrumb navigation on a hypothetical web page*

They are easy to use, and they *should* be there (that's for all the designers out there who neglect them). Besides, breadcrumbs don't cause any harm, and the "design costs" don't outweigh the benefits.[9] Additionally, they can help reduce anxiety by providing a complete trail of the site's structure and an easy way to go back to previous pages, or even the homepage, if needed. Put them above the content and below the main navigation[10] and congratulate yourself for being a thoughtful and considerate designer. Oh, and please don't use them on the homepage. Thank you.

---

[9] https://vwo.com/blog/why-use-breadcrumbs
[10] www.nngroup.com/articles/breadcrumb-navigation-useful

Show the User Where They Are

This is something that can be done very easily, and we should do that anyway; change the appearance of items in the navigation menu to indicate that a link is active (Figure 8-13) and this is the page we're supposed to be on (if you're not doing this, then shame on you). Another way to do that is with big headings, which clearly state where we are, and, of course, breadcrumbs.

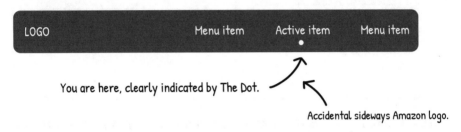

Figure 8-13. *Visual cue that indicates an active link within a main navigation*

Icons and Labels

A potential issue here is that in order to understand what an icon means, you need to rely on previous experience. Unfortunately, not all people have the same understanding about anything, and there isn't a standard usage of an icon for a specific reason (apart from a handful of icons, like a search icon or a user account one, and that's even debatable for older audiences or users with disabilities). So text labels next to the icon are necessary to reduce doubt. By placing the icon on the left of the text label, we force the users to scan that first, so if they know what it means, they don't have to read the label. If they don't, then the supporting text is there for them.

It goes without saying that there are specific situations where the icon is better placed after the label. For example, if you have a "Next" link, you'd probably put an arrow icon after the label. Think about road signs, for instance. You first see the name of the road or a destination and then the icon that indicates direction (or at least I think; I've not traveled for a while, which is unacceptable).

Remember that the focus here is accessibility, as well as usability. And while one research 20 years ago once showed that users were significantly faster when using standalone icons rather than text labels,[11] it doesn't mean that this applies to everybody. Users with disabilities and cognitive decline issues might not always know or understand what icons mean by default. So use some text, be sensible, and don't forget that customary shoulder pat.

In Figure 8-14 the search icon will be scanned first, and if the user identifies it as such, there would be no need to read the label. In contrast, the second example has the icon on the right, after the label, indicating you're going forward. Obviously, if the label was "Previous," the icon would be before it and flipped over to indicate you're going backward.

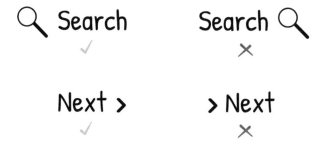

Figure 8-14. *Placement of icons in relation to their text labels*

---

[11] https://dl.acm.org/doi/abs/10.5555/581506.581548

Content Placement

There are a lot of ways a user reads a web page. To begin with, most users don't really read; they rather scan a page to find the information they need. People will just naturally try to achieve their goal by following the path of least resistance, trying to be efficient. This is another reason where hierarchy is key, because that big and bold title will catch the user's attention and, if the user is intrigued, they will stay on that page and read the whole thing.

Eye tracking research has shown a lot of patterns when it comes to how our eyes move on a page. There's the famous F pattern, which is a scanning behavior that basically resembles the letter F; however, that's proven to only be true when a user scans content and not the whole page. Then there's the Z pattern, layer cake pattern (who comes up with these names?), and more.

Common Sense

With having the users always in mind, common sense in design just means that every design element should do just that: solve a particular problem that a user may have. For example, if we want them to view all case studies, we include a "View all case studies" button somewhere prominent in an accessible and usable way. Our design decisions should always be backed up by reason, more than personal preference. Of course we are going to put our personal touches in our designs. And of course we want to make something that is usable but also nice to look at, because we are designers and want to make pretty stuff. But sometimes we go overboard, and it's very easy to go crazy. A good way to keep us on the right path is when we get feedback from other members of our team or other designers in general while trying to keep this feedback away from personal preferences and always provide solid reasoning for it (when you pass on feedback, try to base it on something that you feel might affect usability rather than your feelings and your own personal idea of what looks nice).

Designers and the likes are not your typical user, though. Real user testing would be the best thing to do, ensuring you will catch any design issues early and address them appropriately. Testing will probably include users trying to complete a task unaided (without you giving them any hints on how to do it) on your website while you or some other moderator observes the process trying to identify where they succeeded and where they failed.

Key in testing with actual users is the ability to have a representative audience checking your website, real people facing real issues who can be involved in the process from the beginning effectively showing you how easy, or not, it is for them to use your product. And you don't even have to have loads; five users are all you need really.[12] For accessibility purposes, users with disabilities would need to be involved early in the process.

The clue is in the word "representative." In an ideal world, you'd want your website tested by those who are most likely to use it. And if you're testing for accessibility issues, you'll need users with disabilities and assign them different tasks based on what your users would be most likely to do when on your website. How do you get accessibility testers? Well... that's a great question.

Think of friends or family. Who would be most likely to face an accessibility issue? Think of similar products and try to figure out who would use them and reach out to similar users. There are even specialized recruitment agencies for usability testers. Perhaps you can try your luck there. Aside from that, there are various online platforms where you can

---

[12] Why you only need five users, www.nngroup.com/articles/why-you-only-need-to-test-with-5-users/

upload your designs, assign some tasks to the users, and wait for the results. However, that doesn't necessarily mean that users with disabilities will use your site. So what do you do?

How do you know which people are most likely to use your website, and how do you even begin addressing hypothetical issues that hypothetical people face, before you even begin an iterative process? When talking about accessibility, users are facing very specific problems arising from very specific barriers. This brings us to one of the most important pieces of any product's development process: knowing your audience.

Summary

On some level, you can't talk about web accessibility without mentioning usability and vice versa. By understanding what they both entail, we can be certain our designs will steer toward inclusivity by being both usable and accessible (assuming the content is also in the right direction).

Usability is about how easily you can use something, and accessibility is about making sure that the "something" you're trying to make can be used by users with potential disabilities or limitations. However, it is very easy to get lost through all the available information and definitions out there, so hopefully you'll now have an understanding on where accessibility and usability stand against each other.

Mainly the fact is that even though accessibility practices aim to help those affected by disabilities, the application of these practices actually helps everybody. The examples mentioned in this chapter are not exhaustive as there are numerous situations where certain design choices, such as choosing colors with high contrast and designing with simplicity rather than complexity in mind, can aid both disabled and non-disabled users. A summary of different design techniques was presented in order to understand the basic approach toward solving design and, consequently, user issues.

CHAPTER 9

Whom Are We Designing For?

Definitely not for ourselves, as some people seem to think. We (including our clients) are not the ones that will be using the website, and we are not the ones that will benefit from it (aside from getting paid for our "hard" labor). This is something that a lot of people in the creative, digital, online, or offline industry seem to be neglecting: the importance of knowing the audience we're addressing.

It's kind of (although not exactly) like the old expression, "Read the room." When "reading the room," we look at whoever is in there with us in a particular setting, note their general reactions, and adjust our behavior accordingly. For example, you wouldn't go into a funeral and all of sudden start listening to happy songs on your phone, unless it was that type of funeral. In the same sense, when designing a website for someone to use, we analyze whom these people are, what are their barriers, age, sex, education, and so on, and we develop our product according to their needs. After all, it's them who are going to use it, not us.

But how do we identify them? How can we know who they are? You might be surprised to know that your potential audience is *not* everybody (unless you're Amazon or a similar business with global reach, but even then, you're still limited to Internet users). Everybody on the planet might have potential access to your website, but not everybody cares about what you're offering or selling. People who go to the gym are more likely to land

D. Georgakas, *A11Y Unraveled*, https://doi.org/10.1007/978-1-4842-9085-9_9

on websites that are gym related; people who like fancy jewelry are more likely to visit a jewelry website than someone that doesn't like wearing them. So, based on what you're offering, you can have a pretty good first idea as to whom your *potential* audience might be.

In today's digital world though, that might not be enough. If you have a recruitment website, knowing that your audience are job seekers wouldn't be sufficient, as this is missing some key important elements: what jobs are you offering (also, what is your industry, as nurses wouldn't apply for engineering jobs?) and who is more likely to apply for them based on some of their attributes, like age, education level, or sex.

If we take the preceding example, in the UK currently 16.5% of engineers are female.[1] This would mean that if we had a recruitment website for engineers, the likely visitors would be males since they are the majority. Similarly, if we look into the UK's NHS, the majority of people in managerial roles are women (62%),[2] so we'd have to adjust our website accordingly if we were offering senior NHS positions. These are only top-level examples, as after identifying sex, we would then proceed into narrowing it down even more. What are their ages, what are their interests, what is their education level, and what is their relationship to technology? What is our most likely typical user, and what are some challenges they might be facing? Could they be people with disabilities? Knowing who someone is doesn't necessarily mean that you *actually* know them.

Aside from general info, like "I'm expecting more female than male visitors," it can be quite tricky to narrow down the very specific group that might be your predominant audience, if you're just starting. If you're in

---

[1] www.engineeringuk.com/news-views/
new-analysis-shows-increase-of-women-working-in-engineering
[2] www.england.nhs.uk/2021/03/nhs-celebrates-the-vital-role-hundreds-of-thousands-of-women-have-played-in-the-pandemic/

the business for a while and you have something like Google Analytics[3] set up for your website, it's very easy to get a glimpse of your current visitors – their age, their location, and even the browser and operating system they're using. If you're just starting from scratch, it's okay to make hypotheses that you can validate later. A good way to go about it is by creating a user persona profile.

Personas are something like a representation of your typical user, and they come from having in mind a specific user while developing your product. The persona profile (or profiles, as having an array of typical users would probably give a more all-around view on who will be using your website) includes detailed information about that user: their name, their age, where they are, what are their skills and education, what kind of frustrations or barriers they might be facing, and what exactly they're looking for. You can also include some more background information in the form of a little bio paragraph, and you'll have an overall profile of someone that is most likely to use your website.

They come with all sorts of benefits. They help drive design decisions since by understanding user behavior and their needs, you can discern what you need to put in your canvas to address those needs. If your persona is, for example, someone that's on their phone all the time, then you'd better make those buttons nice and big so they can find them effortlessly and tap them even easier. In addition, they will help you realize what was mentioned in the beginning of this chapter: that you (we) are not our users. By understanding that the needs that require addressing are the users' and not yours, you're getting one step closer to one of designers' greatest values: empathy.

Empathy is basically understanding how someone else feels, acknowledging their thoughts and emotions, without necessarily having

---

[3] If you've lived under a rock and you don't know what this is, it's a service offered by Google (how surprising) that can give you insights about your website traffic (among other things).

experienced them – in other words, how capable you are of putting yourself in someone else's shoes, looking at a situation from their own point of view. By using empathy, a designer can create something that will provide those positive emotions to the user, understand their motivations, and design a great experience, without making any assumptions.

If this all seems like mumbo jumbo, feelings, unicorns, and happy meadows, I can't blame you; it seems the same to me. I've never been the one to blag about my designs, trying to come up with all sorts of weird justifications just to "sell" a certain design decision. During the design process, if you have in mind how the user might feel about a specific situation or how they might feel frustrated by one of your decisions and if ultimately this leads to a design change for their benefit, congratulations! You just showed empathy, and you didn't even know it. You successfully put yourself in someone else's shoes.

Persona Profiles

Remember, though, that the aim is not to randomly profile hypothetical people by writing fictional stories. The aim is to understand your users' mentality, behaviors, and barriers and how to address them. It goes a bit further from just putting down simple demographic information, like age and sex, by digging a bit deeper and providing descriptions of their personalities.[4] Ultimately, personals will be a realistic (to a degree) portrayal of typical users, and hopefully this will help the designers to design something specific for those users and their needs.

Start with hypothesizing who your general target audience might be and work around specific context and user goals. For example, if you're in the process of developing an ecommerce website that sells furniture and

---

[4] Creating Effective Personas for Product Design: Insights from a Case Study. See more in this link: https://uxstrategized.com/Persona_Paper_HCII_2011.pdf

your goal is to sell as much as you can, think about who would be most likely to buy your products, or a specific product, what tasks these people might have to do on your website, and under what conditions.

Students who move away from their home? New couples who just moved to a new house? Older people who just want to renovate? Make a list of potential users, and then the best way to get insight on what exactly they need is to, plain and simple, ask them. The goal here is to get as much information as possible to begin with: use interviews (online or in-person) or questionnaires (send a spam email, go on, others are doing it) or even observe these users while trying to use your product. The more data you get from this and the more you can observe, the more realistic your personas will be. You'll be able to see what their frustrations are and what barriers they will have faced in the future in similar situations.

After you do all that, the next step would be to analyze your results, whether it's data you got from interviews or any information you got from online tools. Try and find patterns within all that information that may or may not validate any hypotheses you might have made in the beginning. List out your findings and the behaviors you might have observed and identify any trends, differences, and similarities. Next comes the fun part (although data collection is still fun): actually putting together the personas.

I say the fun part because it involves some designing. If you're like me and get excited with new things (and then get bored after a while), this is a great opportunity to design something nice that also has substance along with real value for your project. Collect the patterns you've identified, your users' demographics, put your descriptions together, and lay everything on a one-page description for each user (Figure 9-1).

Remember him?

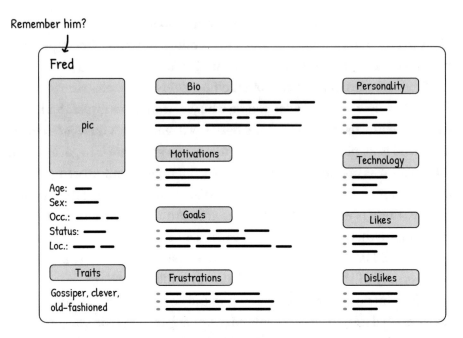

Figure 9-1. Example of a persona profile

All basic characteristics, such as age, location, sex, etc., alongside a small bio and different info on personality, goals and pain points, relationship with technology, as well as likes and dislikes, could paint the picture of Fred, a senior grumpy gossiper next-door neighbor who refuses to go with the flow but occasionally uses the Internet for his crabby habits.

Include a name to make it more realistic. This will also help along the process as you'd be making questions to yourself such as "What would Fred do here?" or "How would Suzan find this approach?" Definitely include a picture, but don't go haywire. I know you're a designer and you want to make fun stuff, but this is the time to be a professional. Suppress your inner child and find a representative image that accurately depicts your user (Figure 9-2). If one of your actual users is willing to allow you to use their image, even better (although if you rely too much on real participant details, it might make you a bit biased).

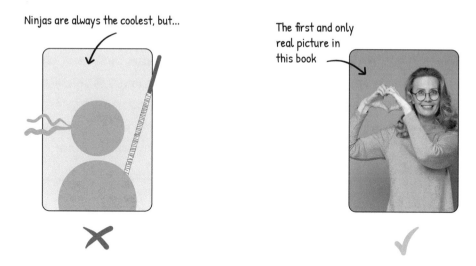

Figure 9-2. _Image examples to be used within a persona profile_

A real image will make the persona even more realistic and help toward building that all-important empathy.

Maybe.

I prefer the ninja dude.

Alongside their demographics, put down a short description for them. Note their behavior and some of their traits. Are they practical? Are they curious, and do they find dealing with technology easy? Include their goals, frustrations, and any barriers they might be facing while trying to complete tasks you've asked them to do.

Finally, no persona has any value unless it's tied into context (otherwise, it's just creepy). That context would be based on you coming up with a scenario that's directly linked to what you're trying to achieve. You set the goals for the users, and then you try to see how your persona would interact in that particular situation, whether it's effortlessly buying a product, applying for a job role, or even using a search form to find specific information. By doing that, you're identifying a task, you pair that persona with the task, you see if there are any potential issues, and then you try to address them through your design. Repeat the process for a couple more personas and prioritize them in order of relevancy.

Persona Profiles for Users with Disabilities

Now after you've done all that, sit back and have another look. Have you included a user with a potential disability in your personas? Within your scenarios, have you thought about certain situations that might pose temporary limitations to your users? Personas will help you understand the user behind the disability, and by addressing their needs in your designs, you will have created something that would be useful for all.

We have already mentioned the vast number of potential users who might be affected by a disability, and this number increases with age. Add the ones that might be going through a temporary disability or limitation, and you can quickly see why you'd need to add additional persona profiles for disabled users. By ignoring the possibility (pretty much *certainty*, to be honest) that these people will be part of your user pool, you're effectively excluding a great number of likely customers. Besides, show some empathy. You can do it.

Developing a persona for a disabled user doesn't mean it will be different than your usual ones. You will still include demographic information and different traits and skills, but you will also account for any potential limitations, the use of assistive technology (if any), and even their level of experience using it.[5] Including disabled users during the discovery process using interviews and questionnaires will help you increase your understanding of their needs, experiences, and frustrations so you can address these in your product, without falling in the trap of stereotyping. Personally, I have never created a persona for a disabled user in the past because little did I know when I first started.

---

[5] Karen Lindsay Williams wrote a great thesis on personas for her master's degree in industrial design. Have a look here: https://smartech.gatech.edu/bitstream/handle/1853/11623/Williams_Karen_L_200608_Mas.pdf

Others, though, have. A great example of personas with disabilities comes from Barclays.[6] By working with accessibility experts, they have created a set of profiles that include users with disabilities such as visual and hearing impairments, loss of motor skills, mental health issues, and learning difficulties. Apart from the usual user description, they've included information about their disabilities, how they arose and how they affect them when trying to use bank products, what devices they use and how, what is their lifestyle like, what are their goals, and what frustrations they face toward achieving them, all in a very detailed presentation of users' bios.

While writing this, I ended up being argumentative as always, even with myself, which is kind of strange and hilarious at the same time. Even after all those benefits that persona profiles offer, "Do we *really* need them?" I pondered. "Would it make such a big difference?" I pondered even more. "Is it actually accurate?" the pondering continued. Turns out I wasn't on my own. Turns out the world is a bit divided (when is it not?).

The most significant drawback that initially came to my mind is that if we base our design decisions (at least on some level) on persona profiles, are we basing them on actual people or making vast assumptions and generalizations based on some interviews we had with a handful of people who we thought would be our representative audience? And what if those people whom we observed and examined weren't enough? What if they weren't even representative? Is simply putting down an average of what someone has said in some arbitrary interview enough?

In reality, an average (typical) user simply doesn't exist, and to work on the assumption that because you have something representative it works for all would be wrong to begin with. Lt. Gilbert S. Daniels, a physical anthropologist who graduated from Harvard University, discovered this during his undergraduate thesis, where he compared the hand shape of 250 male students (this might have been a hoot for an anthropologist,

---

[6] hwww.abilitynet.org.uk/sites/abilitynet.org.uk/files/Barclays-Diverse-Personas-Issue-1.pdf

but it does seem a bit blunt). When Daniels averaged his data, he realized that what he had as an average hand didn't match any of the individual measurements that he had made.

"It was clear to me that if you wanted to design something for an individual human being, the average was completely useless," Daniels said.

Later on (he was only 23, so let's all now feel bad for what we have accomplished so far), he joined the US Air Force, trying to help in the design of a fighter plane cockpit that would fit the average pilot. The US Air Force had a big problem with pilots crashing all over the place, not being able to control their planes. They theorized that it was because of the cockpit's design. In 1950, they measured 4,063 male pilots in an attempt to calculate a pilot's average size and redesign cockpits accordingly. At the end (and to everyone's surprise because of the such large sample), the result was pretty similar to what Daniels had already found. Zero pilots matched the average measurements.[7]

And with this, the era of assumptions was over. Regardless of someone's age, occupation, experiences, feelings, education, and thoughts, all Internet users have the same goals: find information, buy a product, listen to a song, write a book, and so on. Sometimes, there doesn't need to be a need that's deeply rooted in someone's past. Sometimes, we just want to buy that darn teddy because it looks cute.[8] Sometimes, as Harshadewa has put it in an article on uxdesign.cc (2018), people just have a job that needs to be done, and we should stop using personas.[9] Isn't that, though, where the specific scenarios come in? Context that needs to be created and tied in with a persona in order to address a very specific job that needs to be done?

---

[7] www.thestar.com/news/insight/2016/01/16/when-us-air-force-discovered-the-flaw-of-averages.html

[8] Any similarities with real people or real-life events are purely coincidental.

[9] https://uxdesign.cc/
heres-why-you-should-stop-using-personas-63c09a844e67

The following is my brain talking to itself in the span of a few seconds (okay, minutes):

- Scenarios are fine. It's a website after all. How many jobs can one do on it?

- *A lot.*

- But how many? Five? Six? Let's say you have an ecommerce site. You can only look for product info; look into product reviews; add a review; see similar products; add product attributes; delete them; add to basket; remove from basket; buy; pay; add to list; create account; delete account; put details in form fields; read blog articles; share blog articles; read all sorts of information, delivery info, and cancellation info; see product images; return the product; buy more than one product; buy the same product for different reasons; return the used product because you're cheeky; send a message; find contact information.... Wait a minute.

- *Yes?*

- These are too many. It's impossible to account for everything!

- *Yes.*

- So what do we do?

- *Prioritize.*

- AHA!

Okay, I think you got the point. We can't account for all users, and we can't account for all scenarios and tasks. What we can do is prioritize, put our tasks in a hierarchical order, select the major user tasks, and act accordingly. At the end of the day, there is always the risk that the persona we create doesn't exist in the real world, and there is always the risk that some of our design decisions might come from false or misleading information to begin with. That's not a rare occasion. Marouchka Hebben,

147

a human-centered design expert, claims that 97% of personas created are "bullpoop"(to put it nicer), mostly because they have been created without actual user research,[10] rather by people assuming who their users will be, without actually putting in the effort of finding out if that's remotely true.

Persona Spectrums

Even if we put the effort in, things do get a bit tricky as you go along, with and without accounting for disabilities. Imagine a situation where you have to design for users who are deaf. How are you even going to start segmenting this? Are your users mostly completely deaf? Do they use a hearing aid? Are they just hard of hearing? Are they some that might have a temporary hearing loss or just find themselves in noisy environments all the time? All in all, instead of creating a user persona with one characteristic like you intended to, you end up having to put in the equation permanent and temporary disabilities, as well as situational limitations. Well done. You've dug yourself into a really deep hole.

Ultimately, you end up having a spectrum of different users, disabilities, and tasks. Start digging yourself back up and allow me to introduce you to persona spectrums (no, I didn't come up with that). Instead of just defining a user in one dimension, you describe them through situations that they might be facing and what hurdles these bring in their way, whether it's something permanent, temporary, or situational. You won't just design for blind users; you'll design for those who might have lost their glasses (guilty), those who might be looking into a screen under the bright sun, or those who might have rubbed their eye too much because it was dry due to looking at a screen for too long and now they can't see from that eye (also guilty). All of them would be

---

[10] https://medium.com/@hellodesignthinkers/97-of-personas-are-bullshit-heres-why-8b8d9cf67e0

in the visual impairment spectrum. Eventually, you'll end up designing a more inclusive experience with the help of a more diverse range of users.[11] In theory.

Thinking about all that, do persona profiles really matter after all? Of course they do, as long as you do it right, having in mind that you don't design for yourself, unless you're literally designing for yourself, maybe on a personal website. In that case, you can ignore personas, as that would be a bit redundant, let alone silly.

You know what else you can do right, though? Implement web accessibility guidelines in your designs. Let me tell you what to do.

"You can't tell me what to do. I'm an adult!"

("I beg to differ," a 39-year old's mom would say.)

No, I can't. But, based on what some amazing people have done and building on what's already been discussed in the pages before this chapter, there are a few techniques designers can use in their designs to aid accessibility and usability, coming mostly from the web accessibility guidelines.

The remaining chapters present a summary on what we can do as designers to aid toward a happy experience for our audiences, which also includes some design fundamentals we should be aware of. It's purposely not split into accessibility and usability categories as the two usually go together and, more often than not, overlap. It is split, however, in different elements of design, such as animated content, typography, use of color, and so on, while explaining how each element leads to a different accessibility conformance level. Happy reading.

---

[11] https://medium.com/microsoft-design/kill-your-personas-1c332d4908cc

Summary

Who are we designing for is the ultimate question and one that, if answered to a very specific point, will make a designer's life a million times easier. And that very specific point can't come with beliefs and presuppositions. To assume that we know who will be using our website based on some top-level predictions such as more males than females or younger than older audience has the potential of leading us to wrong design decisions.

By analyzing our users' needs, input, and behavior, we can create persona profiles that will give us some form of insight in our most likely users. Who they are, what do they need from us (what problem are we trying to solve), and what might be preventing them from accessing what they need are all questions that hopefully can be answered to a degree when developing user persona profiles.

By including users with potential disabilities or situational limitations, not only are we using our common sense, since some of our users are *definitely* going to be facing issues due to some form of impairment, but we are also closer to creating a more complete and unique experience for the entirety of our audience. In theory, and if we do it right. Accounting for every potential situation and disability out there is kind of tricky (let alone impossible), so being very careful with the context that our persona profiles revolve around and by utilizing persona spectrums can lead to a successful and inclusive user experience.

Persona profiles and their creation are a subject that has been talked about for decades, so hopefully this chapter has helped you get started into understanding what this actually means and also sparked your interest so you can start using them in your own projects, if necessary.

CHAPTER 10

Now You See Me. Now You Don't.

Apart from skipping headings, ropes, and the fact that you can't skip a stone 89 times,[1] one of the most important elements that a designer can have an input on is contrast. Whether it is contrast between colors, contrast between sections within a website, or even contrast between shapes, it is an easy way to identify different elements on a canvas, and it is vital for accessibility and good usability. At least, in theory. And if you're noticing a pattern in me arguing about things that have long been accepted as the norm and have been proven to be correct, you're probably right. Call me argumentative all day long. You would be 100% correct, so there's some data right there. Just because something has been accepted doesn't mean we should not change our minds based on available information, as keeping an open mind to change is exactly what we're talking about. Bottom line is that contrast matters. And it matters a lot.

What is contrast exactly, though? Depending on the context of the conversation, it can have a few definitions. Generally, it is described as a state where one object is strikingly different from the other when you put them side by side. As far as how we are perceiving information, contrast is how different an object is, in terms of its color, shape, luminosity

---

[1] They've said it, not me: `www.wired.com/video/watch/almost-impossible-skip-stone-89-times`

D. Georgakas, *A11Y Unraveled*, https://doi.org/10.1007/978-1-4842-9085-9_10

(brightness), or other attributes, in order for it to be distinguishable and to stand out (Figure 10-1). As long as there is a difference in some kind of attribute and that difference can be clearly seen, you've got contrast.

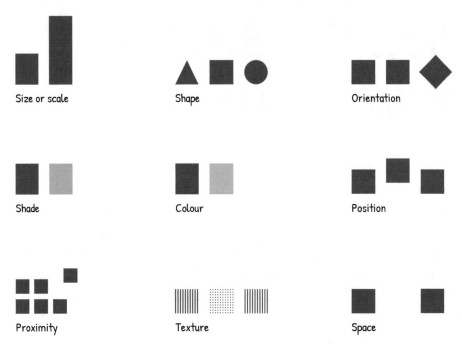

Figure 10-1. *Different types of contrast that you might have come across your design endeavors*

That being said, not all people can perceive contrast in the same way. Visual acuity, or simply how easy it is for people to see clearly and focus on what they see, is what makes us see little details without putting too much effort and is frequently used to assess one's vision. The higher it is, the better we can see and distinguish different objects; the lower it is, the harder it gets to make sense of what we're looking at. Have you ever had an eye test where you were struggling to see the bottom row of letters or the letters looked like they had a halo around them that you couldn't tell what was what? That's exactly that. If you're experiencing something like that now, please stop reading and go have your eyes tested. But, please, come back when you're done.

Every person who can see sees things in a different way, and visual acuity depends on several optical and neural factors, from the health of the retina and how well it functions to how effectively our brain can interpret what we're looking at.[2] People with disabilities who, for whatever reason, cannot see very well and cannot distinguish details in what they're looking at will find it harder to navigate on a website or use a web app if there isn't sufficient contrast between different elements, such as between the text and the background or between the button and the text within the button.

Even though contrast between text and background is quite low in Google's list for rating web accessibility, one needs to be able to read that text whenever they land on a web page. This is a case where accessibility and usability go together. Text needs to stand out from its background color to be readable, and this is really important, as users need to be able to perceive that content on that given page. *How* the text is presented is another matter, which we will discuss further on as the WCAG have a few guidelines as to how text needs to be shown. There are numerous tools online to check contrast between your copy and any background color; however, always remember that your website or product will be used by real people and not by software. In this sense, it's always good to conduct a user experiment with a sample of users who are part of your target audience to determine if the level of contrast between your design elements is sufficient, even if it doesn't conform 100% with accessibility guidelines.

---

[2] Cline D, Hofstetter HW, Griffin J (1997). *Dictionary of Visual Science* (4th ed.). Boston: Butterworth-Heinemann.

What Do the Users Think?

That was the case in the second part of my little comprehension experiment. As before, the control group was presented with a piece of content fully conforming to accessibility guidelines. A second group was presented with the same content, but this time with a twist. The contrast of the text was lowered to a level where it wasn't accessible anymore, based on the AA conformance level (Figure 10-2). The drop in contrast wasn't dramatic (as we might be willing to test a theory, but we're not that crazy as to making the text completely illegible) but low enough to fail accessibility checking.

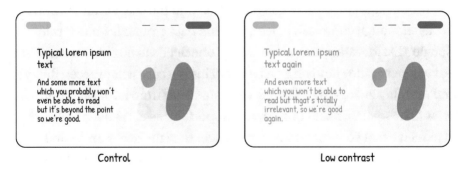

Figure 10-2.   *On the left side, you can see the layout of the website that was used in the experiment*

Text and background have a contrast ratio of 19.92:1, so that's pretty good, I think. On the right side, the contrast ratio falls all the way down to 3.1:1.

This time, the results were ~~different~~ the same, as you can see in Figure 10-3. An average score of 8.1 (±2.68) was not that different from the average score of the users in the low contrast group, which was 7.3 (±2.86), even higher than the score of the users in the skip heading group. Following a simple statistical test, it was shown that there was no statistically significant difference between the average score of the control group and the average score of the users who were presented with a less "contrasty" version of the same content (as mentioned previously, though, there was a significant difference when checking between age groups).

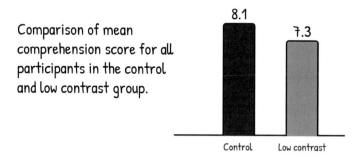

Comparison of mean comprehension score for all participants in the control and low contrast group.

Figure 10-3. *Average comprehension score of participants in the control and the low contrast group*

Could this mean that contrast doesn't matter when it comes to comprehending content? Of course not. The preceding result should only be considered within its own context. Contrast (including all kinds of contrast but most importantly color contrast), in any form, is one of the most important elements of a good design as we need our content to be visible and easily identifiable. What the lack of significant difference in scoring might tell us, though, is that for certain audiences or in specific situations, lowering the contrast a bit, to the level where our digital content is no longer fully accessible (but still readable, in theory), might not have as big of an impact as we might think or expect (plus, in some cases, it might look a bit prettier, and we all like pretty things). What we design should depend on our needs and our audiences and not on some arbitrary contrast ratio (while not exactly arbitrary, these numbers can be considered a bit crude by some people).

What Is This Thing Called Color?

Color contrast is one aspect of design that needs special attention and some tender loving care. Having said that, what is color exactly, and how is it used within a design composition? Some people claim that colors aren't real, but merely constructs of our brain, since the color that we see depends on the wavelength of light that is reflected off a surface (no need to go any deeper in this, as knowledge in physics is not the main point of this book). Color is a characteristic of our visual perception and can be described using three attributes: hue, saturation, and luminance (or value).

Hue and color are sometimes used interchangeably, as color is the term we use to describe every hue, tint, brightness, tone, and shade we see. A hue is the dominant color family of the specific color we're talking about (so pure red and pure green are hues).

On the outside of the circle in Figure 10-4, you can see the hues, pretty much pure colors. Going down toward the center of the circle, gray is added to the color, making it less saturated. If any of you reading this are color experts and this is totally wrong, failure is always an option.

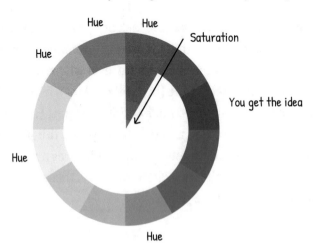

Figure 10-4. *A simple color wheel*

In Figure 10-5, you can see an example of a pure color, in this case red, meaning it's fully saturated (it has all the red in the world), vs. a less saturated version of it, with gray added in. As this is a printed book and not a screen, colors might be a bit different than what you've seen on a screen.

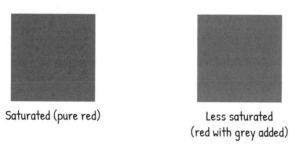

Saturated (pure red)   Less saturated
(red with grey added)

Figure 10-5. *Example of a pure color*

Saturation (or color intensity) is another attribute of color, and it shows how intense a certain color is. A fully saturated color is more intense as it has no gray in it (red is pure red). In this case, we say that the color is pure (e.g., 100% red). A fully desaturated color (0% red, in our example) will show as gray.

Finally, luminance is just a fancy name to describe how bright a color is. Or at least, how bright (or not) we *perceive* a color when we see it. It's quite an important attribute of color when we design pretty things, and if used effectively it's another way to create contrast between different elements, as contrast would be how different the brightness is between two colors. Adding white to a color would increase its lightness, creating what is called a "tint," while adding black would increase its darkness, creating a "shade" (Figure 10-6).

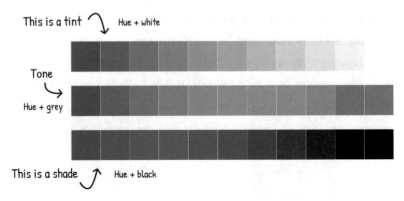

Figure 10-6. *Illustration of a tint, tone, and shade*

Imagine the preceding color is pure blue (so on a screen, it would have an RGB value of 0,0,255).[3] If you add white in it, you're making blue tints; if you add gray in it, you're making blue tones; and if you add black in it, you're making shades.

The difference in brightness is part of the basis for coming up with the contrast ratios needed to conform with accessibility guidelines (who's arbitrary now?).[4] According to a couple of international standards, specifically ISO 9241-3 and ANSI-HFES-100-1988, a typical contrast level that's needed between text and its background is 3:1 (at least that's what the W3C website mentions; I've not looked it up, but I'll take their word for it) for people with standard vision. In a 2004 paper, Arditi and Faye concluded that a visual acuity of 20/40 would mean a loss in contrast sensitivity of about 1.5; in other words, someone with low vision would be

---

[3] In the off-chance you are a designer living in an alternate reality, RGB stands for red, green, and blue, and the whole thing refers to a color model where these three primary colors are added together in various ways to produce all the other colors. It's what your screen uses.

[4] If you want to dig a bit deeper, this is where you can find more info on how the WCAG contrast ratios are calculated (www.w3.org/WAI/WCAG21/Understanding/contrast-minimum.html).

more comfortable with 50% more contrast, meaning someone with a 20/40 vision would be mostly benefited by a contrast ratio of 4.5:1 (since 3 times 1.5 is 4.5). Tadaaa!

Reality Is Not Real

The fact that the WCAG mention that a contrast ratio of 4.499:1 is a failure (I get it; we need to have standards, but still) makes me think funny things about these guidelines, as I cannot imagine someone that can see individual letters at a contrast ratio of 4.5:1, and then when this is reduced by 0.001 point, then the letters become incomprehensible. It's kind of the expiry (or best before) dates on food products. If the milk "expires" on the 31st of October, it will not automatically go off on the midnight of the 30th toward the 31st (I'm hoping there are 31 days in October without looking it up; these months are so complicated!).

You can still drink the milk.

4.5:1 is the contrast ratio recommended for an AA conformance level. A triple A level, so a contrast ratio of 7:1, would compensate for someone with a visual acuity of 20/80. Anything more than that would probably require the use of assistive technology.

Visual acuity of 20/40 is typically associated with users around the age of 80, meaning the majority of people would maintain a decent level of visual acuity up until their older years. This is something mentioned in a paper by Gittings and Fozard published as far back as 1986. And while I can find this paper with no problem whatsoever,[5] for the life of me, I can't find the paper from Arditi and Faye that mentions about contrast sensitivity.

---

[5] Gittings, N. S., and Fozard, J. L. (1986). Age related changes in visual acuity. *Experimental gerontology*, *21*(4-5), 423–433. https://doi.org/10.1016/0531-5565(86)90047-1

I'm not the only one, apparently, that thinks the math, how they ended up in that magic 4.5, and the overall concept of the contrast guidelines are a bit dodgy, as the real world is never that absolute, mainly because of the fact that visual acuity might be something that opticians or eye doctors check by showing you black letters on white screens telling you your eyesight is fine, but then you go back to a colorful world realizing you can't really see very well.

Real-world vision can be better measured by an attribute called contrast sensitivity, which shows how well one can see in low light as well as under conditions of high contrast and measures two variables: contrast and size. And size does matter. Myndex Research[6] argues that, in some cases, contrast in size (as well as font weight) matters even more than color contrast.

Take the example in Figure 10-7, for instance. Overall contrast for text and background is 1.62:1, so a major failure of the WCAG. Every piece of text (font is Open Sans) in this image has the same color, but their perception is different due to their size.[7]

---

[7] Image not directly sourced, but heavily influenced by Myndex Research.

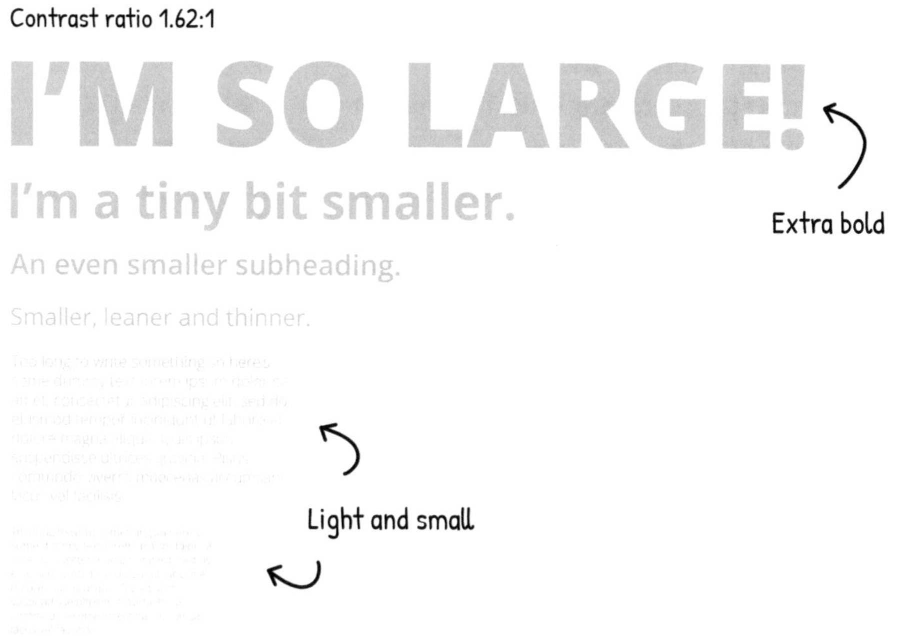

Contrast ratio 1.62:1

I'M SO LARGE!

I'm a tiny bit smaller.

Extra bold

An even smaller subheading.

Smaller, leaner and thinner.

Too long to write something in here.
Some dummy text to wrap up in order to
fill its relevance or whatsoever. Sed do
eiusmod tempor incididunt ut labore et
dolore magna aliqua. Quis ipsum
suspendisse ultrices gravida. Risus
commodo viverra maecenas accumsan
lacus vel facilisis.

Too long to write something in here.
Some dummy text to wrap up in order
to fill its relevance or whatsoever. Sed
do eiusmod tempor incididunt ut
labore et dolore magna aliqua.
Commodo viverra maecenas
accumsan lacus.

Light and small

Figure 10-7. *An example of how the perceived contrast changes with the size and font weight of text*

The text at the top is quite large, and as we go down, we keep the same color but gradually decrease the size and the font weight of the text. Most likely you'll notice that the headline at the top is easier to read than text further below, even though the contrast ratio is the same. As Myndex Research argues, it all comes down to spatial frequency, which in our case has to do with the size and the weight of the fonts. The *larger* the font and the space between lines, the *lower* the spatial frequency. The smaller the font and font weight, the higher the spatial frequency. Perceived contrast is more of a spatial frequency thing, rather than a difference in color brightness.[8]

---

[8]www.myndex.com/WEB/WCAG_CE14weight

That doesn't mean we should fail too much in our contrast ratios, but it *is* something to think about.

What is also interesting is the fact that contrast sensitivity and visual acuity are not mutually affected, and while there is a loose correlation, their relationship can't be classed as linear. In other words, when one is better, it doesn't necessarily mean the other one is better, worse, or vice versa. If you consider that this loose correlation is ultimately depending on types of visual impairment,[9] ultimately this reinforces the fact that we're all different and each approach to design needs to be based on knowledge of our users along with consistent user testing.

How to Design with Accessibility Requirements in Mind

We don't design for software, and having an automated tool tell us that because of a contrast ratio of 4.3:1 we have failed Web Content Accessibility Guidelines doesn't mean we will have failed our users, provided we've done our overall job right. At the end of the day, we need something that is easy to read and not just complies with a guideline. Perhaps these absolute numbers need to be replaced by something that takes into consideration more variables than just visual acuity and contrast in color.

It is, though, generally really, really hard to account for everything and everybody. Hence, we stick to the 4.5. Maybe when WCAG 3.0 comes out implementing APCA (or Accessible Perceptual Contrast Algorithm) that gives more focus to actual human perception rather than blindly following

---

[9] Relationship Between Acuity and Contrast Sensitivity: Differences Due to Eye Disease (2020). This is a free-for-all, great paper in the relationship between contrast sensitivity and acuity: https://iovs.arvojournals.org/article.aspx?articleid=2770151

a number that has come up with questionable math. But that's a long way off yet, and it's a subject that deserves a book on its own. Luckily, there is an understanding and an acknowledgment from the W3C's side that our understanding of visual perception and contrast has been changed and this is something that *will* be addressed in WCAG 3.0.

Another aspect that's not taken into consideration in the WCAG contrast requirements is the brightness of white color, which only adds to the fact that the WCAG contrast requirements mostly fail when it comes to darker colors. When it comes to a website being in dark mode, something that has started being used more and more frequently lately, implementing accessibility standards but, most importantly, making sure that the website is actually accessible is trickier than what one might think.

Dark mode on a website has its obvious benefits: it reduces eye strain and can make an interface easier to understand in lower-light conditions, light-colored text (not white) is perceived as easier to read, and there are less chances of users with sensitivity to light being affected. On the other hand, dark modes are not accessible from the get-go, and as in everything, careful implementation is required.

Such great difference in contrast can create eye strain issues. Using something that's not as intense, like a dark-gray background, can decrease eye strain and increase readability. In Figure 10-8 the pure white text on the far left sits on a completely black background, while the other two examples show how it would look on a dark-gray setting.

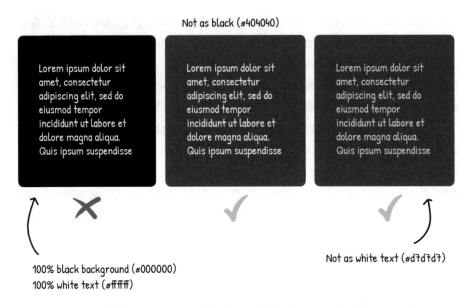

Figure 10-8. *White text on a black and dark-gray background*

Not all colors have high enough contrast with a dark background, which can make site navigation a bit harder (think of the blue border color that comes up as a default when an element receives focus). People with dyslexia or astigmatism might find it harder to read white text on a black background; that's why a light color and not white is recommended for text when it sits on a black background.[10] A font of white color on a black background might also give rise to a phenomenon called "halation," where a little glow seems to be appearing around the letters, which could potentially make the text harder to read.

For users with astigmatism in particular, white text on a black background (meaning a super-contrast) can make it look like something in Figure 10-9, where the text appears fuzzy. Astigmatism is an eye problem that can make your eyes blurry, affecting a large number of the population,

---

[10] www.boia.org/blog/dark-mode-can-improve-text-readability-but-not-for-everyone

so careful consideration is needed. You can have it since birth, but you can also acquire it later on in life. Another reason white text on a pure black background should, ideally, be avoided.

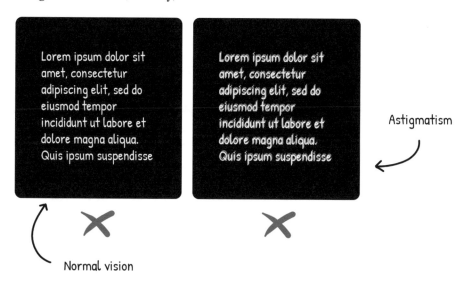

Figure 10-9. *How white text on a black background would potentially look for users with astigmatism*

This could be why white text is easier to read on somewhat lighter backgrounds, even though the WCAG contrast ratio fails. Check out the following example (Figure 10-10). UX Movement did a survey on Twitter[11] a few years back, asking users which button is easier to read. As you can imagine, the one with the white text on the light-blue background was the undisputed winner, even though it fails contrast ratio requirements.

---

[11] https://twitter.com/uxmovement/status/1181306639284080640?s=20

Which button is easier to read?

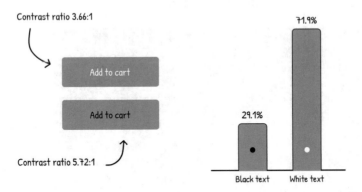

Figure 10-10. *This is a classic example of "we design for the users"*

The contrast ratio of the button with the white text is 3.66:1, which fails the AA conformance level, while the button with the black text satisfies the criterion of a 4.5:1 contrast ratio. Even though it fails accessibility, the button with the white label doesn't fail the users, since the majority of them found it easier to read.

Do you need a PhD and the combined mental capacity of Einstein, Leibniz, and Tesla to just put some text on a canvas? Because that's what all this suggests. No, I wouldn't think so. The takeaway from this is that absolute numbers don't work in the real world, because the real world is not absolute. It's comprised of 8 billion different people (including the babies and the people who don't have access to the Internet) with 8 billion different experiences who might be using a website in 8 billion different ways. Obviously, an exaggeration, but you get the point. Our designs should follow the needs of our users, not the instructions of an algorithm.

Different people see things in different ways. This means that I might perceive red in a slightly different way than you. If we both don't have any vision problems, then chances are the "version" of red we'll see will be pretty much the same in terms of hue, saturation, and luminance.

However, if someone has a color vision deficiency, they might perceive that red as a somewhat different hue of a different luminance. Due to the fact that within an entire population there might be many, many, many different color deficiencies among people, we needed to come up with a way that eliminates (or, at least, diminishes) the factor of color perception (we can't design 12452^{12} different color combinations to accommodate for 12452 color deficiencies). Therefore, simply having sufficient luminance contrast between colors will result in something that can be understood, regardless of *how* we perceive color.

Figure 10-11 shows how different colors can lead to different contrast ratios depending on a common visual impairment, such as color blindness. Some colors, such as the red at the top, would still have sufficient (and even more) contrast for users with protanopia. Others, like the green at the bottom, might be perceived differently, depending on the color blindness type.

---

[12] Randomly chosen number.

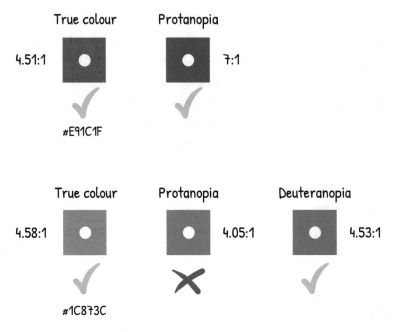

Figure 10-11. *How red and green colors look for users with different color blindness types*

How much difference do we need, though? To avoid making browsing a website look like playing *Tales of Lagoona* (a totally random choice of a hidden object game, nothing frisky involved here, but now maybe I need to check it out. Procrastination, your name is Dimitris), the Web Content Accessibility Guidelines have set out a few requirements when it comes to contrast, based on international standards.

As mentioned, according to success criterion 1.4.3 (this makes me feel like a lawyer; I've decided there are not going to be many mentions of actual criteria numbers to keep this as simple as possible), in order to get an AA conformance level, normal text needs to have a contrast ratio of at least *4.5:1*. This, generally speaking, means that the brightness of the text needs to be 4.5 times higher than the brightness of its surrounding element, be it a background or an image. If you're feeling a bit crazy and want to go for an AAA conformance level, then normal-size text in your content will need to have a contrast ratio of *7:1*.

Notice the word "normal." The WCAG distinguish between text of different sizes. Larger text is easier to read, so the contrast ratio requirements are lower. Specifically, for larger text, you can achieve AA conformance if you have a contrast ratio of 3:1 and AAA conformance if you have a contrast ratio of 4.5:1. When it comes to actual text size, a text is considered large when it's 14 points or larger and bold or 18 points or larger (that translates to 18.67 pixels or 24 pixels, which is an even number and much better).

How precise is 18.67, isn't it? I wonder what will happen if we round it down to 18 px. Hm... You can see these differences in Figure 10-12. Normal text size of, let's say, 16 pixels will fail an AA conformance level if the contrast ratio is less than 4.5:1. Keeping the same color and increasing the font size, however, will pass, as demonstrated in the second row of the image. Despite the fact that contrast is less than the recommended for an AA conformance level pass, the size and font weight make up for it.

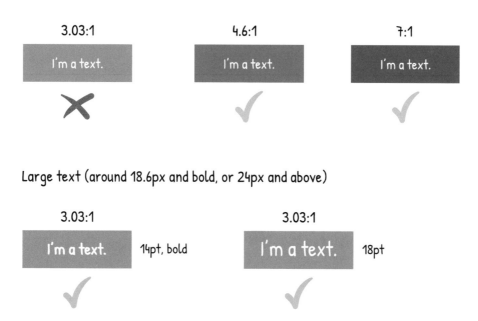

Figure 10-12. *Contrast ratios for regular and large font styles*

In this case, as well, there are some exceptions where text doesn't need to conform to any kind of contrast requirement. These pieces of text include inactive elements (such as an inactive button; if you can't use the button, no one cares about the contrast of the button text), decorative text or text that is part of an image but not important information (such as text on a book that is part of a larger image; that doesn't really affect the user in any way), and text that is meant to be hidden (e.g., a skip link that skips to main content, although when it becomes visible, it needs to have proper contrast).

Finally, when it comes to user interface components, the contrast ratio of 3:1 remains (Figure 10-13). Disabled buttons are one element that doesn't need to conform to contrast requirements, but don't even get me started on those (actually, I do get started in the next chapter).

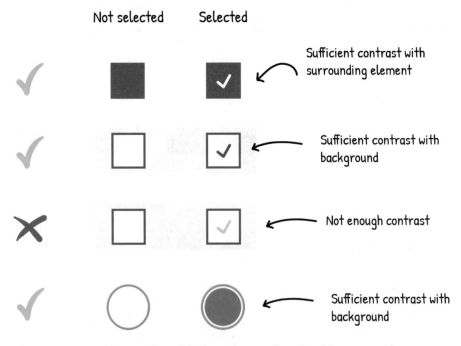

Figure 10-13. *Examples of fail and pass for checkboxes and radio buttons*

The first two elements in Figure 10-13 pass contrast requirements since there is sufficient (at least) 3:1 contrast between the element and the actual check mark, which shows a change of state. In the second example, the white fill of the checkbox doesn't have enough contrast with the element's background, but the dark border compensates for that. The actual checkmark has a satisfying contrast with its background, which makes this pass contrast requirements. In the third example, the check mark doesn't have enough contrast with the checkbox itself, which doesn't clearly show that it is selected. In the fourth example, even though the dot within the selected element doesn't have enough contrast with the border, there is sufficient contrast with its background, which makes it a pass.

Taking these contrast requirements into consideration, any element on your canvas should have sufficient contrast with its surrounding elements. What is frustrating though is the fact that you can't round down contrast ratios (remember that a ratio of 4.49:1 is a failure).

According to our little contrast experiment though, and the work of some very smart people who like to question things, lowering the contrast a bit might not be as bad as we like to think, at least in specific situations. It's a case of following the spirit of the law, rather than the letter of the law. Take Figure 10-14, for example. The red color on the left passes contrast requirements, but the one on the right doesn't. If you ask me, they look identical (although to the hawkeyed people out there, there might be a difference). If you ask me, I'd use any.

Figure 10-14. *Example of how different shades of the same color can fail or pass contrast requirements, even though they look almost identical*

Based on what was mentioned previously about having different elements identifiable as unique, the background of a website section should (ideally) be different, the text on it should be of a color that has high contrast against the background, and a potential image would sit in its own column, properly set apart from the text. One of the biggest "mistakes" designers make (there might be more, as this is my personal assessment and sometimes I go crazy too) is creating a canvas that looks like one big compilation of elements that are not distinct, making the canvas look like a modern art painting.

While there's nothing wrong with that visually, imagine trying to use that "painting" for something useful, that is, when buying a product, signing up for a service, or finding critical information about a project you're working on. Have you seen these "find the hidden object" games? Exactly what I'm talking about.

When we're checking for contrast on a website or a web app, the first thing that needs to stand out is the different sections of our interface. Imagine that you're on an ecommerce website that has a few different sections: a navigation, a header, the content area where the product and its details are, perhaps a section with more information below that, maybe even related products further down, and then a footer. Each of these sections will need to be clearly defined to avoid confusion and elements mixing with each other. Besides, it's science.

Our brains need to be able to distinguish fast and effortlessly separate elements of what we're looking at, and as such, they pay more attention to something that stands out, like things that contrast with their environment or with whatever came before them, if we're talking about sections on a website.[13]

When we see things clearly, we are more relaxed, and it's easier for us to function in a given setting. This is an evolutionary trait as when our ancestors were walking in the jungle, distinguishing a snake from a twig on the ground was paramount when walking through unknown territory. Making out a predator before they saw us was vital to our survival as it enabled us to prepare for a fight or just run away like cowards. Nevertheless, alive cowards.

Regardless, there is a part in our brains that needs clear contrast so it can make quick decisions. Some like to call it the "lizard brain," which just puts an emphasis on the fact that it's the same regions in the brain that are doing the exact same thing as when we were reptiles.[14] We might not be looking at a fight-or-flight response when browsing through a website (that would be awkward), but we still need to be able to pick out different elements and make quick decisions to get the best possible outcome.

So how do we achieve proper contrast between website sections? There are several ways to separate them, be it a border or color change, or even a big margin with a small divider can make a difference (Figure 10-15). As long as we can identify each of these parts of the page as unique, we're off to a great start. And when this is achieved, contrast between each element inside a section is the next important bit to worry about. In the same way, this can be achieved either by white space (or whitespace),[15] dividers, color, and so on.

---

[13] https://cxl.com/blog/5-principles-of-persuasive-web-design/
[14] Burnett, Dean (2016). *The Idiot Brain*. Guardian Books, p. 6.
[15] White space doesn't necessarily need to be white. It simply means empty space around elements in an attempt to clearly differentiate between them.

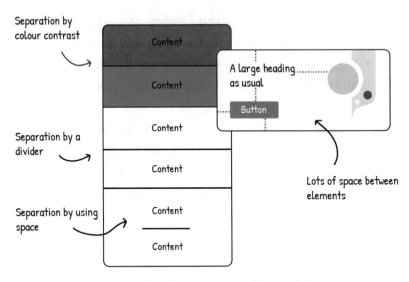

Figure 10-15. *An example of contrast within website sections*

What to Do in a Nutshell

Color

Color is nice and all, but please make sure that information that's conveyed by color also relies on other aspects in order to be understood. For example, if a user tries to fill in a form field and makes a mistake and the field is only highlighted red to indicate an error, someone that can't see red well enough (maybe color-blind) might not understand there is an error there. In this case we can use an icon alongside the color change, such as an exclamation point, to notify the user that there is definitely something wrong there. What's even better is if you use text alongside those two. Displaying information in other ways as well, rather than just color, will count toward your A level conformance.

In the example in Figure 10-16, if you only used a red border to indicate error, someone with a visual impairment such as color blindness wouldn't have a clue about what has happened.

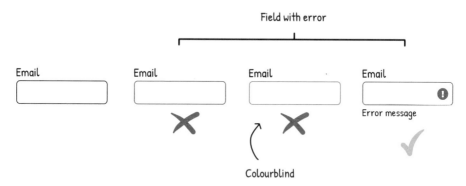

Figure 10-16. *Error indication on a form field*

Adding an icon to it, and even an error message, would up your chances of someone picking up the fact there's an error.

Check your design in grayscale or in color deficiency mode by using a relevant plugin. This can potentially help reveal parts of the canvas that might not be as well understood.

Perhaps it's worth adding an underline indicator on hovered links (Figure 10-17). Some users might not perceive the color change on hover as sufficient to understand that an action can be performed there, so adding some kind of indicator on hover would make it clearer that an element has been somehow interacted with.

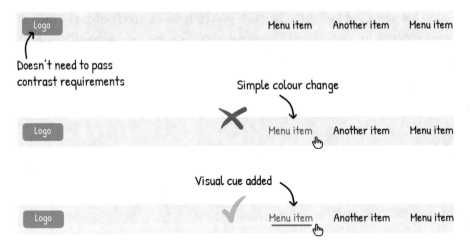

Figure 10-17. *Visual cue when hovering over a main navigation link*

When hovering or focusing on a text link, a visual indicator (like an underline, but it can be anything) would provide the clue that this text is actually a link. Although this is enough to pass the contrast requirement, ideally and based on what we discussed previously, you'd need that underline there by default (Figure 10-18).[16] The WCAG recommend blue color for links, since people with color blindness would be less affected.

When having links within text, a simple 3:1 contrast is enough to pass the WCAG requirements, as this would make the links stand out from the rest of the text.

---

[16] The WCAG recommends only doing that when you have only a few links within a body of text. Otherwise, having a trillion underlined words within a paragraph would create other problems. For most situations, and for all intents and purposes, a simple contrast difference is enough.

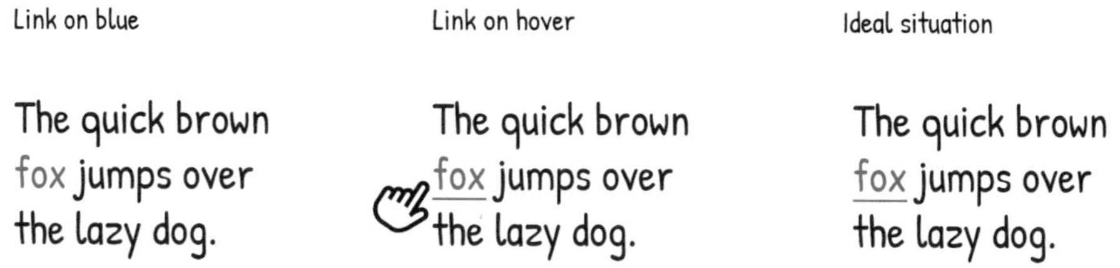

Link on blue   Link on hover   Ideal situation

The quick brown   The quick brown   The quick brown
fox jumps over   fox jumps over   fox jumps over
the lazy dog.   the lazy dog.   the lazy dog.

Figure 10-18. *A link within a body of text*

Separate colors in groups and use each one in specific circumstances to ensure consistency and to avoid confusion. Create hierarchy and use the brand's primary colors for the most important actions; for instance, all primary actions should use the brand's primary color, and all secondary colors should be used for secondary buttons and backgrounds. Make sure that these colors don't clash and have sufficient contrast between them.

In other words, use common sense and act within context.

Contrast

Sufficient contrast is not a requirement for an A conformance level. However, that doesn't mean we should put white text on white background as information on a page still needs to be identifiable and legible.

To get an AA conformance level, ensure that text and background have a minimum contrast of 4.5:1. That is, not 4.3, not 4.49, but 4.5. Exactly (I will never get tired of mocking this). Otherwise, the universe will collapse (only joking, but I won't be the one to try it in case something bad happens). To make that happen (proper contrast, not the collapse of the universe), think simple: Dark background? Light text! Light background? Dark text! There are some exceptions, though. If your text is large enough, then the contrast ratio requirement falls into 3:1. How large? Well, research shows that a satisfying size is about 15 c— Sorry, wrong study.

If your text is 18 pt large (24 px) or 14 pt bold (about 18.67 px), then the contrast requirement falls to the preceding ratio. Also, decorative text has no contrast requirements since it's... well, decorative, so it plays no part in delivering important information. In Figure 10-19 even though there is some form of text on the right side of the image, as it's purely decorative, it does not need to conform to any contrast requirements.

Text on logos or on any image also doesn't have a contrast requirement. If your logo is faint and can't be seen even by people with normal vision, then I'm sorry; that's on you.

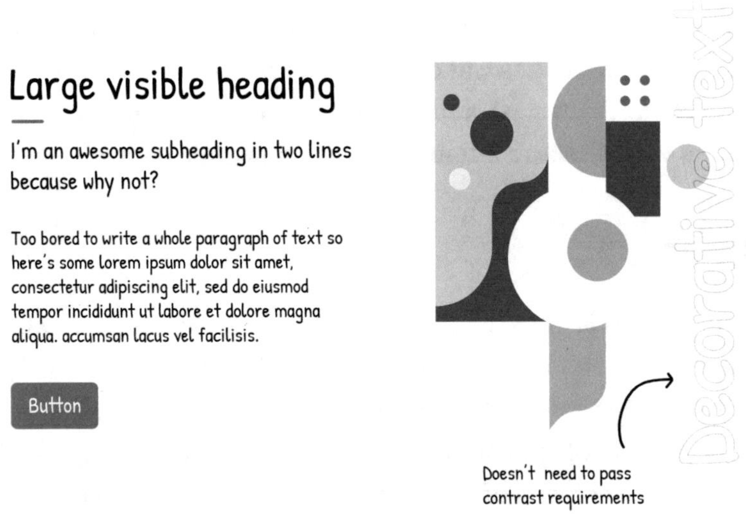

Figure 10-19. *Hypothetical website composition with copy on one side and an image on the other*

This applies to all text used of all colors (aside the exceptions) throughout the whole website, that is, navigations, links, visited links, headings, text in content, and so on.

For a super heroic AAA conformance level, replace the 4.5:1 with a 7:1 ratio and the 3:1 with a 4.5:1. In other words, good luck.

For any elements that are not text, a contrast of 3:1 is required with the color of their surrounding environment, but only the surroundings that are required to understand the meaning of the element.

In the example in Figure 10-20, the only contrast that matters is the one between the icon and its background, in this case, the red disc. That's because the telephone icon is necessary to understand content, so it needs to stand out. The overall contrast with the red disc and *its* background is irrelevant, provided the icon is large enough to see, though.

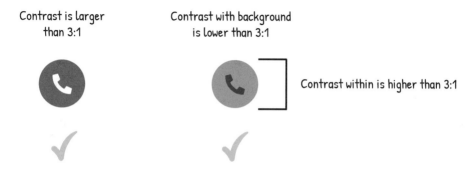

Figure 10-20. *Hypothetical phone icon with contrast requirements*

Have a red button? Make sure it sits on a background that is light enough with sufficient contrast (depending on the situation, if you can tell that a button is a button from context, then there's no need for sufficient contrast), such as in Figure 10-21. This contrast needs to be carried over when the button is interacted with. However, the contrast between the color of the two states (default and hover) is irrelevant, as long as the contrast with the button labels remains. In fact, you don't even need the background of the button to have sufficient contrast with *its* background, as long as the user can understand from context that this is a button.

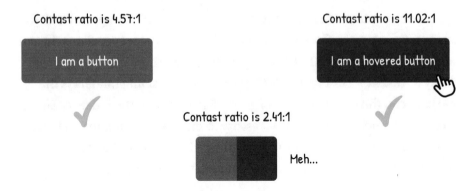

Figure 10-21. *A button with sufficient contrast between its background and label in the default and hover state*

Have a border around a field? Make sure the color of the fill or the border has sufficient contrast with its surroundings. Have an icon? Make sure there is at least a 3:1 contrast ratio between the icon and the space around it.

As before, any logos or any items that are not required for understanding information do not need to have that contrast level.

Summary

As contrast and color are two of the most important things a designer has input on, they deserve their own chapter. We have looked into what contrast is and its different types. Any significant change in an attribute that causes a visual difference can be considered as contrast when putting two elements together, be it color, shape, texture, and so on.

Following a comprehension experiment and the fact that visual acuity is better measured by contrast sensitivity, as important as contrast is, depending on the color used and the size of the element, we can afford to fail accessibility guidelines, to a degree. Having elements that have a contrast ratio that fails the requirements would be okay, if these elements were large enough to stand out in their environment.

However, we still need to think about different disabilities when designing our product and the fact that "no size fits all," as well as the fact that guidelines are there as a starting point. There are some issues when it comes to color contrast requirements, mainly from the fact that people perceive things in different ways and depending on circumstances.

Some of these circumstances in our case are the different issues that users might be facing. When it comes to color blindless, for example, we should check how our colors are perceived by users with different types of the condition. A few examples were given on how certain elements would look (and need to look) when it comes to designing our mockups, from color to size. Hopefully, these were enough to give you a starting point and make you think even more when laying down similar, or other, elements in your canvas.

How we use color is very closely related to how much contrast there is on a given web page or web app. Generally speaking, most of the things we put on a design and that are indicated by color need to have another way for them to be identifiable, and we shouldn't rely on color alone. Users who can't tell the difference between colors because they might have problems with their eyesight (hence, they can see no or low contrast) or have a monochrome display (or even an old one that doesn't display colors properly) will find information received only by color a bit useless. So we need to make sure that information conveyed with color is also available without color, for example, from context or markup.

This can be particularly important to the one item everybody has spent countless hours testing and experimenting with, trying to identify what works best and for what audience: calls to action, as the posh people call them, clicky things like Ɨ some might refer to them or just... buttons.

CHAPTER 11

Click Me Like You Mean It

Buttons here, buttons there, buttons everywhere. Buttons are one of the most important elements on a website or any digital product. They help us navigate and perform actions, they frustrate us when they don't work, and they amaze us when it's time to buy the gift we've always wanted to give to ourselves (or our wives, but mostly to ourselves). They come in all colors and in all sizes. Some even come in weird shapes, but who are we to discriminate? Out of the gazillion different buttons, I'm pretty sure I'm displaying the ugly ones in Figure 11-1, but you get the idea. All shapes and sizes, even though all shapes and sizes are not really needed.

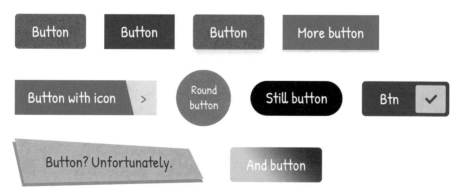

Figure 11-1. *Different types of buttons just for the sake of some context*

© Dimitris Georgakas 2023
D. Georgakas, *A11Y Unraveled*, https://doi.org/10.1007/978-1-4842-9085-9_11

At this point it's important to differentiate between buttons, links, and the different types of buttons (Figure 11-2). Why? Because why not add some more confusion to a subject that is not really needed? Buttons are graphical elements that should be used when we want the user to act on something, be that send a message, buy a product, delete something, and so on. Links are usually text elements used primarily for navigation, to go somewhere (or so they say). Nevertheless, links and buttons serve a common purpose: they allow us to do something and, if done correctly, they provide a positive user experience.

In other words, buttons will perform an action that will affect a website, such as a transaction or sending a message. A link would be used to just browse content. Or so they have you think, since we (for some reason) have text buttons, which are buttons that look like text – which is exactly what a link looks like, text. But it's a link, not a button.

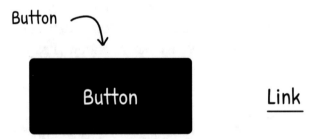

Figure 11-2. *Buttons are... buttons and links are... links*

In order to do something though, the buttons (or links) need to be found. And to be found, they need to stand out from their surroundings. Remember the contrast bit we talked about before? This is another area where sufficient contrast should be applied as you can't use a button if you can't see it. And if a user can't see your button fast enough, they'll go someplace else where their buttons are easier to find. It's not them; it's you.

These buttons can be just like text links, or text buttons if you will. The text will usually describe the action that can be taken when we click or tap them, and they're mainly used for actions of secondary importance, as they are not that well defined and so they seem to play a less important role (Figure 11-3).

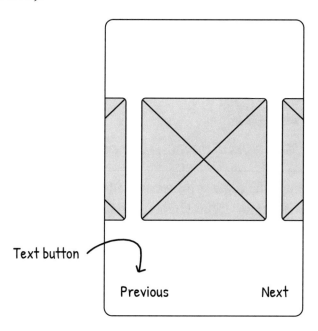

Figure 11-3.   *Text buttons don't necessarily look like buttons. It's just a text label without a surrounding container*

Ghost Buttons?

Then there's this button that people refer to in many names, but at least we all agree on how it's supposed to look: an outlined shape with no fill that surrounds some text. I'm referring to the ghost button, otherwise known as the outlined button, otherwise known as the invisible button, otherwise known as that "button you put in your design if you want people to miss it." Only joking. It's not that dramatic. At least for me. Angie Schottmuller on the other hand, a conversion optimizer, clearly states: *"Ghost buttons drive me crazy [...] Ghosted buttons have ghost conversions."* While that's far from the truth, it's not exactly wrong either.

Figure 11-4 shows the normal button we all know and love on the left side. On the right side, the ghost button we all know but not all love. Unlike how it seems, there is no white fill on this button.

Figure 11-4. *Two types of buttons: normal and ghost*

In 2019, a marketing agency in Texas called CXL conducted a set of three experiments to determine if ghost buttons have any significant impact on conversions. In the first experiment, they ran the test on their own website in an effort to find out if and how a ghost button affects user experience. They carried out a simple A/B test where one version of their homepage had a button with a solid fill and the other one had the infamous ghost button. After more than 10,000 visits to their webpage, the results were in: there was a 20% decrease in clicks on the ghost button. Besides that, the overall user behavior on the homepage was pretty much the same. This result indicates that perhaps a ghost button is less attractive or less prominent than a solid one.

The second part of the experiment was a click test. Users were asked to perform an action on a set of three web pages, such as "Where would you click to buy a ticket?", and they measured the amount of time it took the users to click the buy button as well as the user errors, meaning they clicked somewhere on the page where they weren't supposed to. The results were quite consistent and showed that ghost buttons were a bit harder to spot. Users were about 10% faster on average in clicking the solid button compared with the ghost one. This means when it came to solid buttons, users were about 1 second faster in clicking them.

If you think 1 second is nothing, let me remind you that according to a study published on *Behaviour & Information Technology* magazine in 2011, it takes about 0.05 seconds, or about 50 milliseconds, for a user to form an opinion about a website and that opinion determines whether they'll stay or leave.[1] So, as you can see, seconds (one, in this case) are important. The average error rate was also higher on the pages that had the ghost button. And if able users with no impairments can't make this work, how would users with disabilities perform?

Something to note here though is that out of the three websites they tested, the one that performed the worst had the ghost button on the top right instead of the middle of the screen, which might be giving an indication as to where to place it. If you have to use it, might as well place it somewhere that a user is more likely to look at.

The third and final part of the experiment aimed to see if different types of buttons change the users' behavior. This test was conducted not with actual people but using the services of an online tool called EyeQuant. It's an AI tool that uses a predictive model developed from about 1.6 million real experiments, and the company claims to have 90% accuracy when it comes to results, in comparison with a real user test. I've not tried it; it looks really cool, but it's probably really expensive as well.

One of the suite's tools can analyze a design and show you what they call as "regions of interest." In plain words, you can measure how eye-catching a region of your design is, and that measurement comes from actual quantitative data. CXL highlighted the buttons to identify them as regions of interest, and the tool measures how eye-catching the average pixel of the region is, compared with the average pixel on the whole screen.

---

[1] You might want to have a look at this, dear reader: https://doi.org/10.1080/01449290500330448

The results from this tool showed that ghost buttons are less eye-catching and as such their score was lower. In one of the tests, the ghost button had a score of 38% compared with 60% of the solid button. This means that the ghost button is less likely to attract a user's attention.

But Ghost Buttons Are So Pretty!

Clearly, based on these experiments, there is a pattern that points toward the fact that ghost buttons are less likely to convert compared with traditional, solid-fill buttons. However, this is only an indication. Ghost buttons look beautiful (subjective, but still) and if used in the proper context can really make a design pop.[2]

The data suggests that a ghost button's impact on usability is likely negative; however, this will probably depend on how they're used. Ultimately, what needs to be considered is why we use each of these two buttons: solid or ghost. The ghost button could probably do just fine as a call to action of secondary importance, next to our main button. To determine what's best for your case, don't just rely on past experiments that other people have done because they are only isolated tests done within a different context of their own. Instead, it might be a good idea to use them as a starting point and then test your product to see what works for you. Or not.

Chances are users with visual impairments will have a hard time using a ghost button if it doesn't have sufficient color contrast with its background. When it comes to buttons with a solid fill, some lack in contrast ratio can be compensated by the fact that these buttons are solid objects. And if their size is sufficient enough, they can still be seen and understood. Ghost buttons on the other hand consist of a thin border and only a text label, so careful implementation is needed.

---

[2] I'm using terminology we've all heard at some point in our professional journeys: "Can you make it pop?" (If you can relate to this, raise your hand.) The other one is the famous "wow factor," which everybody mentions, but no one can explain what it is.

Types of Buttons

Putting the ghost button aside and thinking of it as just a particular style of a standard button, Adam Silver, interaction designer and author of *Form Design Patterns*, distinguishes between four types of buttons and links (Figure 11-5): the submit button, which does what its name says, submits a form (like when signing in or adding a product to a basket); a normal link that's used for navigation purposes; a button (a button button?); and calls to action, which are like normal links, only styled to look like buttons.[3]

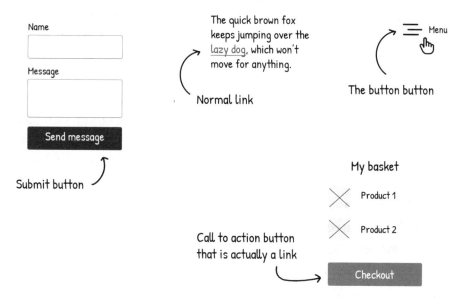

Figure 11-5. *Types of buttons according to adamsilver.io.[4] Check it out. There is a great case on the use of button names and if they actually matter. But please check it after you finish this book*

---

[3] https://medium.com/simple-human/but-sometimes-links-look-like-buttons-and-buttons-look-like-links-9b371c57b3d2
[4] https://adamsilver.io/blog/but-sometimes-buttons-look-like-links/

If you ask me, I don't really get why we need so many labels for so many different things. A button in real life is something you press or something you put through a slit to make your clothes pretty or functional. I guess buttons in web design look like real-life buttons, which you somehow "press," and so are named as such. But the only real buttons we have are the ones on our keyboards, mice, or whatever we use to navigate a page. Why aren't buttons just links that have a background around them to make them stand out? Oh, wait… Designers are so weird sometimes. Why do you have to label everything?[5] I guess we need a name for things so we can distinguish them. But do users care? That's the ultimate question.

InVision, a digital product design platform, states other types of buttons: text buttons, which are just that, text that doesn't have a container and describes an action that will happen when a user clicks or taps it (looks like a link, but it's actually a button[6]); the infamous ghost button that was described previously; and raised buttons that are like any other button apart from a drop shadow that makes them look like they're raised (come on). This adds weight to the button and makes it look more clickable as it's an easy way to make it look more distinct in a busy layout. Toggle buttons are used to group options together, and only one of them is active at a time (e.g., the buttons used to justify text in a word-processing document).[7]

You can see Google's Material Design 3[8] button types in Figure 11-6. Google keeps the text button, renames the ghost button into an outlined button, and brings in a new name for simple buttons, which is filled buttons. Raised buttons are also now called elevated (a bit posher I guess). These are like any other buttons, similar to the raised buttons of InVision. There is a text label surrounded by a container, which could be filled with

---

[5] You will never know if I'm joking or not.

[6] If it looks like a duck, sounds like a duck, and walks like a duck…

[7] www.invisionapp.com/inside-design/comprehensive-guide-designing-ux-buttons/

[8] https://m3.material.io/components/buttons/overview

color (isn't that just a normal button?), elevated with a slight drop shadow, or even have an icon next to the text label as a visual aid alongside the standard label.

Figure 11-6. *Different types of buttons from Google's Material Design 3*

Material Design also mentions tonal buttons, which are kind of a middle ground between filled and outlined buttons, basically a filled button where the fill is of lower opacity than the button label. That's what it looks like, at least. That button is supposed to be of lower priority. Surprisingly, disabled buttons are not in their own category, which is great! Remember a few pages up when I said I wouldn't get started on them? Now is the time for this.

Disabled Buttons

Disabled buttons (Figure 11-7), apart from creating a potentially confusing and poor user experience, can also exclude people with disabilities, making a web page less accessible. These buttons will normally have a text label on them, like on any other button, but it will be really transparent, to the point even a user with normal eyesight won't be able to see what it says.

Figure 11-7. *Example of a disabled button on the right vs. a button with a fully opaque fill. Supposedly, the light-gray color (or a black with reduced opacity) signifies that a button can't be used*

Surprisingly, the WCAG don't require a specific contrast ratio on inactive user interface components. To be honest, even the fact that they're there creates confusion as some users might think, "Wait a minute. Why can I not click this?" Most of the time, users won't even get feedback as to why they can't click or tap that button. Obviously, the reason is that some requirements are not met yet, but it might not be as obvious for some people, especially if they're new to technology or have cognitive disabilities.

Hampus Sethfors, a UX and accessibility specialist at Axess Lab, gives a great example as to why disabled buttons can be problematic for web accessibility reasons.[9] As illustrated in Figure 11-8, a user who can't see very well might zoom in an interface to see something, let's say a registration form, much clearer. In the off chance that this form has two fields side by side, the user is very likely to miss the second column (for instance, two columns side by side for First name and Last name). The Last name field becomes pretty much invisible. It's very easy to forget what you were doing, thinking there's only one column to fill in.

---

[9] https://axesslab.com/disabled-buttons-suck/

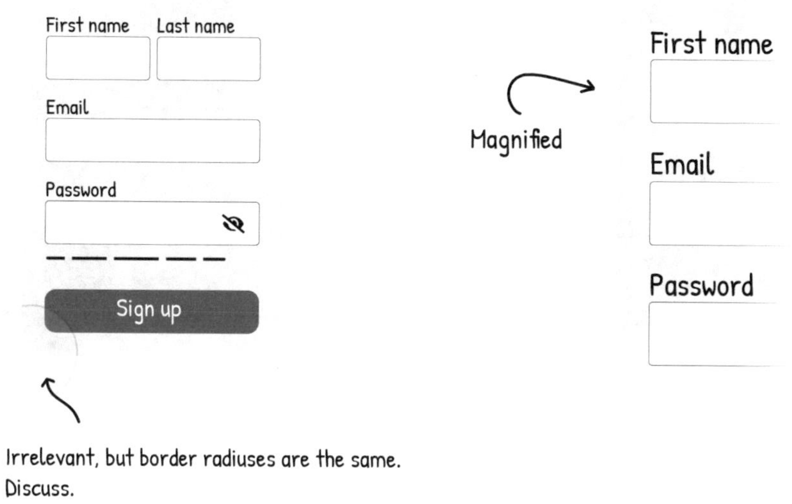

First name   Last name

Email

Password

Magnified

Sign up

First name

Email

Password

Irrelevant, but border radiuses are the same.
Discuss.

Figure 11-8. *In the preceding example, a user who can't see very well has zoomed in to see the form fields better*

You will then happily fill in all the fields in your view, and thinking you were done, you will proceed to click or tap the register button (Figure 11-9), and nothing will happen. You will then tap it again, and still, you'll get nothing. The number of times you will click or tap before you quit depends on your level of tolerance for things that don't work as they're supposed to.

Actually, that button does work as it's supposed to. It's disabled because you haven't filled in all the fields, so it prevents you from registering. And as mentioned previously, there is a great chance this button will not be focusable if you're trying to get to it using your keyboard. What's even worse is that you won't get any kind of feedback as to why it's not working, and by the time you realize it, you'll probably have moved on to a different website that works properly.

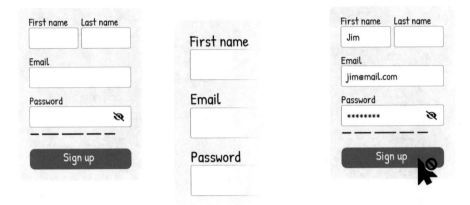

Figure 11-9. *Illustration showing the missed field in a hypothetical registration form. According to the example from Axes Lab, due to magnifying the user interface, the user will have missed one of the form fields, preventing them from submitting the form*

Instead, if the button was not disabled (meaning a user would be able to interact with it), an error message would give the user the reason as to why they couldn't submit that form. Ideally, disabled buttons or other components should not exist or, at least, should not exist in this form. If you really need to have a button that is disabled, a good alternative might be to make it look like it's disabled by using CSS while keeping it active in the code. This way it would still be focusable, clickable, and able to provide feedback if interacted with a mouse or a keyboard.[10]

When all the fields are filled in correctly, then with some code magic, it could turn to its proper color signifying it's ready to be clicked or tapped. If you really have to use a disabled button, might be worth providing some context next to it, as to why it's disabled or what the user needs to do for

---

[10] As always, when it comes to things design, some user feedback will help eliminate any confusion.

the button to become clickable. Personally, I prefer active, nice-looking buttons that users are always able to interact with and real-time validation whenever a form is filled in. Buttons, not links.

A Button Should Look Like a Button

Someone once told me, "A button should look like a button, and a link should look like a link." But we have so many names for basically the same things, so how can we be sure what a button looks like? At the end of the day, all that a button or a link does is perform an action when interacted with. And if that control element is prominent enough with a clear text label as to what it does, is there any point to how it looks?

Does anyone really know how many types of buttons are out there? The issue comes from the fact that a standard, everyday user doesn't care about the terminology we use or, for example, if a link is styled as a button (in this case what do we call it, link or button?). All users are concerned about is that the things that are supposed to do a specific action or take them somewhere specific do so.

If a button has text on it that says the very descriptive "Click this to buy this product," a user couldn't care less if it's a link styled as a button, a button styled as a link, or a duck disguised as a goose. They probably don't know how links work. It's most likely none of their concern, and it shouldn't be. They just want to buy the darn thing. To be honest, even for designers, I'm not sure if it would make a difference in their (our) work if they knew that this eye-catching, accessible, and usable button that they've designed is going to be coded as a link styled as a button. It wouldn't for me. As long as I know that what I've designed is usable and accessible in its specific situation, that's all that matters.

Sometimes designers and web professionals forget what it is like to be a normal user. Every day, we look at different websites and play around with code or design systems, trying to figure out what works best and in what situation, that we sometimes forget how a user actually uses a website or a web app and what exactly they want out of it. They just want it to work as expected with as little friction as possible. What happens behind the scenes is irrelevant to them. I really don't have a clue how my mobile phone works and have no idea about what happens when I tap a certain place on a screen that makes things work. I know how to use it though, and that's enough for me. We are not the average users, but we need to think like them.

And what do users want? Well, that's the million-dollar question. For now, though, let's just focus on buttons. In terms of accessibility, and usability, the way we design buttons should adhere to a small set of guidelines to make interacting with them easy for everybody.

Normally, buttons should be big enough to allow for easy clicking (or tapping, if you're on a mobile device); be static, meaning they shouldn't be moving or floating around on your canvas; and have enough space around them, if they have to be side by side. This includes other control elements as well, such as radio buttons or checkboxes, as if they were too close to each other it might be harder for some people to choose different options (Figure 11-10).

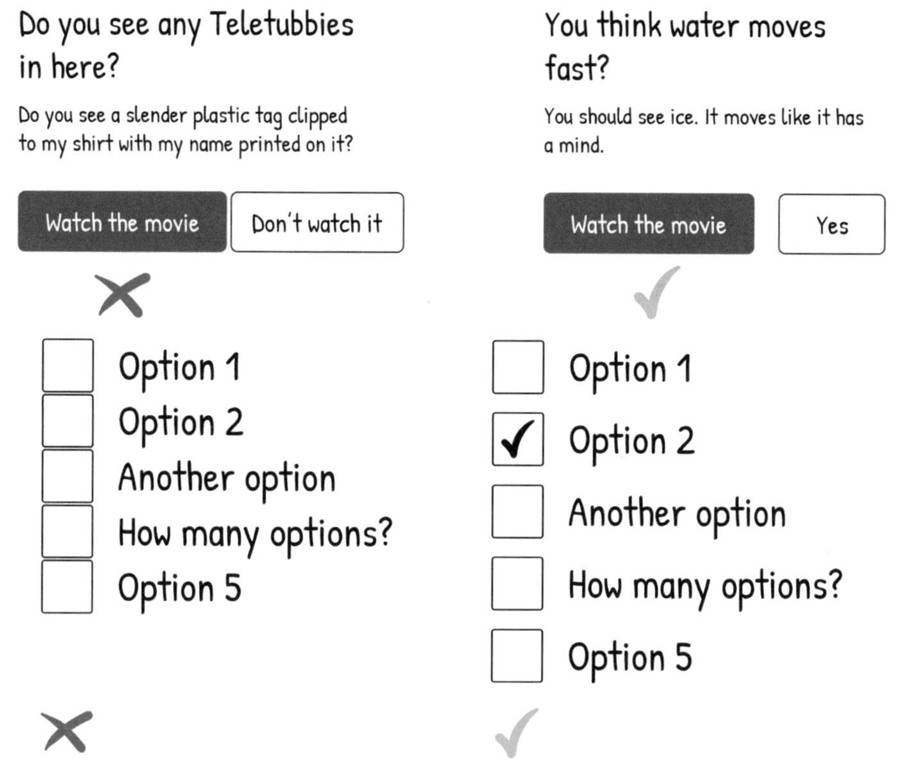

Do you see any Teletubbies in here?

Do you see a slender plastic tag clipped to my shirt with my name printed on it?

| Watch the movie | Don't watch it |

✗

☐ Option 1
☐ Option 2
☐ Another option
☐ How many options?
☐ Option 5

✗

You think water moves fast?

You should see ice. It moves like it has a mind.

| Watch the movie | Yes |

✓

☐ Option 1
☑ Option 2
☐ Another option
☐ How many options?
☐ Option 5

✓

Figure 11-10. *What to do and what not to do, when it comes to laying out buttons or other interactive controls*

When it comes to actually building something that needs to be accessible, what we use matters. A link should be built as a link and a button as a button. And this is not just semantics, as screen readers and any other assistive software will treat each tag differently. For example, an element that is surrounded by an *<a>* tag will be treated by a screen reader as a link, and it will respond when the *Enter* key is pressed on the keyboard, and a *<button>* will respond to either *Enter* or the *spacebar*.

Recommendations for Buttons and Other Controls

Make sure your buttons or any other controls have sufficient contrast with the background they sit on, according to the WCAG requirements (Figure 11-11). Even if this is a gray area, and in some cases where the control is easily identifiable as such, and contrast requirements don't apply, who's to say what's identifiable or not? And who's to say that your users will actually understand what you're trying to convey? To reduce ambiguities, ensure the label of the button and its background have a 4.5:1 contrast and the button's background has a 3:1 contrast ratio with its own environment.

Figure 11-11. *Example button illustrating the different contrast requirements for the button itself as well as the background it sits on*

Buttons could use hierarchy as well. As such, if a particular button is the one we want users to click the most, it should (visually) be the dominant one and stand out more than any other button in our interface (Figure 11-12).

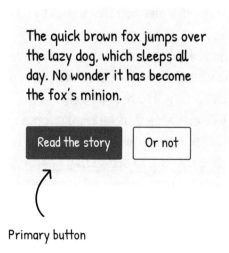

Figure 11-12. *Example of two buttons side by side, a primary and a secondary*

No need to be fancy with names; primary, secondary, tertiary, and so on all signify hierarchy, and that should be reflected in a design. At least, if it serves your purpose, as no design guide, recommendation, advice, suggestion, or principle should be absolute in my opinion. In Figure 11-13, the buttons on the left don't seem to have enough visual difference to create hierarchy, unlike the ones on the right.

Figure 11-13. *Illustration of button hierarchy*

A button is an interactive element that needs to be very distinct and easy to identify. As such, if we want people to find them and use them, we need to make sure they stand out enough from their environment and ensure they're eye-catching to attract attention. Don't overdo it though, as simplicity as a rule can be applied here as well.

When it comes to something that we want people to use, it makes sense to have it in a familiar, easy-to-see place. Don't make people scan the entire screen to find that call to action that's associated with what they've just read. Figure 11-14 illustrates what to do and what not to do when it comes to button placement. Ideally, buttons need to be closer to their content so they can be easily seen and understood and have a clear label and also a familiar shape.

Ensure consistency is maintained in your buttons. Stick to the same design for buttons that have the same significance. For example, all primary buttons that are considered more important and are higher up in the hierarchy ladder should look the same, all secondary buttons should look the same, and so on. Consistency is key to usability.

Users with mild cognitive impairments will benefit from familiar and simple layouts, as well as an easily understood hierarchy. In other words, put things where they are expected. You will make the lives of your users easier, and you'll get a lot of praise from people you don't know for doing pretty much what's expected.

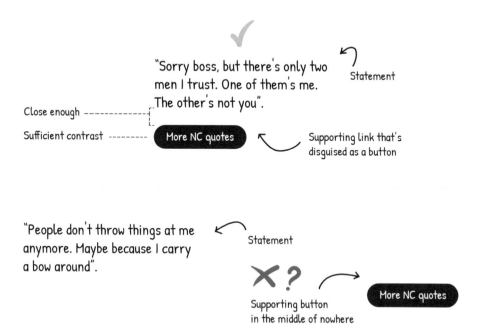

Figure 11-14. *Illustration of a pretty common way to place buttons (top) and one that doesn't make sense (bottom)*

Avoid generic button text, like "Click here" or "Read more," as whatever text sits on a button should have meaning outside of its related content and should always tie back to what that button will do for the user. Instead, it might be a better idea if you preferred phrases like "Read article" or "Send your message" instead of "Submit."

Button labels need to make sense without having to read all the content that supports them. If someone is using a screen reader and lands at a button without having listened to the context, a "Read more" announcement will mean nothing. As shown in Figure 11-15, a generic button label might make you miss the wealth of wisdom that the best actor who has ever lived has to offer.[11]

---

[11] That's Nicolas Cage for the unworthy among you.

Think simple and answer simple questions during a design: Can the users see the button and its label? Has the label got a clear meaning? Is there priority when two buttons are side by side? (I mean, if you want to prioritize a goal over another, if you want a hypothetical 50/50 click ratio for both buttons, then go ahead).

Figure 11-15. *Example of a generic button label and a more specific one*

If you have to use disabled buttons (as if we want to use them, but still), you could have a disabled cursor when hovered over and some supporting text stating why the button can't be interacted with at that point, as illustrated in Figure 11-16. Also, your disabled buttons do not need to conform to contrast requirements. Finally, don't do these and don't have disabled buttons or components in your product.[12]

---

[12] Don't disable buttons.

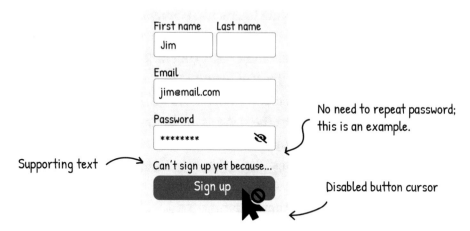

Figure 11-16. *Example form showing a disabled cursor pointer over a button that can't be interacted with yet*

Give the users some visual feedback. Don't leave out a design for all button interactions (Figure 11-17), from an active to a hover and all the way to a focus state, as they all deserve your love and attention. Ensure that the design of focus state passes contrast requirements when the button is on a light and a dark background.

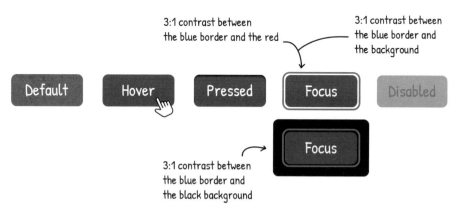

Figure 11-17. *Typical button states*

Last but not least, buttons are interactive elements, and any interactive elements, if not supported by HTML, should always have semantic meaning by using proper labels and roles, in our case <button>, aria-label, as well as <u>aria-describedby</u> if you need to add a button description. Screen readers like that, and screen reader users will love you. Ideally, an accessibility label should be the same as the button label to avoid confusion, for both the developer and the user. Moreover, imagine an icon button, like an "Add to favorites" that's shown in Figure 11-18. It doesn't have an actual label next to it, so the accessibility label should describe what will happen if you click that button.

Figure 11-18. *Example of a card with content and an Add to favorites icon button*

Summary

This chapter provided an overview of what a button, a link, and also a button button are. I would like to hope that you got an idea of how to design accessible and usable buttons. However, the most important thing to remember when it comes to dealing with accessibility issues is simply keep it simple.

If you need to name your buttons a million different ways, go forth. You are the owner of your work anyway. Remember that the user doesn't care about our nomenclatures and how we do things. They only care about getting a job done and that the things that they use work to do what they're supposed to do.

Buttons, links, and any kind of control, like a checkbox or a slider control, need to be of adequate size, have explanatory labels and be correctly coded, and have sufficient contrast with their backgrounds in all of their different states and clear and distinct focus states, ensuring that the user is always informed of what's happening and what has happened regardless of how they're using your website. Don't make their lives hard, and they'll love you for that.

Actually they won't. The best user experience is one that you don't even know you're experiencing, when you use something totally without thinking and you know it works. Users will love that new t-shirt that they bought through your website, and they'll love that they could find that piece of information they wanted really quickly. And they'll come back for more, because it works. Oh, and before I forget, don't use disabled buttons.

You're Going to Tell Me What to Do, Aren't You?

Yes. I mean, kind of.

After all this mumbling about web accessibility and what it all means (or should mean), the following present rules and guidelines, as deciphered from WCAG 2.1 and 2.2, that aim to make a website as accessible as possible.

But remember that they are just that, guidelines. And they should be treated as such. Always check with your users to make sure that you are actually doing the right thing and not blindly following rules and regulations, just because you want to be compliant. I'm not saying these things; others are, based on what is deemed more accessible. Here goes nothing!

Animated Content

No content should start out of the blue without the user expecting it (ideally). In reality, who doesn't love things popping out here, there, and everywhere while blinking and flashing like a carnival? The truth is that some people find it hard to concentrate and read if there are things moving

D. Georgakas, *A11Y Unraveled*, https://doi.org/10.1007/978-1-4842-9085-9_12

left, right, and center. These distractions can sometimes make it hard for our users to complete the goals we want them to complete. So proceed with caution.

On the other hand, some people might find flashing or flickering objects rather disturbing to the point it could cause them dizziness or even seizures, in some cases. People who could be affected the most are the ones with vestibular disorders, epilepsy, and migraine sensitivities. The vestibular system includes parts of the inner ear and brain, and it's responsible for the processing of sensory information and spatial orientation, meaning it lets us know if we're upright, sideways, upside down, and so on.[1]

People with vestibular disorders can experience symptoms such as motion sickness, issues with their balance, chronic dizziness, headaches, and even nausea when looking at motion on the screen. However, anyone can experience similar issues if subjected to excessive motion on the screen for a longer period of time.

In other words, don't design something that might cause seizures in people. To conform with accessibility, do not include anything that flashes more than three times a second.[2] If you want to be a web accessibility superhero, though, do not include anything that flashes to begin with. You might think to yourself, "If I make this button flashing, people might notice it easier and use it more" (as in Figure 12-1). In reality, people will indeed notice it; however, they will immediately close that web page because looking at this thing will make them feel dizzy and uncomfortable.

---

[1] Purves D, Augustine GJ, Fitzpatrick D, et al., editors. Neuroscience. 2nd edition. Sunderland (MA): Sinauer Associates; 2001. Chapter 14, The Vestibular System. www.ncbi.nlm.nih.gov/books/NBK10819/

[2] www.w3.org/WAI/WCAG21/Understanding/three-flashes-or-below-threshold

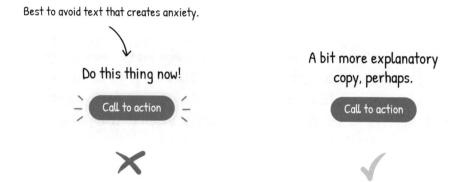

Figure 12-1. *Flashing buttons, or any kind of content, should ideally be avoided*

There are exceptions, though, so if you want things to be flashing around, maybe reduce their contrast so they're not as visible (enhancing the experience rather than causing people to faint, such as in Figure 12-2) and make sure you don't use fully saturated red as apparently it's more likely to cause problems. In addition, rather than have them flashing, perhaps a slow fade in–fade out animation could be easier on the eye. Perhaps. As always, I'm not telling you what to do.

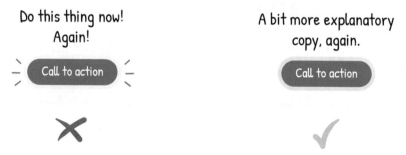

Figure 12-2. *Example of a slowly animating (I know this is a book and you can't see things moving; use your imagination) border around a button, rather than a flashing one*

Always make sure that any animated or moving object does not interact with the content or overlap important information (Figure 12-3). After all, all the user wants is to digest your content, and if there are things moving around preventing them from doing just that, you'll be starting off on the wrong foot. In that respect, it would be a good idea to stay away from flashing lights and geometric patterns that might be of high contrast (like repeated patterns of dark/white lines or grids).

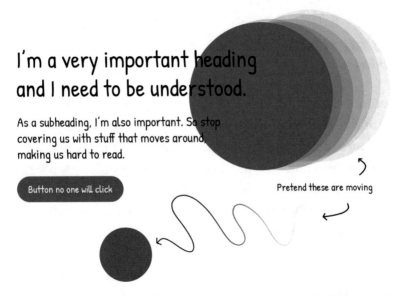

Figure 12-3. *Attempt in illustrating moving shapes behind and around important information*

Any animated image needs to stop moving within 5 seconds. Additionally, please stop auto-scrolling carousels (or if you have to, provide a simple and intuitive way for the user to play/stop the scrolling on command; more on that in the "Carousels and Sliders" section a few pages down).[3] Another way to go around it is to pause the scrolling on hover or when an item in the carousel is receiving focus.

---

[3] www.w3.org/WAI/WCAG21/Understanding/pause-stop-hide.html

Some people might find it hard to concentrate while objects are moving within their field of view. On top of that, the movement might make it harder for them to read what's on, for example, a card with text on it, since the card will be moving automatically. Finally, users with motor control problems will find it harder to select a specific object if that object keeps moving, as the users' movement would be slower.

To get a spectacular AAA conformance level, you'll need to *not* use any kind of (decorative) motion animation on your website, and also you need to make sure that users can somehow disable animations that are not essential either by completely disabling all or using a pause button in certain circumstances, like a carousel on auto-play (what is essential is up to you, though).

All these should be taken within the context of what you're trying to achieve, your purpose, and the specific requirements of your audience. If, for example, your needs require an image to be flashing for more than 3 seconds or an animation to be on loop forever while being annoying, make sure you have a valid reason for it and explain it thoroughly on the page where that (irritating) animation sits on, as well as in a statement around your website's accessibility level.

If you want to be accessible, that is. If not, then the court's waiting. :)

Content

Have you ever come across a, let's say, ecommerce website that sells a product (this is just an example; if any similarity with real websites happens, it's purely coincidental) and when you land on the page you see a very big, bold, and inspirational heading saying something along the lines of "Reach for the stars"? There's nothing wrong with this quote necessarily, but if the website sells clothes, that line is a bit out of context. Is it a shop, or is it an online therapy website?

Someone that will reach that page will want to know immediately what that page is about or if that page satisfies their search query. Having clever text on a website or a digital application might be giving users the wrong idea about you if it doesn't contain at least a hint of what you do or what you offer (Figure 12-4) and can ruin the experience for users with cognitive impairments. Or for anybody, for that matter.

Figure 12-4. *Illustration of a clothes shop displaying disjointed content*

Ideally, you'd want to ensure that your first heading (hopefully a H1 if you have your structure correctly set up) gives to the users some form of hint of who you are and what you can do for them. This not only gives the user clear perspective but will also contain keywords that could potentially be beneficial for your product if they are relevant to a user's search query. Something like in Figure 12-5, where the introduction is relevant to the image. For all intents and purposes, this should be an online shop for clothes.

Figure 12-5. *Illustration of a clothes shop displaying relevant content*

All in all, avoid being *too* fancy with your content.

Use easy-to-understand language and avoid complicated sentences (Figure 12-6). Although that's a requirement for an outstanding AAA accessibility conformance level, no one wants to scratch their head every time they read your content. Head-scratching leads to injury and website abandonment (even if the more you scratch, the more you want it).

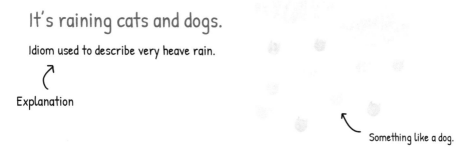

Figure 12-6. *Example of a complicated sentence against an easy one, with the same meaning*

If you have to use idioms, complicated images, or weird phrases, it might be worth having both text and image that might help people with cognitive deficits understand your content better (Figure 12-7).

How delightful to make
your acquaintance!

Nice to meet you!

Figure 12-7. *Depiction of the cats and dogs idiom*

If you want to get a mere A conformance level, then all you must do is
define the default language of the website by using the "lang" attribute in
your HTML document. Again, this is not because someone at some point
decided to make developers' life harder (although how hard is it really? It's
just a few characters of code, you lazy....) but because screen readers or
any other assistive technologies that convert text on the screen into speech
are more accurate when the language of whatever they're trying to read is
properly defined.

If you're aiming for an AA conformance level and your content consists
of passages of different languages, then each passage will need to have
its language identified separately. For example, if your main content is in
English but somewhere in there, for whatever reason, you decide to put a
sentence in Korean, then this sentence will need to be identified as Korean.
A text-to-speech software will have a very, very, very hard time trying to
identify Korean characters if it thinks it's in English. Far-fetched, I know.
You can do this by simply adding to the different language text the code

```
<span lang=kor">
```

(Note that this is for Korean. Your example might be different, so don't
start splashing Korean stuff everywhere if your language is English.)

If you're writing in English, try and make each sentence 25 words or
fewer. According to gov.uk's guide on content design,[4] users with learning
disabilities will not look at a sentence as a whole, identifying chunks of text

---

[4] www.gov.uk/guidance/content-design/writing-for-gov-uk#how-people-read

and filling in the blanks based on what they already know (which is kind of the way people read). Rather, they will read letter for letter, and they won't be able to understand a sentence if it's too long. Having sentences that are 96 worlds long, such as the one depicted in Figure 12-8, would be hard to people with moderate learning disabilities. Saying that, I have no clue if there are sentences in this book that are longer than 25 words. So busted if there are!

"As he crossed toward the pharmacy at the corner he involuntarily turned his head because of a burst of light that had ricocheted from his temple, and saw, with that quick smile with which we greet a rainbow or a rose, a blindingly white parallelogram of sky being unloaded from the van—a dresser with mirrors across which, as across a cinema screen, passed a flawlessly clear reflection of boughs sliding and swaying not arboreally, but with a human vacillation, produced by the nature of those who were carrying this sky, these boughs, this gliding façade."

Figure 12-8. *An excerpt from Vladimir Nabokov's The Gift. The preceding sentence has 96 words*

To put it simply, if your content is such that cannot be understood by a 12-year-old and you want to get that elusive AAA conformance level, then you need to also provide an alternate version of the same text in plain and easy-to-understand language (e.g., by using a summary). Users don't read a web page fully. Nielsen Normal Group mentions a 2008 study that identified that users will only read around 20–28% of a website's text content[5] (although this is 15 years old, so things might have changed).

In this sense, put your most important content first using headings and subheadings and try to use as few words as possible to convey meaning. In Figure 12-9, you can see an example of this. The content on the left uses fewer words in a more to-the-point approach, while the content on the

---

[5] www.nngroup.com/articles/how-little-do-users-read/

right expects you to read whole sentences to understand what they offer, rather than just simple words.

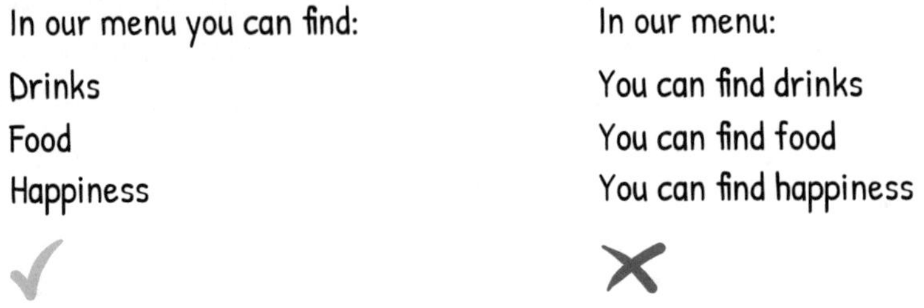

In our menu you can find:	In our menu:
Drinks	You can find drinks
Food	You can find food
Happiness	You can find happiness
✓	✗

Figure 12-9. *Fewer words and simpler sentences make content easier to understand for all users, including ones with learning difficulties*

Cards

An accessible way to present cards is within *<li>* elements.[6] That's because screen readers announce the number of items, so the user knows how many there are (Figure 12-10).

Use cards to group together related elements. Grouped cards can appear complicated to some users, making it harder to concentrate on just one. Use with enough space around the cards and make sure there is a distinct heading and any primary call to action sits at the bottom of the card. As said by Heydon Pickering, a simple card design that doesn't resemble a mini website is always preferrable.[7]

---

[6] How nice would it be if there was a <card> element?
[7] https://inclusive-components.design/cards/

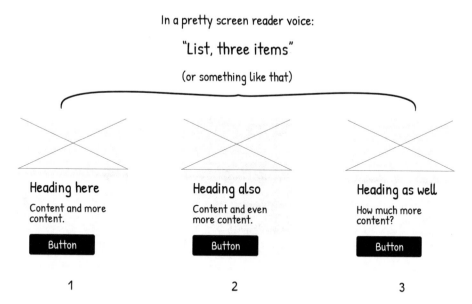

Figure 12-10. *Three cards grouped together as list items. The screen reader would announce to the user the number of cards*

Use an appropriate hierarchy of content within the card making the content easier to scan. A common pattern for a card (although there are a gazillion types of cards) could be an image at the top, followed by a heading, sometimes some supporting text, and then a call to action (Figure 12-11).

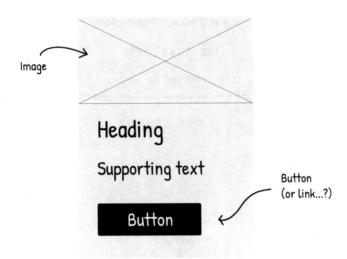

Figure 12-11. *Structure of a common card on a web page*

When the website is finally built, check that said content doesn't break when read on smaller devices and that lines don't wrap (Figure 12-12).

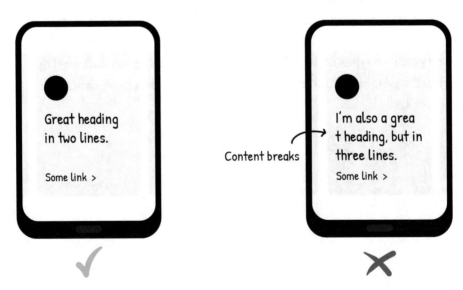

Figure 12-12. *Example of content breaking when a card is viewed on a smaller device*

If the whole card needs to be interactive, make sure it receives sufficient focus, the mouse cursor changes to pointer when hovered across the whole of the card, and there is a distinct hover state (Figure 12-13).

Figure 12-13. *Illustration of different card states*

There is a caveat though: if your whole card is a link, then all the content that's within it is a link. And if all that content is a link, when a screen reader gets to it, it might announce the heading, any subheading, *and* the button content all together, which, if your content is descriptive enough, might not be as bad, but it definitely adds to the complexity of using a screen reader in the first place.

Graham Ritchie, a developer specializing in web accessibility, sets out another great example why having a whole card clickable might not be a good idea for some people. If you're on a mobile device and you suffer from a disability that affects your fine motor skills or have any kind of coordination problems, you might touch the screen hoping to scroll down, and then all of a sudden (because the whole card is a link), you end up on a different page.

As already mentioned, use descriptive language in your primary calls to action and avoid words or phrases that could be taken out of context, such as "Read more" or "Click here." Imagine four cards in a row with four "Read more" links and no context. Some screen readers may navigate a web page by going through all the links, so that can end up being pretty useless for the user.

If the whole card is *not* interactive and there are different links within the card, make sure they receive sufficient focus in a logical order, starting from the link at the top and going down, as expected (Figure 12-14).

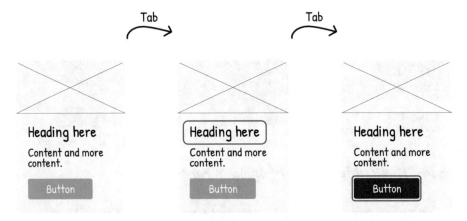

Figure 12-14. *Focus order inside a card with multiple links*

Finally, if an image inside the card is purely decorative, it doesn't need an alternative text. However, *alt=""* should remain, as if it was missing, screen readers would pick the image up and read all or part of the source attribute[8] instead.

Carousels and Sliders

Make sure you prioritize and show important items first. General research has shown that around 1% of users engage with carousels and most of them only do so with the first slide. When it comes to mobile usage, things are a bit trickier. Mobile users generally go through a website faster in their

---

[8] As in the location of the server where the image is located, which sometimes can be a really, really, really long link.

search for specific content, and they might not even notice you have a carousel in there.

When your website is built, check that all functionality, including navigating through each carousel item (e.g., an image) and through each element within the carousel items, is possible through a keyboard. In other words, make sure that all carousel elements receive focus (Figure 12-15). Focus should remain on that element until moved, and no unexpected change should happen.

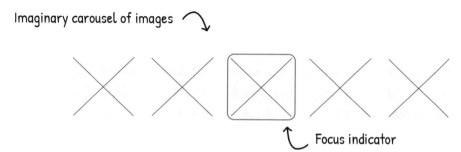

Figure 12-15. *Focus indicator around a carousel item*

Before your website is built, and while you're designing pretty things, don't forget about the fundamentals: check and verify that all elements in a carousel item have sufficient contrast according to the WCAG for text and non-text contrast.

Make sure there is a way to pause animation when the carousel is on auto-scroll. You can do this either with a pause/play button or a pause on mouse hover or when an element receives keyboard focus.

Add next/previous arrows *and* ensure they have semantic meaning. Check that arrows receive sufficient focus. If an item within the carousel is focused, the carousel should not continue forward as this can create confusion and frustration, while the item you thought was selected is slowly going away from the screen. Figure 12-16 shows a hypothetical carousel with arrow controls and a pause button.

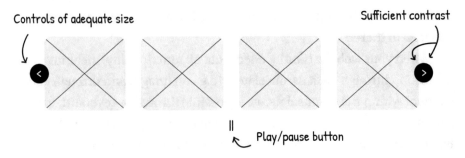

Figure 12-16. Hypothetical carousel with arrow controls and a pause/play button

Ensure any controls are of appropriate size, they don't cover any important content, and they have enough space around them for ease of use. Controls should be at least 44 × 44 px in size (see "Touch Targets (Size Does Matter)" for more info). Check that they receive sufficient focus when navigating with a keyboard (Figure 12-17).

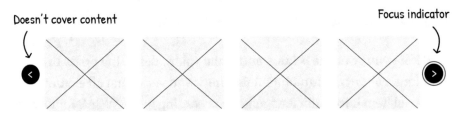

Figure 12-17. A carousel with a focused arrow control

If you're using status indicators (such as little dots along the bottom of the carousel or even a slider bar), make sure the indicator for the active slide or element is distinct enough from the other, inactive indicators, and give them a clear hover state too, as depicted in Figure 12-18.

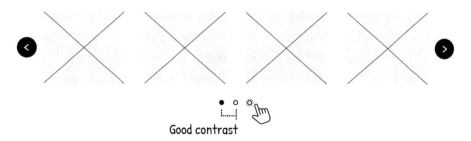

Figure 12-18. *Carousel showing an example of a hover state on a status indicator, in this case a dotted outline*

A very valid point made by Nielsen Norman Group is that even if your carousel is on auto-play (which you shouldn't do), by the time you see a different carousel element, the user will have already scrolled down since a mobile page is small by default. If you're using cues to indicate more content (which you should), a good idea is to create what is called the "illusion of continuity" by having text or half of the slider element look like it continues off the side of the screen, which will make users quickly understand that there is more content there (Figure 12-19).

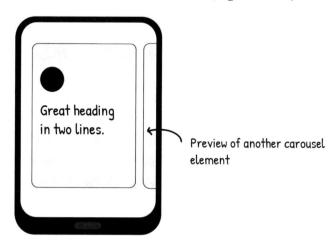

Figure 12-19. *Illustration of the "illusion of continuity," where part of the element is shown on the side of the screen*

Dots are generally considered weak visual cues since they're quite small to begin with. Obviously, to make the illusion of continuity work, make sure that your carousel supports control by swipe. If you go down that path, ensure that you use a low number of items in your carousel since a user would have to scroll all the way to the end to discover your 52nd element. And they won't.

If you really want to use arrows or dots on mobile devices, make sure they don't cover the carousel element(s) and that there is sufficient contrast between them and their background (Figure 12-20).

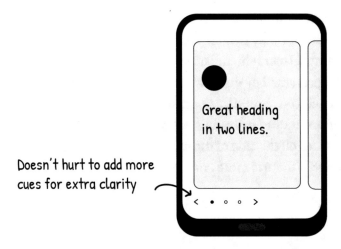

Figure 12-20. *Carousel indicators at the bottom of the carousel, alongside a kind-of-showing carousel item on the side*

To sum it all up, and if you really want to be an accessibility superhero (strictly from a design point of view), include elements in your design that will create clarity rather than confusion: arrows of adequate size with descriptions, visual cues, and even the actual number of items in your carousel (Figure 12-21).

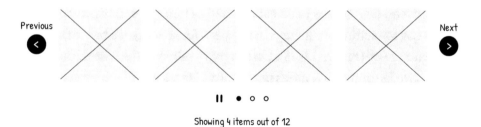

Showing 4 items out of 12

Figure 12-21. *Example of a carousel with all sorts of controls and cues. Notice that the dots are not in the middle. To that I say, "So what?"*

Icons

A good idea would be to use simple and literal icons instead of highly detailed ones (Figure 12-22). The idea of an icon is to illustrate meaning easily or accompany a text label to convey meaning faster. In that sense, an icon with lots of details might create confusion as the user tries to understand what on Earth we are trying to communicate.

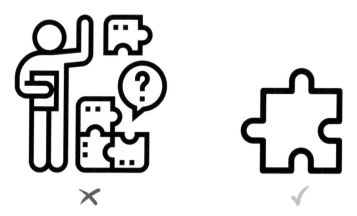

Figure 12-22. *Examples of a complicated and a simple icon*

If an icon has already been established as one of a certain meaning (e.g., a cog for settings or a magnifying glass for search), it's best to stick to it for ease of use (Figure 12-23). Do not try to reinvent the wheel. Users who might have learning difficulties or cognitive issues will much prefer to look at something simple that they've probably seen before than something totally creative but meaningless.

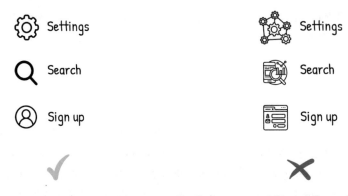

Figure 12-23. *Common icons on the left vs. complicated ones on the right*

Icons that are placed near text labels help the user understand your message as they scan your page. A user looking at a magnifying glass will know that they need to select that to search for something, and they won't have to read the text label next to it, thus reducing the time it takes to use your product. Use the icons on the left side of the text label as people generally read from left to right (at least in countries where people read from left to right because we also have the opposite, like the ones driving on the left side of the road).

Use SVG (Scalable Vector Graphics) icons as they can be enlarged in any size and can be changed or animated with CSS. Also, if a user zooms in to enlarge the screen size because they can't see very well, SVG icons will still look nice and crisp (Figure 12-24).

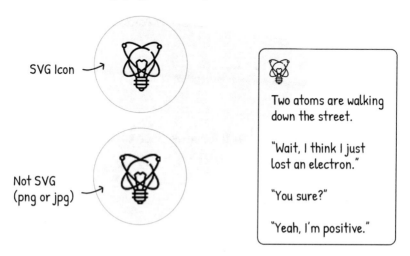

Figure 12-24. *Difference between an SVG and a non-SVG icon when magnified*

If an icon is purely decorative, it needs to be hidden from screen readers, so it doesn't get accidentally announced, creating confusion for the user. A simple *aria-hidden="true"* will do. As well as with all graphics, if it's purely decorative, it doesn't even need an alternative text.

If the icon actually serves a purpose but it's not accompanied by a text label, then it needs to have a *role="img"* assigned to it (assistive technologies might not always acknowledge it) and a descriptive title reflective of what the icon does.

If the icon is wrapped within a link but the link is the one that controls the action, then the icon is purely decorative and needs to be hidden from screen readers. If the icon is the link, then it needs an accessible label, with a simple *aria-label="Good Label"*, for example:

```
<a href="your-link-destination-here" aria-label="I am an
amazing icon">
    <svg aria-hidden="true" ... >
    </svg>
</a>
```

That's enough developing stuff for now. Back to design.

Language Selector

Make sure the language switcher doesn't interfere with the content or the main navigation but it's still distinct enough to be easily identified. Regardless of how you choose to present it – be it some text or a button with or without a dropdown menu – ensure the switcher receives sufficient focus as well as the language options within it (Figure 12-25). Finally, check that you can exit by using the keyboard.

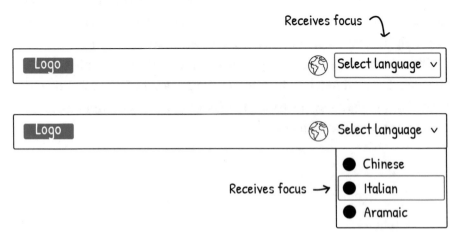

Figure 12-25. *Language switcher items receiving focus*

If you need to use a language selector, a good idea might be to place it early on a page or in the footer, since most assistive technologies would have shortcuts allowing you to jump to the first or last element of a page. To be a language switcher superhero regardless of the situation, include a language switcher button at the top of the page as well as in the footer (Figure 12-26).

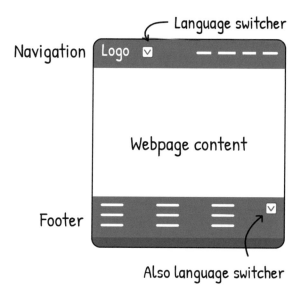

Figure 12-26. *Language selector within the navigation and the footer*

Use a generic icon, like a globe, to indicate that the element has to do something with language or country, as some people might not be able to read your text, especially if they're trying to access your site from their own country but your website's default language is a different one (Figure 12-27). In this case, the use of automatic redirection or translation of the site based on the user's IP might be a good option.

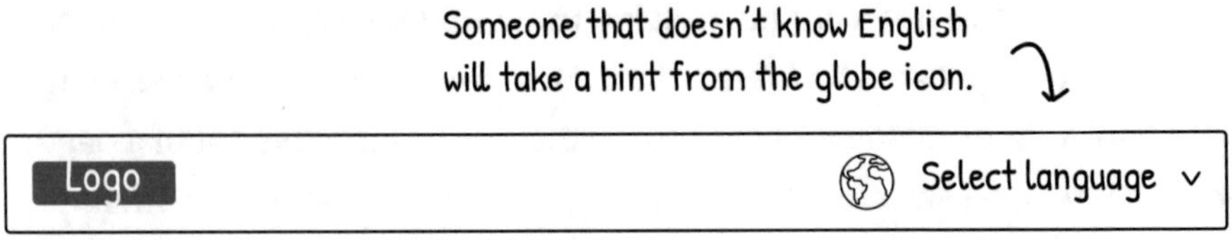

Someone that doesn't know English
will take a hint from the globe icon.

Logo   🌐 Select language ∨

Figure 12-27. *For someone that doesn't speak the language of your site and wants to change language, a relevant icon might have more meaning than the actual text*

To finish things off, make sure your language selector has an appropriate ARIA label, so it's announced by a screen reader. However, any icons or flags should have an *aria-hidden="true"* since they don't need to be announced by a screen reader.

Links

Make sure all links receive sufficient focus when navigating with a keyboard and that the focus indicators have sufficient contrast based on guidelines. Ensure that going through each link follows a logical order (Figure 12-28).

Tab   Tab

Logo   Link   Link too   One more

Figure 12-28. *Links within a navigation*

Every link and its destination should be clear, within the context of their surrounding content. This will give you a mere A conformance level. If you're striving for an AAA conformance level, then each link text and destination should be clear enough regardless of its surrounding content (Figure 12-29). This way, if assistive technology reads out all the links on the page, a user will be able to understand them without having to hear the rest of the content. In other words, stop using "Read more" and use descriptive text.[9]

We are the most awesome company in the world. At least that's what we call ourselves. Because we know better.

Read more >

No, we are the best company in the world. Others call us that. Because they know better. Or something.

Company profile >

Figure 12-29. *Example of a descriptive and a generic link*

It might be best to indicate a link with an additional cue, such as an underline, rather than just color (Figure 12-30). This way, users don't rely on color alone to understand information. Regardless, your links should have sufficient contrast with their surrounding environment, according to accessibility guidelines.

Refusing to use lorem ipsum. How much more can one person come up with?

Figure 12-30. *Example of a link within a sentence*

---

[9] www.w3.org/WAI/WCAG21/Understanding/link-purpose-in-context.html

Avoid linking images. If, however, you need to link an image, make sure that the alternative text describes the purpose and destination of the link and *not* the image itself. This is a case where even decorative images will need an *"alt"* text. Whatever that may be, it might be a good idea to avoid starting with "Link to..." or something like "Click to..." A screen reader will announce that this is a link anyway, so if you don't want your users to listen to something like "Link to link to...," might be best to avoid.

Take Figure 12-31, for example; if your onion image is a link leading to recipes with onions, it would be better to add an alternative text such as "recipes with onions," rather than just describing the image as "onions." This way, a screen reader user will hear something like "Link to recipes with onions" and not "Link to onions."

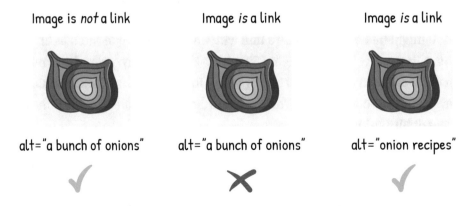

Figure 12-31. *Examples of different alternative text depending on whether an image is a link or not*

Avoid showing links to the same destination next to each other. For example, if you have a blog post snippet with an image, a heading, and a text such as "Read article," avoid having all these three elements linked to the same destination, since assistive technology users would have to navigate through all three of them, even though they do the same thing, and this would result in a bad experience. Instead, use only one element as the link (Figure 12-32).

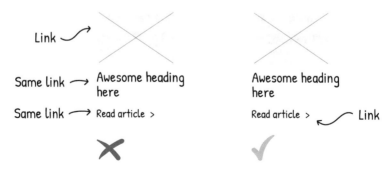

Figure 12-32. *Multiple links and a single one within some type of content*

If you must use short link text such as "Read more," make sure that you give your link a sufficient purpose by adding a description through an *aria-label*. You can also use *aria-describedby* to provide additional text for the screen reader, aside from the link text.

Breadcrumbs should receive sufficient focus and be marked up as a navigation landmark (nav). Make sure that the active page is clear enough and that the breadcrumb trail follows the structure of the page's URL. The breadcrumb trail is usually located between the main navigation and the start of the content, so no need to reinvent the wheel; keep things familiar for the users and make sure that the last breadcrumb that denotes the current page is *not* a link (Figure 12-33).

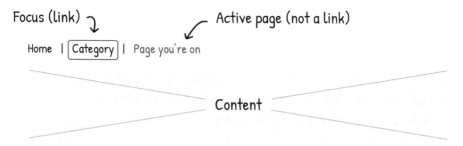

Figure 12-33. *Example of a breadcrumb receiving focus*

In addition, whatever separators you use between links should be added with CSS rather than as text; otherwise, they might be read by screen readers.

On mobile devices a long breadcrumb trail that breaks into multiple lines might create confusion as well as take up valuable real estate on the screen. A possible solution would be to use a single breadcrumb that shows just the last level (Figure 12-34).

Figure 12-34. *Example of a mobile breadcrumb*

Navigation

Where is your office located? Where do I see details of your products? Where do I search for a job? How on Earth do I get there? A paramount element of web design and good usability, web navigation of any kind helps the user move around different pages of a website to accomplish their goals. Your main website navigation would usually be a set of links laid out in a menu, linking to internal or external web pages and representing the structure of your website (Figure 12-35).

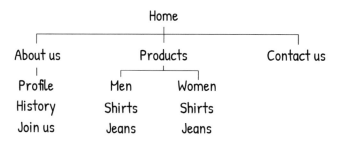

Figure 12-35. *A very simple, and probably none existing, website structure*

I think we have already established that designers like to make things complicated. As such, there is an obvious inconsistency on how many types of navigation there are out there. Some, like Kinsta (a US-based hosting provider), mention three types of navigation: a global, which is the same across the whole website; a hierarchical, which is like a submenu depending on what page you're on; and a local navigation, which is just links within content.[10]

Others, such as HubSpot, identify five types of navigation: a horizontal bar, or just a series of links displayed horizontally; a dropdown menu, where a list of links appear when the user interacts with the main navigation; a hamburger navigation where your links are hidden behind an icon called a hamburger or burger; a sidebar navigation where the different links are stacked in the sidebar; and a footer navigation, where your navigation links are within... the footer.[11]

Now some, like TemplateToaster, mention eight types of navigation depending on content and interaction.[12] But this is getting too far away from the scope of this section. For all intents and purposes, the ones

---

[10] https://kinsta.com/blog/website-navigation/

[11] https://blog.hubspot.com/website/main-website-navigation-ht

[12] https://blog.templatetoaster.com/types-modern-navigation-menus/

mentioned by HubSpot do the trick for web designers, so here's a small preview in Figure 12-36.

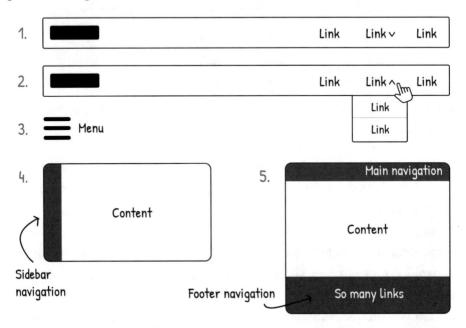

Figure 12-36. *Types of navigation. 1 (top): Horizontal navigation. 2 (second to top): Dropdown navigation. 3 (middle): An icon indicating a burger navigation. 4 (bottom left): Sidebar navigation. 5 (bottom right): Footer navigation*

If all that seems so familiar, it might not be for everybody, as users are not your average web designer who does this thing for a living. According to a survey by Kinsta, only 50% of users managed to find where to go to see relevant content, and that was on a standard navigation.

If that wasn't clear enough, imagine half of your audience leaving your website because they couldn't find what they were looking for. Not necessarily because it wasn't there, but because they couldn't get to it.

The harsh truth is that users will wait for no man. They will not spend more time than they need to, to study your website and figure out your navigation structure. Instead, they will move on to the next available search result. Much like one ex-girlfriend of mine who moved along fairly quickly to a different ~~boyfriend~~ product before she even had a chance to get familiar with ~~me~~ mine.

Part of navigating is not only where you can go from where you are but also knowing where you are in the first place. I'm sure you've noticed in public places, such as a metro station or a famous landmark, maps that show the surrounding area and where you can go from there. This is completely useless unless you know where you will be starting from in the first place, hence the big and bold "You are here" symbol.

These types of maps show great examples of navigation that we can use in our digital products – little arrows, roads, color-coded symbols, names of places, all in an effort to help us know where we are and the possible destinations. Besides, most of the time our users will probably not visit our website straight from the homepage, so we owe it to them to make their journey as easy as possible. Easy and accessible.

Now, the truth is that sometimes we designers like to overdo it (or not do it at all by hiding our entire site structure from our users behind a simple icon and then for some reason call it a burger). A very large and complicated navigation could be as detrimental to our users' needs as a nonexisting one (Figure 12-37). I guess in this sense, less is still more even when we're talking about navigation. Less here doesn't necessarily mean don't add anything to it. More like keep it simple, familiar, and consistent. Keeping the navigation in a familiar place (such as the top or the right side of the canvas) means reduced cognitive strain as users will be able to find it easier.

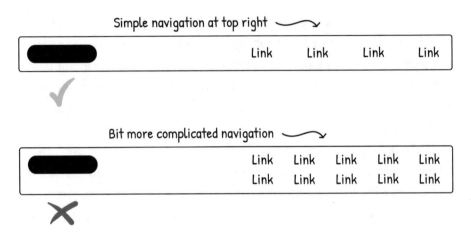

Figure 12-37. *Example of an easier and a more complicated navigation menu*

Practices that can increase cognitive strain (in other words, that will make you think more rather than less, which is what you need) can include having weird rollover submenus coming out only when hovering over a certain point of a thin horizontal navigation (users with reduced fine motor skills might find it hard to hover over a certain point or maintain the mouse cursor on top of that point for a long time) or when nonfamiliar language is used for menu items (Figure 12-38). For instance, if you want to suddenly be creative and rename a perfectly acceptable "About us" to a weirdly vague and out of any context "Upward and onward," you might want to think twice. Descriptive language is good for the users, as well as search engines.

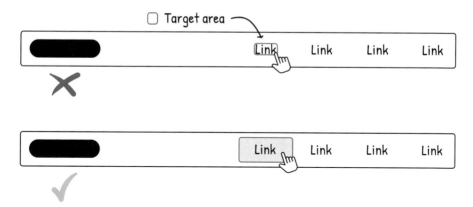

Figure 12-38. *A larger target area for navigation items (bottom) would be more beneficial to users with loss of fine motor skills or any kind of coordination issues*

"Wait a minute. You're telling me what to do!" No, I'm not. I'm only using logic and a very small hint of common sense, which can always be tested and disproven. Logically speaking, when we are presented with something we already know, we find it easier to deal with, rather than when we come across something unexpected.

If you are presented with a car and you are expected to drive it, chances are you already know how to drive a car and you'd have no problem at all. If, on the other hand, someone invited you over for a drive in their new vehicle and said vehicle is a car that has the steering wheel on the other side (like in some crazy parts of the world; I'll let you decide which is the right side for driving), good luck trying to coordinate controlling the car and switching gears at the same time. It will take a while. An accessible navigation, therefore, is one that's simple, easy to access, and consistent.

Make sure that your navigation can be accessed by keyboard and that going through it follows a logical order. Ensure all links receive sufficient focus and that colors used conform with contrast requirements (Figure 12-39). Make sure that focus is never hidden from the user while going through the navigation.

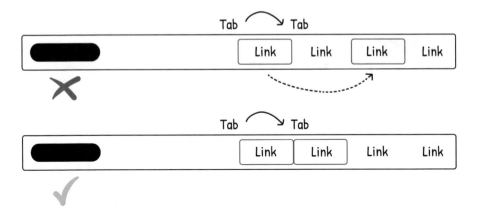

Figure 12-39. *Logical focus order when navigating within menu items with a keyboard*

Include a skip navigation link (Figure 12-40) at the top of the page as early as possible and make sure it can receive focus when someone Tabs on their keyboard. Users will not have to go through every item on the menu list and can skip straight to the content of the page. This link should be hidden by default and activated on keyboard navigation.

First tab ↘

Skip to content				
⬤	Link	Link	Link	Link
	Content			

Figure 12-40. *Skip to content link*

Different users like to use different ways to do the same thing, and according to the WCAG, there must be more than one way for users to locate a web page within a set of pages.[13] Individuals with reduced cognitive abilities might find it easier to scan a full sitemap (in, let's say, the footer of your website) rather than going through all your different menu and dropdown items. In this sense, provide users with alternative ways to find different content. If a full sitemap is not an option, consider adding a search bar (Figure 12-41).

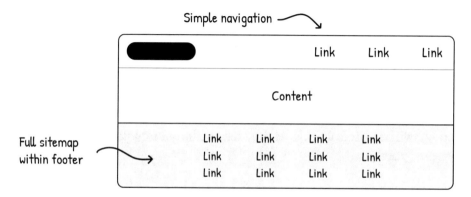

Figure 12-41. *Two ways to locate pages within a web page*

If you use a left-hand-side vertical navigation, make sure it stands out from the rest of the content and that all links receive sufficient focus in a logical order (Figure 12-42).

---

[13] Unless that page is part of a process, for example, the payment page on an ecommerce site.

Figure 12-42. *A vertical side navigation, with clear contrast from the rest of the content, demonstrating focus order*

Leave sufficient space around different navigation elements. Users with difficulties in their motor skills or dexterity or ones that use a touch screen will benefit from this, as they require larger targets to interact with (Figure 12-43).

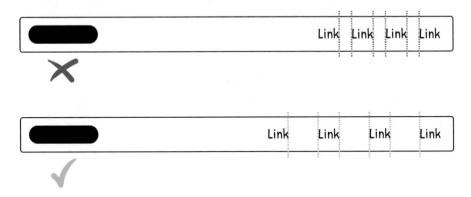

Figure 12-43. *Space between main navigation links*

If you're using dropdowns or fly-outs, make sure that all links receive sufficient focus and that the expanded menu doesn't disappear straight away after the mouse cursor is away from that area. Ensure that any submenu is also visually indicated, for instance, by using a nicely designed arrow, such as in Figure 12-44. Dropdowns are annoying as they are, as they can appear out of nowhere, and if there's no indication that they're there, we're making the experience more complicated than it should be.

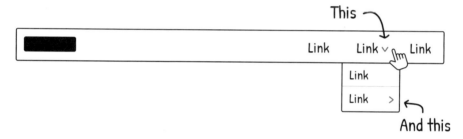

Figure 12-44. *Simple dropdown and fly-out menu indicators within navigation*

Make sure that all states of navigation items (including the active one) are distinct enough from one another as users with a short attention span will benefit from an easily identifiable hover or focus state (Figure 12-45). A change of color (along with a visual indicator), a thick underline, or even a color change in the background (again, along with a visual indicator) would usually be just fine.

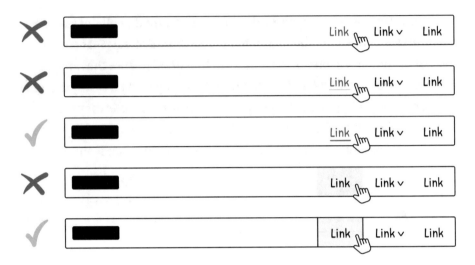

Figure 12-45. *Pass and fail examples of hover states in a main menu navigation*

Identify menus using a *<nav>* tag and include your navigation items within a list. This will allow a screen reader to announce the number of items so the user will know what to expect.

Navigations should be labeled accordingly with the *role='navigation'* attribute. This defines the navigation landmark. If there is only one navigation, then this is enough. However, if more than one navigation exists, then each one needs to have its own distinct label. This can be achieved with *aria-labelledby=""*, where inside the quotes you put the name you wish to assign to that navigation, that is, "nav1," "nav2," and so on.

On mobile devices, the trigger should be a *<button>*. If for any reason another element is used, then a *role='button'* should be used as an attribute as this will allow screen readers to pick up that the navigation is clickable.

Tabs

Tabs can be considered as a form of navigation as they take you through different views of the same kind of content with only one of the tabs active at a time (ideally). However, I've left them outside the "Navigation" section since not everybody agrees on that and, frankly, they do deserve their own dedicated section, albeit small, since they can be very helpful in grouping similar content and presenting it in a compact way that's not too overwhelming (Figure 12-46).

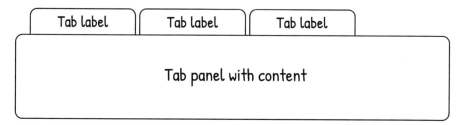

Figure 12-46. *Simple illustration of a tabbed interface*

Generally, I would be against any kind of design that includes hidden content, since you're running the very high risk of users not seeing that content. However, if it fits your purpose, go for it. To make things a bit easier for users, label your tabs clearly and avoid long descriptions. Make sure that active and inactive tabs are clearly indicated (Figure 12-47).

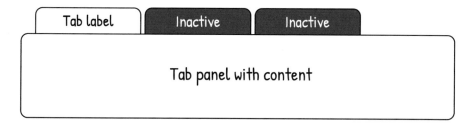

Figure 12-47. *Clearly indicated inactive tabs*

The tab itself is called... tab, but the content that's revealed when you click that tab button is called a tab panel. These should be properly marked up with the required ARIA roles and controls. For instance, the container the tabs are in needs to have the role <tablist>, and each tab that is contained within that tab list needs to have the role.... <tab>.[14] Similarly, the content panels for each tab will need the very self-explanatory and obvious role of <tabpanel>.[15]

Using keyboard navigation, when you get to the tab list, the first focus should be on the first active tab element, as shown in Figure 12-48. The next focus should be the tab panel if the tab panel has not already been revealed automatically. Arrows on your keyboard should be used to navigate through the different tabs, each time with sufficient focus on each tab (right arrow takes you to the next tab and left arrow to the previous one). This navigation should be circular; if you're on the last item by pressing the right arrow key, then if you press "right" again, the focus should move to the first tab. In other words, make sure the tab order makes sense for your users.

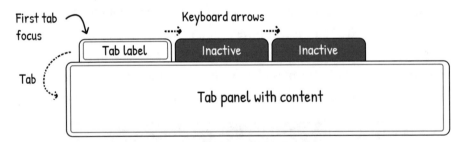

Figure 12-48. *Keyboard navigation within a tabbed interface*

---

[14] How intuitive.

[15] www.w3.org/WAI/ARIA/apg/patterns/tabpanel/

On mobile, a good technique is turning tabbed navigation into an accordion (Figure 12-49). Some developers might argue that it might be too complicated to turn something that has tab structure into an accordion; however, usability-wise, it can be a great way to compact content and save space. It doesn't come with no disadvantages though (is it ever easy?). It still contains hidden information, and if the content within the accordions is too much, then this can result in a long, long scrolling. One possible solution would be to make the header of the accordion sticky, so the user always knows where they are and can always collapse that panel to go to the next one, without having to scroll all the way up.

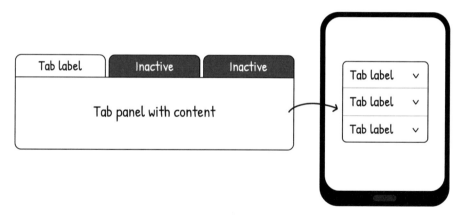

Figure 12-49. *A tabbed interface can turn into an accordion on a mobile device*

When using accordions, each content should be revealed under its own heading and not at the bottom of the element, similar to Figure 12-50, on the right side. The one on the left is something I've seen quite often, and it can become quite frustrating if you are a user with anxiety or cognitive disabilities or just someone in a hurry that just wants to get a job done.

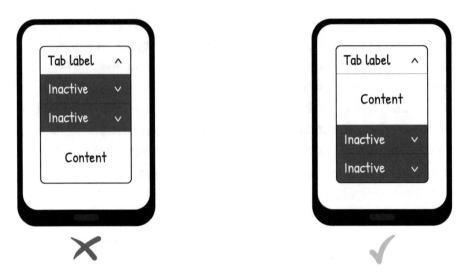

Figure 12-50. *Incorrect and correct placement of content within an accordion on a mobile device*

Focus States

A focus indicator (Figure 12-51) highlights an interactive element (like a button, a form field, or a link) when it is selected by using either a keyboard or a voice command. It pretty much is just a shape on or around the element emphasizing it, and this emphasis could be an outline or a shaded overlay.

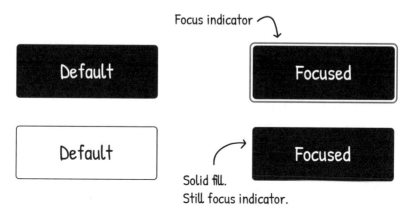

Figure 12-51. *Simple focus indicators*

There is a default style that browsers adapt to show those indicators, but it's really not very nice-looking, and in most cases it won't fit the overall style or brand of the page we're designing. Having said that, if it gets the job done, does it matter how it looks?

Focus indicators need to have high visibility, a good contrast that stands out from the rest of the surrounding content. Some developers (we don't like them) sometimes decide to disable focus states overall, either because they find it too tedious working on them since they should apply them to each element in a way that makes sense or because the designer hasn't included these states in their deliverables toward the developer (we don't like them either).

And we don't like them because a lot of people benefit from them. Users who navigate our page only with the help of a keyboard can easily identify where they are when visible focus indicators are provided. People with mobility issues might also resort to using a keyboard to navigate, and they too deserve to know where they are. Users who are blind or whose low vision doesn't allow them to easily track a mouse cursor will only find them helpful. And if the heart-warming gesture of making people's lives easier is not enough, a visible focus state is a requirement under the accessibility guidelines. So... ha!

Don't forget to design focus states for any interactive element, such as buttons, links, cards, form fields, and so on (Figure 12-52). If you can interact with an element with a mouse, it needs a focus indicator. Elements that are *not* interactive do not need a focus state. A good idea might be to start with a list of all your interactive elements and see what focus indicators you need to apply and where.

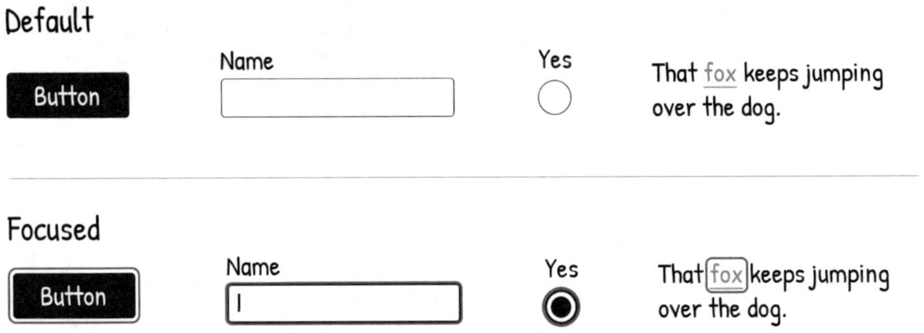

Default

Button · Name · Yes ○ · That <u>fox</u> keeps jumping over the dog.

Focused

Button · Name · Yes ◉ · That [fox] keeps jumping over the dog.

Figure 12-52. *Some interactive components and their focus states*

Don't overthink it. Sometimes, a great and acceptable focus state could be just the same as a hover state, as long as that has a nice contrast and the change is visible enough.

Test and then test some more. Make sure that all functionalities can be performed through a keyboard, all focus states are visible enough, and going through all the functionalities follows a logical order, depending on how your content is structured (Figure 12-53).[16] This is really simple, and it will go toward your A conformance level. If you really want to be thorough about it, unplug your mouse and see how far you can get. If you feel frustrated in any way, then something is wrong.

---

[16] www.w3.org/WAI/WCAG21/Understanding/focus-order.html

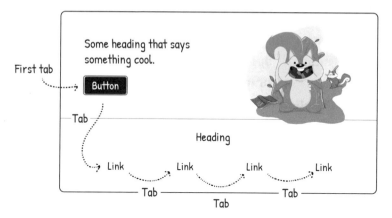

Figure 12-53. *Logical focus order when navigating with a keyboard*

Another requirement for a mere A conformance level is that when an element receives focus, then there shouldn't be an unexpected, automatic change. For example, if you navigate to a "Submit your form" button, then the form should not be submitted when the button receives focus, but rather when the button is actually clicked.

Links should not open automatically when they receive focus, popups should not appear out of nowhere, and nothing changes focus automatically. No one likes a haunted user interface. However, this doesn't apply when the focus doesn't change the context (e.g., if you navigate to a menu item that has a dropdown list of links and that menu drops down automatically when you focus on its trigger).

Who wants a basic A level, though? We are not peasants. We are trying to be accessibility heroes here, so an AA level is what we should be at least aiming for. When we have content that appears on focus (e.g., a tooltip or a popup), then this content needs to be dismissible. In other words, we need to be able to get out of it. Imagine if you open up a hidden menu, navigate through some links, and then decide you want to go out of it. You hit the *Escape* key with all your might, but nothing happens. Congratulations! Your element is not dismissible, you're stuck in this menu forever, and you have probably broken your keyboard in the process.

For an AA conformance level, the focus indicator of an element needs to have a 3:1 contrast ratio between its focused and unfocused states, *and* that focus indicator, apart from enclosing the element completely, needs to have the same contrast ratio with its surrounding environment, for example, the button it belongs to. If that seems a bit confusing, have a look at Figure 12-54. When the button is not focused, the focus indicator is invisible. In other words, it's white (as the button's environment). So, when that button gets focus, the outline needs a 3:1 contrast with the white background (the unfocused state), as well as a 3:1 contrast with its adjacent colors, in that case, the color of the button.[17] For an AAA conformance level, the preceding contrast ratio should be 4.5:1.[18]

What this basically tells us is that the focus indicator needs a 3:1 contrast ratio with its environment. The red outline has high contrast between the white environment as well as the color of the button. Either option from Figure 12-54 would pass the requirements.

Figure 12-54. *Focus indicators that pass the WCAG contrast requirements*

Additionally, when a component receives focus, the focus indicator mustn't be hidden (or obscured) behind another element, for example, a banner or a sticky header or footer (Figure 12-55).[19] If it's partially hidden, then all is well, as users are still going to be able to see that element; if it's

---

[17] www.w3.org/WAI/WCAG22/Understanding/focus-appearance.html
[18] www.w3.org/WAI/WCAG22/Understanding/focus-appearance-enhanced
[19] www.w3.org/WAI/WCAG22/Understanding/focus-not-obscured-minimum

not hidden at all, you'll be reaching the accessibility superhero ninja level (meaning an AAA conformance level, but I like to overdo it).[20]

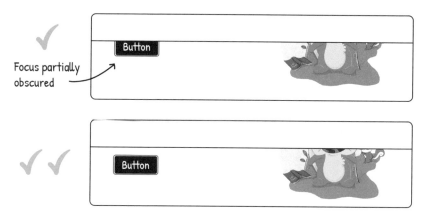

Figure 12-55. *Illustration of the "Focus not obscured" success criterion*

When it comes to how they actually need to look in terms of the area they cover, the WCAG try to explain the concept in a way that a 12-year-old probably won't understand, although 12-year-olds are probably not their audience and it's not meant for them, so technically it's not a failure.

According to the guidelines,[21] the area of the focus indicator needs to be at least as large as the area of a 1 px–thick perimeter of the unfocused component or to be as large as a 4 px–thick line that goes along the shortest side of the component. It obviously needs to have the same 3:1 contrast requirement between a focused and unfocused state, and if that's not there, then the border cannot be less than 2 px.

Then there is mention about the perimeter of a hypothetical rectangle shape. For example, if the shape (a button) has two sides of 100 px and two of 50 px (Figure 12-56), then its perimeter is 296 px. The WCAG mention that the requirement for the area would be a focus indicator of at least 296

---

[20] www.w3.org/WAI/WCAG22/Understanding/focus-not-obscured-enhanced
[21] www.w3.org/WAI/WCAG22/Understanding/focus-appearance.html

px or more. But that's the perimeter. Right off the bat, there is a comparison between apples and oranges, in this case, areas and perimeters. The issue comes with how areas and perimeters are defined.

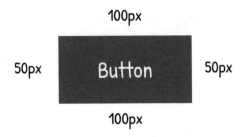

Figure 12-56. *A button shape*

Take a look at Figure 12-57 for some area and perimeter definitions. A surface area is the total area that a shape occupies, and a shape's perimeter is a closed path that surrounds it.

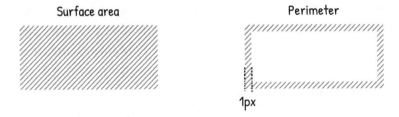

Figure 12-57. *Surface area and perimeter*

To calculate a perimeter, you need to all add the length of all the sides; in our case the button's perimeter would be 100 + 50 + 100 + 5 = 300 px. We would then need to subtract the overlapping pixels of the four corners, so our perimeter becomes 296 px.

To calculate a surface area, however, you'll need to multiply the length of the two sides, so in our case, the surface area would be 100 × 50 = 5000 px^2. Throughout the whole explanation, there is a bit of confusion around areas and perimeters, with some of the content making sense only when it's accompanied by actual graphics. Figure 12-58 shows an example of a focus indicator that passes the requirements. It's 1 px thick, and its surface area is larger than the button it focuses on.

Figure 12-58. *Button and its focus indicator*

If that red outline was inside the button, similar to Figure 12-59, its surface area would be smaller than the button (since it's a smaller shape). Its perimeter would also be smaller. But a 1 px–thick border wouldn't cut it, even with a successful contrast requirement, as it wouldn't be very visible at a glance.

Raising the thickness to 2 px makes the indicator easier to see. According to the WCAG, increasing the pixel thickness from 1 px to 2 px would also increase its surface area. But that doesn't make sense, as the length of its sides would remain the same. It seems to me that when they say area, they mean just the area that the border covers and *not* the inside of the shape. In that sense, yes, it would increase its area, but not its perimeter.

Figure 12-59. *A fail and pass focus indicator for a button component*

If you ever go on the guidelines to have a read, forget about areas and perimeters, as these are very well-defined terms in math and are not explained clearly for someone that is just beginning their journey in web design. If all these seem like Greek to you and you're thinking they *really are* trying to deliberately confuse us, if you ever need to design custom focus indicators, think simple and don't make your brain bleed: just make them thick and visible enough.

Figure 12-60 shows some examples of focus indicators that pass the requirements for a simple rectangle shape. Luckily for us, not all of these need to be true at once. As long as the focus indicator is clear enough for all to see, it doesn't matter what it looks like.

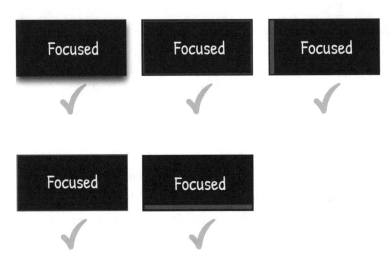

Figure 12-60. *Various focus indicators that pass the WCAG requirements*

For the love of anything you believe in, *do not* remove focus states, and if you need to, change them to something unique and perceivable if they're not easily identifiable. Browsers don't always do a good job on this.

Hover States

A hover state appears on an element once a user runs a mouse cursor over it. This might be because they actually want to interact with that element or simply because they'd like to check out if there is any fancy hover effect that they can ~~steal~~ incorporate into their own project. It is basically a change in styling that helps the user identify that element as interactive. It's a member of a larger group called "states" that Google's Material Design defines as "visual representations used to communicate the status of a component or interactive element." You might be thinking of active states, visited states, disabled states, and so on.

One might argue that for usability hover states are not really that important or do not need to apply everywhere, since a hover state on a link or a call to action will only appear for a split second once the user has already made the decision to interact with that element, meaning they are already engaged.

When it comes to accessibility, a hover state can be as important as the normal state of an element. The change from the normal to something different potentially signifies that the element is interactive and that something can be done with it. Have a normal mouse cursor change to a pointer, and this will give enough visual feedback, meaning we can definitely click that thing, be it a button or a simple text link.

A hover effect will happen when the mouse is on the target, and it needs to be clear enough and easily identifiable, so the user won't have to focus on the cursor, but rather on the content itself. That being said, changes on hover should be clear and distinct. If an individual will use a screen magnifier to read a button, a link, or a table row, the state of the element will swap into hover, so an easily recognizable change makes perfect sense.

Make sure the hover state is quite distinct from the normal state of an interactive element. In other words, it needs to have sufficient contrast with its surroundings according to accessibility guidelines. When it comes to buttons, a simple change of color or a shadow could be enough (Figure 12-61). Consider using CSS to change the hover state of an element rather than an image, as the additional hidden image might interfere with a screen reader.

Figure 12-61. *Examples of button hover states*

Sometimes we have elements moving up a bit on hover. Posh designers like to refer to this as changing the elevation of an element. This makes perfect sense to a user with no disabilities as they can clearly see movement, which could mean that element is interactive. If someone is using a screen magnifier or has a visual impairment that prevents them from seeing your 5 px elevation, they can potentially miss that very slight movement, so always pair it with something else: a color change or any other style change in your element (Figure 12-62).

Figure 12-62. *Button elevation as a hover state*

Links need tender loving care as well. A distinct color change on hover along with a decorative element such as an underline can make a real difference. Avoid making fonts bolder on hover. Even though it's a clear and distinct change (in most cases), it can sometimes be clunky and not very smooth.

Hover states can potentially apply to anything that is clickable, even a checkbox or a radio button. Consider context, your audience, and your goals and design accordingly. Having said that, hover states offer visual simulation and don't always apply to clickable elements. Consider other elements that might be "out of the norm" and in need of a clear hover state such as draggable items, like in Figure 12-63.

Figure 12-63. *Hover state on a draggable button*

As a last word, don't rely on a hover state alone to indicate something as interactive. Ideally, a button should look like a button without the need of a hover over.

Lists

Dear developers, please use unordered lists when the order of the items is not relevant (these will be marked with a bullet) and ordered lists when things need to be in order (these will be marked by sequential numbers).

Use programmatically formatted lists. Screen readers require list items *<li>* to be contained within a *<ul>* or *<ol>* element. If lists are coded correctly, a screen reader will be able to announce the number of items and correctly identify any nested lists.

Similarly, any definition lists should be wrapped within a parent *<dl>* element.

Make sure that the only content within an ordered or unordered list is contained within a *<li>* element (you can also have *<script>* and *<template>*). Dear designers, keep it simple and don't stray too far from a simple bullet list. Simple always wins.

Touch Targets (Size Does Matter)

It does indeed. But mainly when you're trying to touch something. And interact with it. On a (touch) screen device. If you're one of those superhero wannabes and trying to achieve a breath-taking AAA conformance level, then you probably need to amend your target sizes. And by target, we mean the region on a screen that is interactive and accepts an action. Sufficient size in target areas allows for easier access of a control (especially if it's used quite often) and prevents unintentional activation of targets that might be close together.

Users with hand tremors or any kind of mobility impairments, ones that use a small mobile device and may or may not have larger fingers, or anyone that finds it hard clicking that little dot you call radio button will benefit from large enough targets with sufficient space between them.

For an AA conformance level, the size of your target must be at least 24 × 24 pixels. If that's not possible for various reasons, then the targets can be smaller, as long as there is space around them to equate to 24 px at least. If you can't do either, you need to ensure that whatever function you're preventing your users from performing can be done from somewhere else on the page as well.

If your target lies within text, you don't need to follow these. Targets that are contained within some bodies of text are excluded from this requirement since in responsive design these targets can end up anywhere on the screen and obviously that content needs to remain unchanged, regardless of the size of a screen or the orientation of a device.

Compared with how focus indicators are presented, these instructions seem logical enough. Figure 12-64 shows a few examples of target sizes for icon buttons that fail and pass the WCAG requirements.

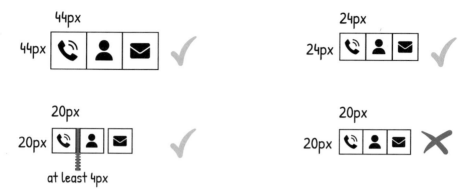

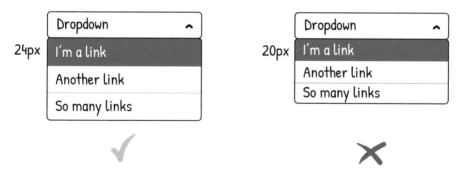

Figure 12-64. *Examples of targets showing how to pass the WCAG requirements*

Even though the target size is irrelevant when it comes to links within text, if that link is within a dropdown menu, then the requirements still apply. Figure 12-65 shows how to pass or fail, depending on the size of the target.

Figure 12-65. *A dropdown menu that passes (left) and fails (right) target size requirements*

For an AAA level, increase the preceding number to 44 px. Again, your target doesn't need to be 44 px large, as long as the element and the space around it equate to a size of 44 px. This means that if you have an interactive icon that is 24 px wide, it needs to have a 10 px padding on each side to meet this requirement (because 24 + 10 + 10=44, just in case).

Sufficiently sized touch targets are especially important for users who might have mobility impairments, loss of fine motor movements, or bigger fingers than normal, ones that use a small mobile device with one or two hands, or anyone that finds it hard clicking that little dot you call a radio button.

The W3C recommends having a touch target that is no less than 44 × 44 pixels for an AAA conformance level. That seems quite specific, doesn't it? I must admit that initially this number looked a bit too precise. "Why not 43 pixels?" I wondered, being naturally argumentative. Turns out there are a lot of recommendations out there when it comes to how big a touch target needs to be.

An MIT and The Touch Lab collaborative study by Dandekar K., Raju B., and Srinivasan M. (2003) showed that the average size of a human finger pad is about 16–20 mm.[22] According to Smashing Magazine,[23] this translates to about 45–57 pixels. And that seems adequate. Apple, on the other hand, recommends a 44 × 44 *points* as a minimum for a touch target for iOS devices. In their guidelines for a touch target, Microsoft suggests a minimum size of 7.5 × 7.5 mm or about 40 × 40 pixels. Android recommends a minimum touch target size of 48 × 48 (about 9 mm in physical size). Global Experience Language (GEL), which is BBC's design system, suggests that a touch target should be at least 7 mm (with 5 mm in some cases), which means we're looking at a minimum size of 24 × 24 px sometimes, based on their conversion from millimeters to pixels. Lastly, Nielsen Norman Group recommends a touch target of about 1 cm in size.[24]

So what gives? Should we all go and buy some rulers to start doing digital work by using a tool that's meant to be used on another medium on any device that we design for? Of course not (unless you're into this

---

[22] 10.1115/1.1613673

[23] www.smashingmagazine.com/2012/02/
finger-friendly-design-ideal-mobile-touchscreen-target-sizes/

[24] https://adrianroselli.com/2019/06/target-size-and-2-5-5.html

stuff). This only re-enforces the idea that touch targets need to be of a sufficient size, depending on the situation and our purposes. This will not only help out the users by making it easier for them to use our product, but it will also make them use it faster, since the bigger the target, the quicker someone will find it and tap it.[25]

Multimedia

Make sure that all images that are part of the content have an *alt text* description. Images that are purely decorative don't need the *alt* text. However, the *alt* tag should still be there and left null (empty) as otherwise a screen reader might start reading the source text that shows where the image is located.

There are a variety of reasons you need that alternative text for your images. A screen reader will read that text out loud when a user gets to the image providing blind or visually impaired users with information on what that image is about without having to actually see it. This text will also be displayed if, for whatever reason, images won't load, because of a slow Internet connection or even because some people prefer to disable images when browsing.

Your *alt* text should be brief and to the point – a short sentence or phrase is enough – and should describe the image, rather than its purpose (Figure 12-66). If an image is a link, though, then the *alt* text should describe the purpose of the link and not the image itself.

---

[25] www.nngroup.com/videos/fittss-law/

Figure 12-66. *A family of ducks*

When it comes to complex images, like illustrations, graphs, or diagrams, an alt text might not be sufficient to describe all the information on the images accurately. In that case, we need to make sure that the information on these images is also presented as additional text on the page. Figure 12-67 shows a bar graph with a text link that leads to a page with a longer description about the image.

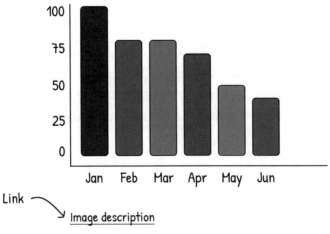

Figure 12-67. *Image of a graph with an associated link that leads to a longer description of the image*

Ensure that any video that has audio or any standalone audio is accompanied by a transcript or captions so users with hearing loss or hearing impairments will be able to understand what it is about without having to look at it.[26] That doesn't mean that transcripts need to be necessarily on the video itself. If that's not possible, even a link that leads to the transcript is enough (Figure 12-68).

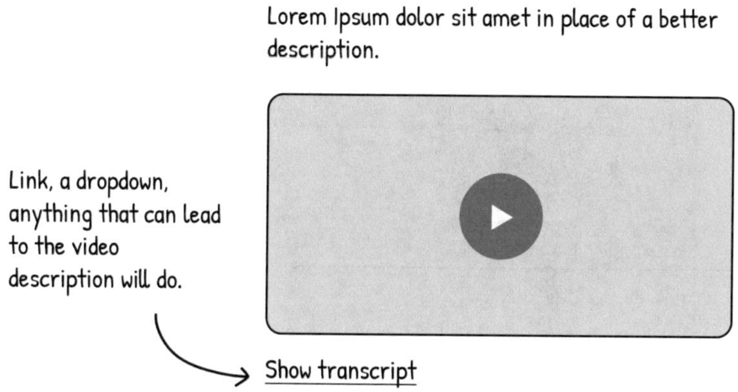

Figure 12-68. *Hypothetical video element with a text link leading to a new page*

Remember one of the most important guidelines: there must always be an alternative way to access information for people who cannot perceive it. Besides, transcripts are beneficial to everybody. I dare you to recall the last time you watched a video on mute and relied only on the subtitles. I bet it was pretty recent.

These are sufficient for an A conformance level, and any extended information aside from the standard transcript will give you an amazing AAA conformance level. You will get extra bonus points if you're presenting live audio or video with captions as well.

---

[26] www.w3.org/WAI/perspective-videos/captions/

Any audio or video should not be on auto-play, and controls for play, pause, and stop should always be provided (Figure 12-69). And if you're still on the path to the light side aiming for an AAA conformance level, make sure that any pre-recorded audio is clear enough and that any background noise does not interfere with important content. Generally, guidelines require a background noise of at least four times quieter than your main audio.

Figure 12-69. *Illustration of a video frame showing video controls*

Still on the path of enlightenment? Have a sign language interpreter on your video, and we will love you forever, you and your little AAA conformance level badge (if there is one; I'm not sure).

Tables

In the not so old days, HTML tables were used to achieve a certain layout. A few cells here and a few cells there were enough to place elements on a page, either in rows or columns. Well, we've got CSS now for this, so this use of tables is a bit obsolete nowadays, since CSS allows for cleaner and simpler code. Now, tables should only be used to present data that can be structured into rows and columns. However, tables still need to adhere to certain guidelines so they can be as accessible as possible.

If you have to use a table, assign a *role="presentation"* attribute to it.

You should always (pretty much) include table headers (Figure 12-70). If your table is small enough or kind of self-explanatory, then column headers and not a *<th>* should be enough. Separating headers visually (e.g., with a different background color) is also beneficial.

Table header

#	Name	Level	Height	Status
1	Lauren	43	164	Active
2	Ipsum	39	178	Active
3	Dolores	40	153	On hold

***Figure 12-70.** Example of a data table*

Include scope attributes: *scope="col"* for the column headers and *scope="row"* for the row headers. This is helpful for assistive technologies as it can make the logical relationships in the table easier to pick up.

Make sure you use table captions (Figure 12-71) to announce what the table is all about. This is also beneficial to sighted users since they can get an insight into what the table contains without having to rely on trying to identify your headers. On the other hand, a screen reader that would read the caption would provide enough context for the user so they can decide if they want to read the whole thing. Use the *<caption>* element to give your table an accessible name.

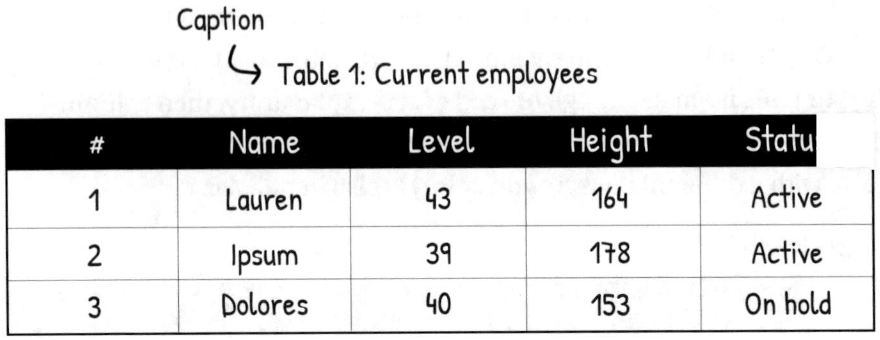

Caption

↳ Table 1: Current employees

#	Name	Level	Height	Statu
1	Lauren	43	164	Active
2	Ipsum	39	178	Active
3	Dolores	40	153	On hold

Figure 12-71. *Example of a table with a caption at the top*

It goes without saying that any elements of the table should have enough contrast with their cells and their background. For example, if your table has borders, they need to have sufficient contrast with the color around them, based on the WCAG contrast requirements (Figure 12-72).

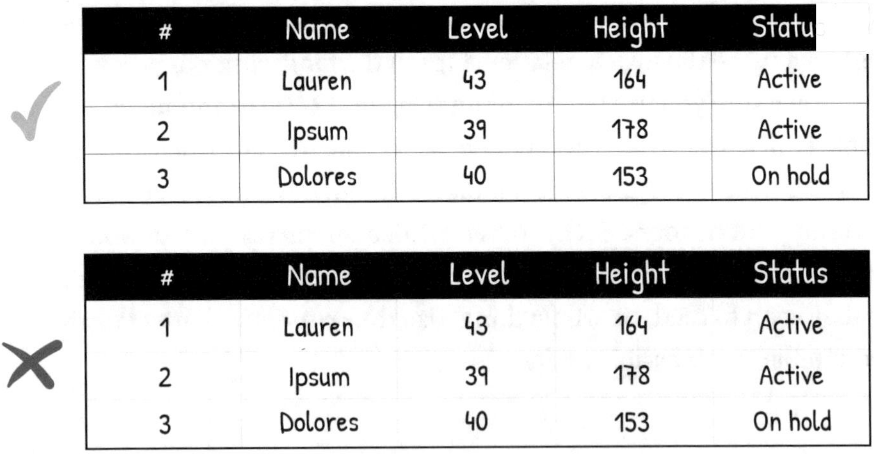

✓

#	Name	Level	Height	Statu
1	Lauren	43	164	Active
2	Ipsum	39	178	Active
3	Dolores	40	153	On hold

✗

#	Name	Level	Height	Status
1	Lauren	43	164	Active
2	Ipsum	39	178	Active
3	Dolores	40	153	On hold

Figure 12-72. *How to style table borders*

If you have to use icons within a table, make sure that you don't solely rely on visuals to convey information. A screen reader would have a hard time identifying a checkmark without any kind of context, and the user will be even more confused.

Avoid using empty cells to format your table. That will create unnecessary confusion for users who rely on screen readers. Use multiple tables instead. Actually, your tables should be very simple to begin with, so don't even go there.

Style odd and even rows differently, as this can be another visual aid for people to easily understand your table layout (Figure 12-73). Another helpful aid is highlighting table cells on mouse hover and keyboard focus so users can identify where they are.

#	Name	Level	Height	Status
1	Lauren	43	164	Active
2	Ipsum	39	178	Active
3	Dolores	40	153	On hold

Figure 12-73. *A table with different background colors on even/ odd rows.*

If, for whatever reason, you decide to create a table layout, make sure that elements such as *<caption>, <th>,* and so on are *not* used since a screen reader might interpret this as data table when, in fact, is a layout. But seriously, don't do that.

When it comes to mobile, make sure that when device orientation changes, there is no loss of data or horizontal scrolling. Tables with data are a bit tricky to translate to a smaller device, especially if they are too wide to begin with. There are various tricks you can try to keep them usable and accessible, such as turning your rows into separate cards, if your content allows it, such as illustrated in Figure 12-74.

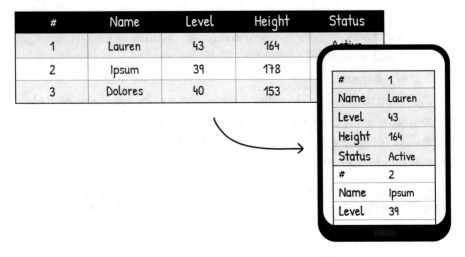

Figure 12-74. *How to translate data tables to a mobile device*

Typography

About 90% of a website's content is pure text. And that makes sense, as people browse websites to find out any information that they need in the form of text, be it trying to find information about a project, buy a product, just browse silly videos, or figure out what to write in a weird book about web accessibility.

Even more important than having text on a website is how this text is presented, as good typography would impact the overall user experience, from someone's mood to the readability of your content. Have you ever tried to read a doctor's prescription before they became electronic? Long, incomprehensive characters joined together in a scrambled mess that only made sense to the doctor and the pharmacist. Arguably, these are the only two people who need to be able to read that information, but still, not very accessible.

Your website needs to convey meaning to its online visitors, and the simplest way to achieve that is by using simple, easy-to-read fonts and by laying out your typography by following a simple set of guidelines aimed toward an effortless online experience.

And talking about effortless experiences, organizing a web page with headings will give the user a sense of structure and logic (Figure 12-75). Headers should, ideally, be presented with larger font than the rest of your copy so they can be distinct and easily identifiable as this will help users with cognitive disabilities, as well as anyone else, to make sense of what you're trying to present.

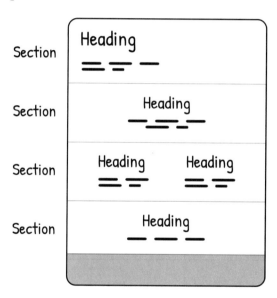

Figure 12-75. *Sections on a website organized by headings*

Properly structured headings are especially important for individuals who use a screen reader. A 2017 study conducted by WebAIM[27] identified that almost 70% of users of a screen reader use headings when trying to find information on a web page. Another interesting thing this study points out is the usage of landmarks (basically a section of a website identified as such). Landmark usage as a means of navigation through different sections

---

[27] https://webaim.org/projects/screenreadersurvey7

has been continually decreasing since 2014 for reasons unknown. It could be the fact that this practice is not being used properly or perhaps that navigating through headings is more efficient (or more familiar).

Headings in a web page are ranked from the most important one (a *<h1>*) to the least important (*<h6>*). As per guidelines a proper logical order would be to use a *<h1>* for the main purpose of the page and then identify each unique section with a *<h2>* tag, which can then be subdivided with a *<h3>* and so on. Remember that you can't skip headings (although as we have already seen sometimes it doesn't matter), for example, you can't have a *<h4>* after an *<h2>*, but you can have an *<h2>* after an *<h4>* as this would have closed the previous section.

And as always, in the quest for creating meaning, your headings should be descriptive enough to match the content that comes after them. To put it simply, if you're changing a topic, start with a heading. It will help create structure, and this will help users with slow reading abilities, short-term memory issues, or any other cognitive limitations understand what your content contains and what it's all about (Figure 12-76).

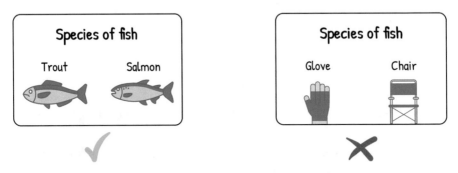

Figure 12-76. *Example of headings with relevant (left) and non-relevant supporting content (right)*

Make sure you're flexible with your typography to ensure your design works on any device and in any way the user will choose to view your content. A requirement for an AA conformance level is that text needs to be able to resize up to 200% without any loss of content or function

(Figure 12-77). The use of a typographic scale could help with that, making your text content appear normal in just about every situation.

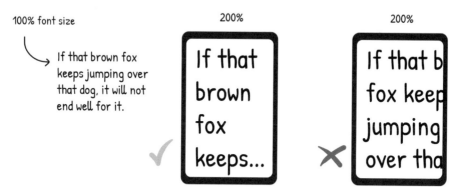

Figure 12-77.   *With a 200% magnification, your text should remain legible and your content read in a logical fashion (right side)*

Prefer the use of simple fonts in an adequate size as they're easier to read, and avoid fancy, decorative fonts with complex characters that make someone's eyes cry from too much effort (Figure 12-78).

Figure 12-78.   *Example of a fancy illegible font (left) and a proper one (right)*

Apart from that, the WCAG have set out a few guidelines on how text needs to be presented on the screen to be easily understood and read by people with different cognitive abilities. More specifically, if a user changes the appearance of text, this needs to remain legible and visible in full. Your content and its function should be unaffected should a user choose to change line height to at least 1.5 times the font size, spacing between paragraphs to at least 2 times the font size, spacing between letters to at least 0.12 times the size of the font (so specific), and, finally, word spacing to at least 0.16 times the size of the font.

That's a lot of numbers, and you might be (rightfully) wondering: *"How on Earth do I do all these things?"* The reality is you probably don't have to, if your website is written in clean HTML and CSS code; all these should already be there in some way. The important bit is *not* to prevent the user from making changes to letter spacing. And this will give you a desired AA conformance level.

If you want to take it one step further, you can include these in your design; make sure line height for all copy is at least 1.5 times the font size and the space between paragraphs is at least 1.5 higher than line height (Figure 12-79).

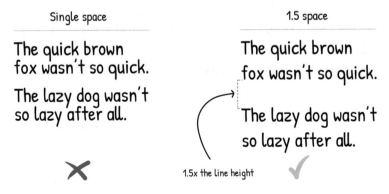

Figure 12-79. *Examples of a single and 1.5 space between lines and paragraphs*

In addition, there are four more criteria you need to pass to get a breath-taking AAA conformance level; the user needs to be able to change background and foreground color (high-contrast mode perhaps?), any blocks of text should be no more than 80 characters long, and text should *not* be fully justified and can be enlarged up to 200% without the need for the user to scroll horizontally.

It goes without saying that we shouldn't use images of text instead of text. Images of text don't allow a user to change the appearance of them in case they don't understand them (e.g., change their color, size, or letter spacing). Moreover, it's an AAA success criterion. However, if that text is part of a logo or decorative or if there is no other way to achieve the desired effect with text, then this criterion doesn't apply.

Avoid using all capital letters in your content, as it reduces readability (especially in long pieces of text), and don't underline text as this ideally should be reserved for identifying links. Organize headings in a logical order, starting from the more important (*<h1>*) to the least important (*<h6>*). Headings *must* have heading tags as screen readers will rely on this.

If you need to do something nice and decorative with your text, do not rely on heading tags but rather use different text styles.

Finally, do not use headings as subheadings, for a nicely done slogan or for anything else that doesn't signify the *start* of a section or specific piece of information.

Forms

A few years back, I was part of the marketing team of a company that did a little bit of everything. Later on that marketing team moved on, working for a design agency under the same management, and during those years I must have seen more forms than I could handle. Especially when the ugly ones were the ones that usually worked better. And the reason for that was obvious: they were simple to use, as what's pretty and what's not clearly depends on the observer.

When users use a form, they fill in some data, and then something happens. They log into their personal profile by typing in a username and a password, subscribe to newsletters, send messages, apply for jobs, and so on. They are simple interactive elements that usually comprise form fields that the user fills in. They have labels that explain what field is the one you're trying to complete and maybe some feedback and some validation if you do it right, they could be one or two or more columns if you're feeling adventurous, and finally they have a button that performs an action.

When it comes to designing accessible forms, there is a clear road to follow: simplicity, clarity, and obvious ways to identify errors. Users with disabilities might find completing forms challenging. A simple layout will help users with cognitive disabilities understand what they're looking at easier, and large fields or controls such as checkboxes will help users with dexterity issues complete it faster. Clear and properly coded labels will help users who use a screen reader understand what is required of them in order to complete the form successfully.

A simple, one- or two-column structure[28] with no fluff is usually what will do the trick, so try to avoid overcomplicated form layouts and provide your users with something easy to use that follows a logical order. Figure 12-80 shows an example of a form where similar information is not grouped together (left side) and one where the flow makes sense (right side). No one likes giving out personal details anyway, so might as well make the experience as frictionless as possible.

---

[28] There is a lot of debate about whether a one-column form performs better than a two-column form. Luckily for us there are arguments for both, so before you give a definite answer, might be better to experiment for yourself for your specific situation and see what happens.

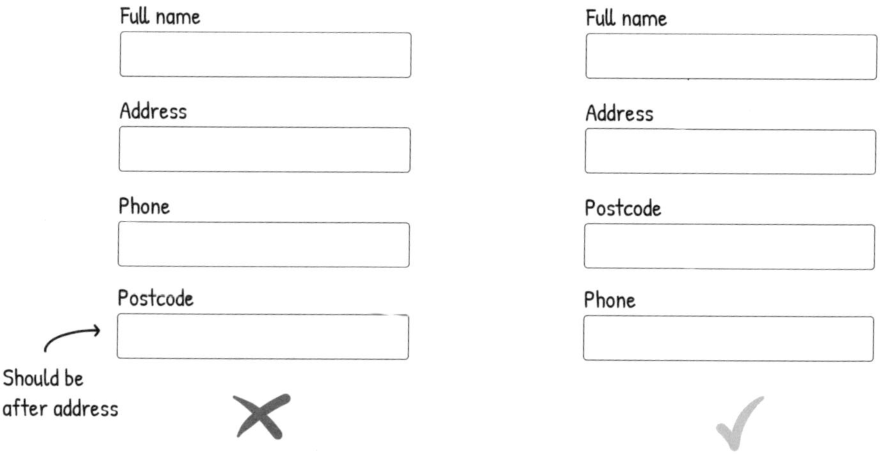

Full name

Address

Phone

Postcode

Should be
after address

Full name

Address

Postcode

Phone

Figure 12-80. *Illustration of two forms. The one on the right correctly groups address and postcode together, as it's similar information*

If you have to use mandatory fields, usually that's denoted with an asterisk "*". However, to avoid creating confusions for your users when someone doesn't know what an asterisk means or when they can't see the little "* required field" that's hidden in the middle of nowhere, it might be best to also include a clear instruction by simply adding the word "Required" or "Optional," depending on how you want to approach it (Figure 12-81).

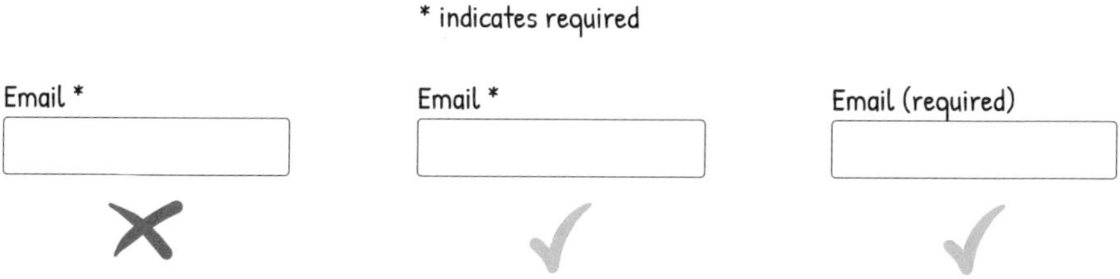

* indicates required

Email *

Email *

Email (required)

Figure 12-81. *How to design a mandatory field*

Mandatory or optional fields are not the only time you might have to give instruction to people on how to use the form. For example, you might be instructing a user how to fill in a date or letting them know that their password needs to be eight characters and include every possible weird combination out there. These instructions also need to be picked up by screen readers, so make sure you use appropriate ARIA labels (with aria-describedby, for instance).

As always, make sure that the form and its fields have sufficient contrast with their background. Adding a visible border around each field that has a 3:1 color contrast ratio with its environment can make them visible enough for most people (Figure 12-82).

Figure 12-82. *Color contrast around the border of a form field*

It should go without saying that as an interactive element, a form with its fields needs to receive sufficient focus so people know where they are if they happen to use their keyboards (Figure 12-83). Ensure that tabbing through the form follows a logical order, taking you from one field to the next, all the way down to that action button.

Full name
[Darth V...]

Full name
[Sith L...]

Full name
[Lord V...]

✓

Full name
[   ]
············ Tab

Address
[   ]

Postcode
[   ]   Tab

Phone
[   ]   Tab

Figure 12-83. *Example of sufficient focus around a form's text field and illustration of logical order when navigating the form with a keyboard*

All fields and controls need to be clearly labeled (Figure 12-84).[29] There is a bit of a debate as to whether you need to put labels on the right of the field or above the field. At the end of the day, this is something you can experiment with, and see what fits your needs best. As long as the labels are close to their associated elements, you should be up for a great start.

What is your relationship to the applicant?

✗ ☐ Father

✓ ☐ It's complicated

✓ ☐ Jedi tutor

✓ ☐ Not sure / Won't disclose

Figure 12-84. *Placement of labels with an example form's controls*

---

[29] www.w3.org/WAI/tutorials/forms/labels/

When it comes to what a user actually enters in a field, validation is needed to avoid errors and frustration. For example, a text field is expected to receive text, and a numeric field (such as for a telephone number) is expected to only receive numbers. Validation, however, is not as important for web accessibility, as long as a potential error can be clearly identified so it can be corrected.

Depending on how the website is built, the check for errors can be client-side, meaning there is some code that checks for errors in real time, as you input your data, or server-side, meaning the form has to be submitted first and analyzed by some server and then a message of error or success is returned.

If you have real-time validation, a good technique would be showing the error message next to the field you're trying to interact with, alerting the user that something is going wrong (Figure 12-85).

Figure 12-85. *Error message with inline validation. The error appears as the user types in the field*

Otherwise, displaying an error message at the top of the form, clearly communicating to the user that there are errors on the form that need correcting, is another way to do it (Figure 12-86). That error message should be very clear about what errors have occurred *and* how to fix them.

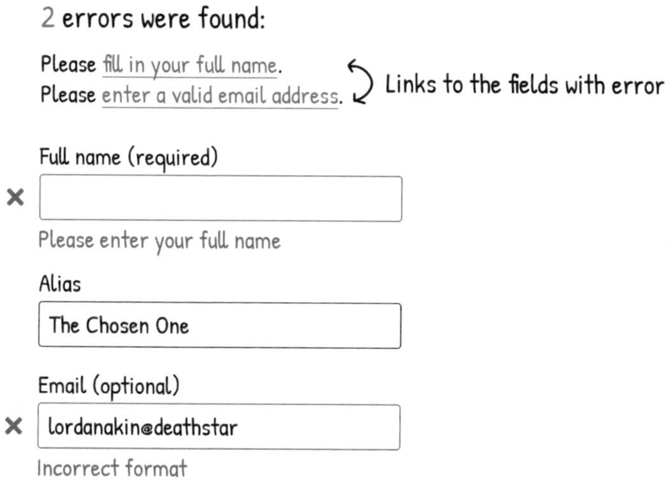

2 errors were found:

Please fill in your full name.
Please enter a valid email address. ↰ Links to the fields with error

Full name (required)

✗ [   ]

Please enter your full name

Alias

[The Chosen One   ]

Email (optional)

✗ [lordanakin@deathstar   ]

Incorrect format

Figure 12-86. *An example form communicating error messages*

If the user has finally managed to complete your accessible form and ends up with a button that says "Submit," that form wasn't bulletproof after all. It's very easy to forget what you're doing online, especially when dealing with long forms. A generic "Submit" button label doesn't provide any context as to what you've been doing, so it might be preferable to include labels such as "Send your message," "Pay now," "Create account," and so on (Figure 12-87).

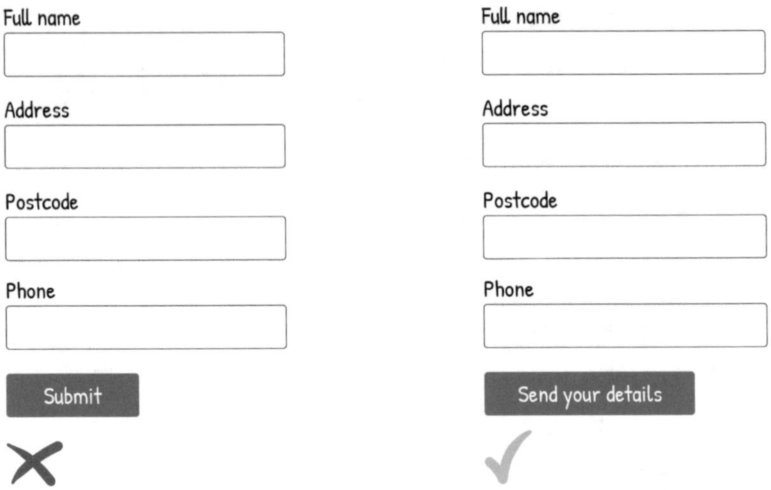

Figure 12-87. *Two forms with different text labels on their submit buttons*

Users with anxiety will love you if you constantly provide them with reassurance that what they're doing is working. Consider indicating clearly that any kind of form has been successfully submitted (or not) by providing a success message on the button itself (Figure 12-88) or a new page that the user is redirected to after the form's submission.

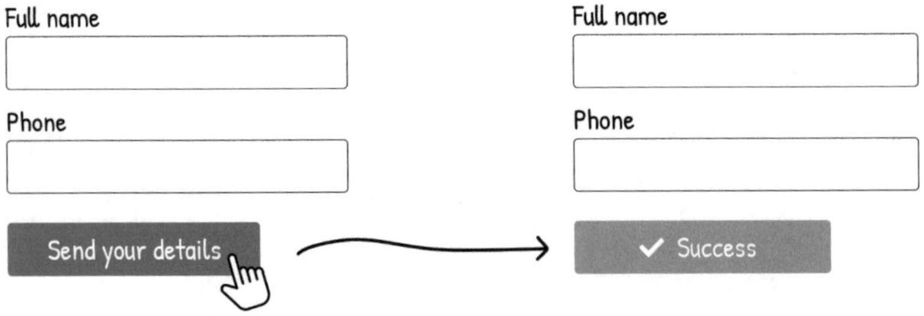

Figure 12-88. *Example of a success message after a form submission*

Summary

Phew! That was a long one! This was the longest chapter in this book, and that makes sense, as there was information provided on accessible design for a number of elements, from animated content to forms and carousels. Hopefully, you have an idea of what to look for, if you managed to finish it.

It's very easy to neglect little details in our designs, such as carousel arrows, a play/stop button, or even a show transcript link. Details though are what matter, and when it comes to web accessibility, these little details can make or break a user's experience. If you haven't managed to finish the whole chapter and you're one of those who like to read the ending of a book to see if it's worth it, even though it's completely out of context, here is a summary of what you can do.

When it comes to animated content, auto-play is discouraged. Nothing should flash more than three times a second, and if you have to have stuff auto-playing, make sure there are controls, such as play and pause.

Content needs to be clear, concise, and logical, with all interactive elements able to receive sufficient focus. Don't forget to put alternative descriptions in your images when needed as well as captions and transcripts to your videos. Use visual cues on text links when necessary and avoid overly complicated UI elements and page structure.

Typography needs to be clear and legible. No one likes to put effort into reading in the first place, so if we make it harder than it actually is, then we are more or less guaranteed a failure. Your forms should ideally be easy to understand with all the fields following a logical order when presented to the user. Any errors need to be easily identified and explained so the user knows what to do to correct them.

Lastly, make sure that your whole website can be navigated with a keyboard and that going through the different elements makes logical sense. Who knew "everything" fit in one page after all?

CHAPTER 13

So What Is the Verdict?

Congratulations if you've made it this far. I'm sure it wasn't easy (although I kind of hope it was). Hopefully, some of the clutter and confusion of the web accessibility guidelines has been resolved, and you are now in a better position to tackle any web accessibility issues that come from bad or not-as-well-informed design decisions.

The truth is, though, we've not answered one of the most important questions: Does any of this matter? Would websites be less successful as products if they implemented fewer accessibility guidelines or if they didn't conform fully? That's a tricky question, and one that I suspect is not easy to answer as we'd have to come up with an experiment that aims to answer it fully.

It should go without saying that for users with disabilities, having a proper structure, sufficient contrast, large target sizes, keyboard navigation, clear content, and clean and accurate code will enable assistive technologies to present a website clearly to them, helping them achieve whatever they want to achieve. Someone that is blind or has severe visual impairments should be able to order a pizza online, as much as the next person. Someone that can't use a mouse deserves to navigate a website properly so they can get to the information they want. Even if they don't use assistive technologies but are presented with a variety of obstacles in their everyday lives, these practices will still make a difference.

D. Georgakas, *A11Y Unraveled*, https://doi.org/10.1007/978-1-4842-9085-9_13

Taking that aside, do these practices offer anything to users with no disabilities? We've already mentioned that when implementing accessibility guidelines, the lives of all users become better. Everybody can see content more clearly, and everyone can use a web product under difficult or inconvenient situations. But what if they weren't there for users with no disabilities? Would it affect the success of a product? Would it mean that most people would not be able to buy that product as efficiently or find information easier?

If we take a look at big brands and how accessible their websites are, the results make you think: Nike's website, a multibillion-dollar company, has a lighthouse score of 73. On the other hand, dominos.co.uk has a score of 99 on their homepage. Similarly, Amazon's homepage has a score of 98. Rakuten's shop has a lighthouse score of 90, and random Wikipedia pages have a score that ranges between 85 and 90. Could they all be crazy? (Apart from Nike, they might need to do some work.) Obviously these scores show half of the picture since I've not done a full accessibility audit, but it's a good starting point to get an idea of what's going on.

Apart from tricky, the question around whether these practices matter might seem like a dumb one (it isn't), but these are the ones that usually come to my mind! What's interesting though is that others have asked the same questions in the past. It's easy to blindly follow rules and guidelines, but ultimately there needs to be a reason for this. In this case, the reason is *it works.*

A 2017 study by Sven Schmutz, Andreas Sonderegger, and Juergen Sauer showed that implementing web accessibility guidelines led to increased performance and a more positive experience for users with visual impairments as well as non-disabled users.[1] A similar 2018 study by the same people showed a clear advantage for non-disabled users once

---

[1] Schmutz S, Sonderegger A, Sauer J. Implementing Recommendations From Web Accessibility Guidelines: Would They Also Provide Benefits to Nondisabled Users. Hum Factors. 2016 Jun;58(4):611-29. doi: 10.1177/0018720816640962

more, with accessible websites having the effect of faster task completion and overall higher satisfaction ratings than when using non-accessible websites.[2] Another 2013 study showed that users who were blind and others that had significant visual impairments were able to complete tasks on accessible websites that they were otherwise unable to do in sites that were not accessible. When it came to both disabled and non-disabled users, both groups reported overall higher satisfaction when using an accessible website.[3]

If we consider elderly users, as the older you are, the more the chances of physical as well as cognitive decline,[4] it makes sense to assume that implementing accessibility guidelines would have a direct positive effect on older people's online experience, especially since older users wouldn't be as experienced with technology compared with younglings. When putting some of WCAG 2.0 to the test, a 2009 study[5] showed that older users didn't really care about keyboard navigation as they preferred to use a mouse because it made them feel included (even though they had difficulties). A 2013 study showed that elderly users preferred visual presentation of text in accordance with accessibility recommendations; even though it didn't lead to faster completion of tasks, they liked looking at it better (so increased satisfaction).[6]

---

[2] Schmutz, S., Sonderegger, A., Sauer, J. 2018. Effects of accessible website design on nondisabled users: age and device as moderating factors. Ergonomics 61, 697–709. doi:10.1080/00140139.2017.1405080

[3] Afra P., Mireia R., Toni Granollers, Jordi L. C. 2014. Impact of Accessibility Barriers on the Mood of Blind, Low-vision and Sighted Users. Procedia Computer Science, vol.27. https://doi.org/10.1016/j.procs.2014.02.047

[4] Arch, A. 2009. Web accessibility for older users. In: doi:10.1145/1535654.1535655

[5] Sayago, S., Camacho, L., Blat, J. 2009. Evaluation of techniques defined in WCAG 2.0 with older people. In: doi:10.1145/1535654.1535673

[6] Petrie, H., Kamollimsakul, S., Power, C. 2013. Web accessibility for older adults. In: doi:10.1145/2513383.2513414

What this tells us, considering the thousands (potentially; I've not counted them, but there are a lot) of web and academic articles that have been written on the effects of web accessibility guidelines on user performance and satisfaction, is that these practices, to a lesser or a higher degree, work. At least in the contexts of the various studies, although there is no reason to assume that they don't work in real-life scenarios. On top of that, they show that some accessibility guidelines are irrelevant when it comes to specific context and specific users, meaning that under certain situations we could indeed afford to fail and that wouldn't affect the success of our product.

Usability should not really be considered here, and that's because it should be a given and we can't afford to fail there. There is no automated tool to check for usability as a user always needs to be involved in any UX testing. But if we follow best design practices, we can be sure that when the website is done, it's at the best possible state it can be, usability-wise. An easy and enjoyable experience for the users needs to be there if we want our websites to be successful and the users satisfied. So that should not be taken for granted.

On the other hand, I'm (fairly) positive to say that web accessibility does matter (d'oh!) although the degree of implementation depends on your audience and that, yes, we can afford to fail accessibility checks and it won't matter to how our users use our websites, to our audience, or to how successful the client will be, because at the end of the day, we don't design for our clients' egos or taste or our own personal preferences and we don't design for the whole world (even though our audience is potentially global).

We shouldn't even be designing to avoid lawsuits. We design for specific and very well-defined users. It is our users' needs and expectations we need to fulfil and not our own. And that needs to be made really clear to the people we work with or for, especially if that work is on a consultancy level. We need to make sure that our experience and knowledge is put into use in order for them to get the best result. And if that means getting an accessibility score of A or AA, -ABGW, or 40%, then so be it. And that won't mean that we won't have done a good job. We will have done the best possible job for that specific client with that specific audience.

You can think about it like having a meat store, for example, and you only sold meat and you only wanted to sell meat. Would you go out of your way to cater for vegans when they're not your potential customers? It doesn't matter, right? Although expanding your product range could potentially bring in more customers and consequently more revenue. But if you don't care or if it doesn't add any value to your business, it's irrelevant.

Accessibility guidelines are there to help us designers design websites that are accessible (obviously). But the only thing that can tell us if something is accessible or not, to give us a definite answer, is not an audit from Google or a color contrast checker but is, again, the users themselves.

Final Word

Despite the fact there is a really important case in favor of implementing web accessibility guidelines, it seems that there is still much work that needs to be done. Considering the number of disabled Internet users and the potential positive outcomes that can come from implementing these guidelines (positive both in terms of user satisfaction and financial gain[7]), there is still room for improvement.

WebAIM's 2022 report on web accessibility shows that little has changed in the last few years.[8] While evaluating a million homepages, they found about 50.8 errors per page, which is a bit over 1% increase from the previous year's report. They also found an increased complexity

---

[7] https://sitemorse.com/blog-article/10016/18-key-statistics-about-web-accessibility-for-2021/

[8] https://webaim.org/projects/million/

on how a homepage is presented, and what's even more alarming is that about 97% of all the pages they tested failed in one way or another on web accessibility guidelines (most common errors were low contrast, empty alt text descriptions, and empty links).

Especially when it came to "skip links," only 14% of the homepages had one, and of those, one in eleven didn't work for some reason. Well, at least the thought was there.

It seems that when designing and developing a website, there is a certain lack of awareness and implementation of the proper techniques[9] as well as a relatively low number of web professionals who can actually test for these kinds of problems.[10] Luckily though, there seem to be an increased number of articles and resources available online (and offline) for designers and developers that aim to reduce that gap in knowledge and instill that desire to be part of the solution rather than the problem. So maybe it's just a matter of time to get there.

And if you don't want to do it out of the goodness of your heart, do it for the goodness of your pocket and your sanity, as there are thousands of lawsuits happening on lack of website accessibility in digital products (in 2020 about ten lawsuits a day were filed for digital accessibility problems[11]), and you could very easily end up on the losing side, you lawbreaker. It doesn't take a long time, it doesn't cost much, and it will make you look good in the eyes of your users.

---

[9] Abuaddous, H.Y., Zalisham, M., Basir, N. 2016. Web Accessibility Challenges. International Journal of Advanced Computer Science and Applications, 7. doi:10.14569/ijacsa.2016.071023

[10] J. Brown and H. Scott. "The challenges of web accessibility: the technical and social aspects of a truly universal web." First Monday, Vol. 20, No. 9, 2015.

[11] https://blog.usablenet.com/a-record-breaking-year-for-ada-digital-accessibility-lawsuits

Final Word v2

What could be hindering our ability to design and develop accessible websites even though we can find out the benefits of these practices? One answer could be that web professionals are still not very aware of accessibility practices, of all the standards they need to follow in order to make something as accessible as possible. It could also be that they've done their research and found out that in fact, their audience doesn't warrant them implementing those practices. Although, somehow, I doubt that.

Could it be that we live in a digital world where advertising and fancy graphics are in the center of every website out there? That increased need for complex graphics and even more complex pages that show the "wow factor" (that leads to a complicated way of developing) could be a reason accessibility is an afterthought rather than a priority in developing a digital product.

To put it simply, maybe we are putting image over function. Maybe we've come to a point where we make creativity complicated, combined with a difficulty to find simple solutions to tough problems.

It definitely can't be time and cost. It is quite easy to learn the fundamentals and use your common sense to design and develop something simple, something pretty, and something that works. If the difference in developing an accessible version of a website is a day or two days more in development, that's pretty much nothing in the grand scheme of things, or in the grand scheme of how long and how much it costs to develop a website. Besides, the more you do it, the more it becomes second nature, and the more you'll be implementing accessibility, and usability, practices to your websites. So might as well start now rather than later.

Final Final Word (If You Know, You Know)

Totally irrelevant with the concept of this book, but if you've wondered about my use of font for the images throughout the pages, I've deliberately used a font that resembles Comic Sans in the images within these pages.[12] I like to pick on designers and their displayed sense of a weird authority.

Discuss!

Summary

"Who needs a summary after a summary?" you ask. You, I'd answer. It wouldn't be a book written by a designer of all things digital if it didn't include a final final word v2.

In this book we've covered initial definitions on web accessibility, laying out principles that need to be followed. In a nutshell, whatever you're designing and/or developing online needs to follow a certain set of practices in order to be accessible to people with disabilities or potential situational limitations. Eventually, this would extend into improved usability for all.

As all people are fundamentally different (but yet so much the same), a one-size-fits-all approach wouldn't be appropriate. In other words, know your audience and what disabilities they might be facing and understand what you can do to help them. We talked about the importance of being aware of who is going to be using your digital product in order to develop it in a way that addresses their specific needs.

We also covered why you need to do it, as aside from ethical, financial, and "just doing a good job" reasons, you also have to think about your family if you ever go to jail for not complying with web accessibility guidelines. As these are now part of legal frameworks around the world, knowing what to do and doing it is essential for a digital product's success.

---

[12] It could be worse. I could have actually used Comic Sans.

Following on, we laid out a number of practices and guidelines that have to do with specific design elements, such as forms, typography, carousels, images, layout and structure of a web page, and so on, and how to approach design decisions when it comes to using color and contrast.

I hope that throughout this book the impression of following the spirit of the law rather than the letter of the law was made clear. Simply following some guidelines and design practices will not be enough to make something truly accessible as user input and barriers that they face should always be at the forefront of any design decision. Even though I kept referring to it as "it" (I've done it again), accessibility practices are not just one thing you can implement and hope for the best, but rather a continuous process of acknowledging problems, implementing solutions, testing, and repeating the process.

Hopefully, some of the information in this book was new to you and beneficial in some way or another. If some of the content was incorrect, apologies. I blame ~~my technical reviewer~~ myself for not giving you the correct knowledge. If anything, being wrong can spark a conversation, so there's always an opportunity to learn something from it.

Now go on and make something pretty. And usable.

And accessible.

Index

A

AA conformance level, 96, 154, 159, 166, 168, 214

A/B test, 70, 186

Accessibility, 13, 14, 119, 136, 149, 151

Accessibility guidelines, 115, 154, 158

  operable, 22

  perceivable, 22

  perceive, 27

  robust, 23

  understandable, 22

Accessibility standards, 18, 19, 163

Accessible Perceptual Contrast Algorithm (APCA), 162

Accessible Rich Internet Applications (ARIA)

  accessible name, 91

  components, 85

  elements, 83

  focus, 91

  modal window, 83, 84

  native elements, 89, 90

  properties, 86–88

  roles, 85

  screen reader, 84

  states, 86–88

  tab role, 90

  users, 91

  web developers, 83

Advanced Research Projects Agency Network (ARPANET), 2, 3

Alt tag, 127, 263

Alt text, 263, 264

American Speech-Language-Hearing Association, 44

Americans with Disabilities Act (ADA), 106

Animated image, 210

Animated object, 210

ANSI-HFES-100-1988, 158

ARIA labels, 80, 83, 87, 101, 278

Assistive technology, 23, 35, 42, 83, 93

Astigmatism, 164, 165

Audio transcripts, 127

Authoring Tool Accessibility Guidelines (ATAG), 16

Autism spectrum disorder (ASD), 61, 63

Automated tool, 68, 77, 79, 162, 288

Auto-scrolling carousels, 210

Printed in the United States
by Baker & Taylor Publisher Services